SPIELBERG

THE FIRST TEN YEARS

To Laurent,
who is there?

Steven Spielberg

2074-71

©Universal Pictures

SPIELBERG

THE FIRST TEN YEARS

WRITTEN BY
LAURENT BOUZEREAU

FOREWORD BY
JOHN WILLIAMS

INTRODUCTION BY
GEORGE LUCAS

INSIGHT
EDITIONS

SAN RAFAEL · LOS ANGELES · LONDON

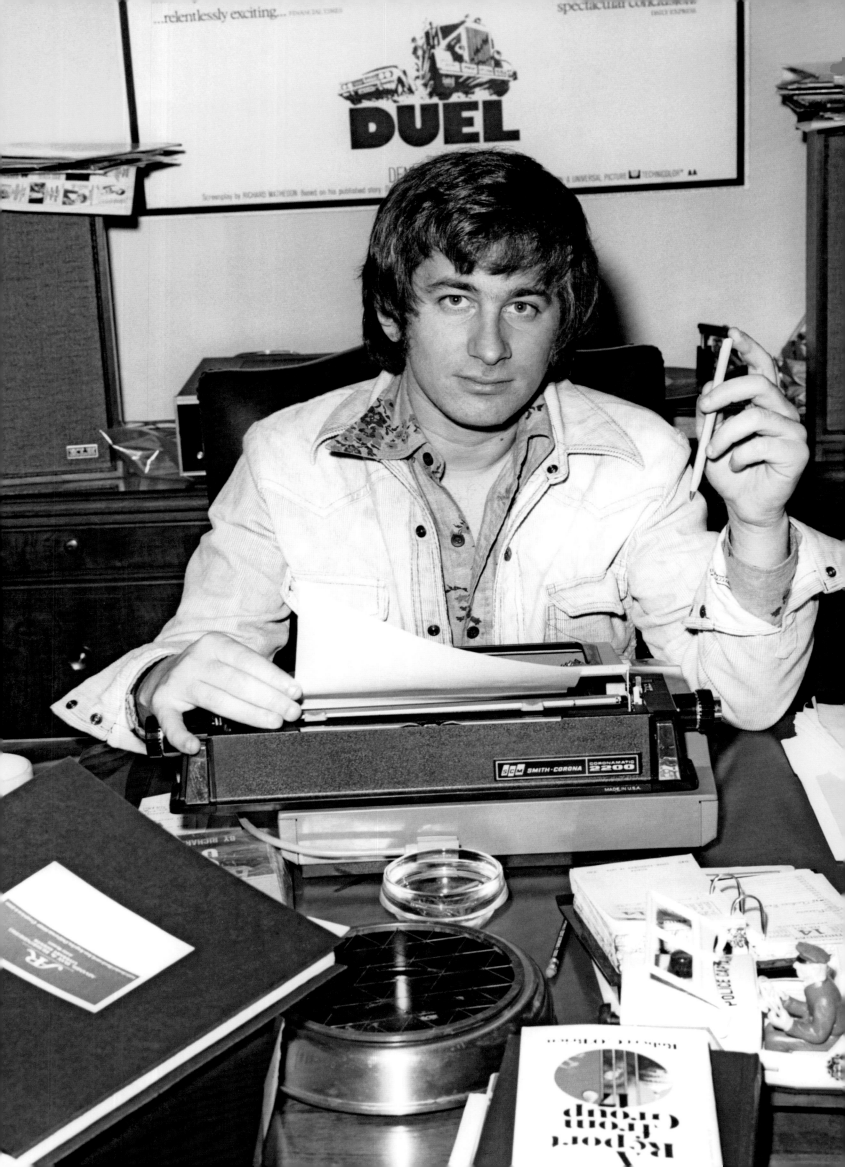

CONTENTS

FOREWORD by JOHN WILLIAMS

Sometime in 1973, Universal Studios arranged a lunch meeting for Steven Spielberg and myself to discuss my composing the musical score for *The Sugarland Express*. I'd heard wonderful things about his first feature-length film *Duel*, and so on meeting Steven I was surprised and very impressed by his youth. During our ensuing conversation, he displayed an amazing maturity for such a young person, as well as an encyclopedic knowledge and love of film music… even to the point of remembering some of the themes from my early work that I'd forgotten myself. I was truly impressed by his razor-sharp mind, and it was only a little later that I realized I'd had lunch with a young man who was about to become one of the greatest filmmakers of all time.

Within a short span of months, Steven lit up the world of filmmaking like a comet, and his brightness has never dimmed. Hollywood, and indeed the world, immediately recognized that this was the arrival of a genius, artist and craftsman of an extremely rare order.

Not surprisingly then, Steven has contributed one great film after another, creating a body of work that may never be surpassed by one person: *Close Encounters of the Third Kind*, the *Indiana Jones* series, *E.T. the Extra-Terrestrial*, *Saving Private Ryan* (possibly the greatest World War II film ever made) *Jurassic Park*, *Schindler's List*, *Munich*, *Lincoln*, *West Side Story* and many more. He's taken us to the depths of the ocean… the highest reaches of the sky… and everything in between.

Steven, of course, is a great many things. He is an entrepreneur, an important philanthropist, a studio executive, a writer and director, and an inspiration to young people around the world who themselves aspire to be storytellers, filmmakers and, through their work, servants of beauty and truth. We can be thankful to Laurent Bouzereau for this wonderful book, which not only is an invaluable document of Steven's early career, but which also serves as a unique love letter to a truly great man.

John Williams

OF THE THIRD KIND A

INTRODUCTION by GEORGE LUCAS

The first Steven Spielberg project I ever saw was *Duel*. I had heard about both him and it, so while at a get-together at Francis Ford Coppola's home, I ran upstairs and tucked away watching it while everyone else was partying. Here was a young filmmaker of my own generation clearly talented with an eye for bringing gripping tension, emotion, and adventure to the screen. I was in the midst of making my first feature film, *THX 1138*, and needless to say, was impressed. It spurred me on even more.

Fittingly, Steven and I had first met at a screening of my short student film, *THX*, and would later be reintroduced through fellow filmmakers Matthew Robbins and Hal Barwood who were writing *The Sugarland Express* with him. Fast friends, we were always talking about our films and what we wanted to do next. When *Sugarland* was released, it was a revelation of great performances and narrative. Steven's talent was boundless.

We happened to be in a period when the business was changing; the studios were being bought by conglomerates, becoming more corporate and, in many cases, less creative in nature. In that setting, a small group of us happened to be making our way into the film industry at the same time: Steven and I, Martin Scorsese, and Brian De Palma among others. We weren't trying to change the industry, we just wanted to make movies that we liked and would want to see ourselves…that would hopefully appeal to other moviegoers too.

By the time *Jaws* came along Steven and I were creative compatriots. I would go over to the studio to see what he was up to and watch the progress as the shark was being built. I was well aware that during production nothing ever goes quite as swimmingly as one would hope, sometimes literally. Challenges behind the scenes can become even bigger beasts than the ones that make it to the screen. Steven was under a lot of pressure on that film and some days he would say "Oh, it's not going very well." I was supportive and certainly empathetic. He pressed onward and when I later saw the film at a preview screening, it was just as fantastic as I knew it would be. His personal fortitude was always deeply ingrained.

Over those early years we'd also chat about the people we were working with, not realizing working together on a shared project wasn't that far down the road. I was directing *Star Wars* at the same time Steven was working on the great *Close Encounters of the Third Kind* and he had recommended John Williams as a composer for *Star Wars*. After that, Steven did the unexpected and directed a comedy, *1941*. Funny with a wildness brought on by youth, it was a different genre for him. He was always moving forward, growing his cinematic craftsmanship across each of his films.

We first collaborated on *Raiders of the Lost Ark*. I'd been working on it for a while – I had finished *Star Wars* and was prepping *The Empire Strikes Back* as executive producer. Steven and I were talking about the kinds of movies we wanted to make next when he said, "I really want to make a James Bond film." I told him, "Well, I have a James Bond film. It takes place in the '30s, but it's still a James Bond action-adventure film. It's in the spirit of the Republic serials." I told him about *Raiders* and he said, "It's great, I'll do it."

Everyone kept saying it would cost thirty, forty million dollars and I said it wouldn't, that we'd do it for twenty and I'd pay for the overages. When I told Steven my plan, he told me, "Oh my God, I could bankrupt you if I go over budget." I said, "Yeah, you can, so don't do it!" Even then, we were in complete sync and knew the kind of movie we were making.

After the success of *Raiders*, Steven directed *E.T.*, and we were in what people called the blockbuster business. Everything Steven touched became successful and deservedly so. I always say I don't really have favorite movies. It's akin to comparing your children…you love each for their individual characteristics that make them unique. Looking back on that time, I will say that out of the many classic films from the first decade of Steven's career, *E.T.* shares in its theme, scope and heart the essence what I was also striving to create with *Star Wars* - a children's film that can remind adults alike of the wonder of storytelling with sincerity and that shared experience touches us all.

Steven has had an undeniably great impact on the film industry and cinematic history, from those first ten years that shaped and defined his career through to his most recent works. At the end of the day though, I will always look back on those early years, glad that I got to work with my friend and watch plenty of great movies along the way.

George Lucas

OPPOSITE George Lucas and Steven Spielberg during shooting of *Raiders of the Lost Ark* (1981).

PAGES 10–11 During filming of *Close Encounters of the Third Kind* (1977), Steven Spielberg directs Richard Dreyfuss as Roy Neary.

PREFACE

BY
LAURENT BOUZEREAU

"I don't dream at night, I dream at day, I dream all day; I'm dreaming for a living."
—Steven Spielberg

For nearly three decades now, I've had the great pleasure of being Steven Spielberg's documentarian, first making retrospective films on his early work, and then later being invited on set to capture the unique magic of his filmmaking process. Even after all these years, the privilege of being able to work alongside Steven has never lost its significance to me and continues to be the fulfillment of a lifelong dream.

I was born in Eaubonne, a little suburb north of Paris, in 1962. I was always interested in film, and at ten I announced to my parents that I wanted to be a movie director. Even at that very young age, it was somehow at the back of my mind. There was a little movie theater in Taverny, the town where I grew

up, and whenever my parents took me, I was always looking behind, rather than at, the screen, because I wanted to know how this spectacle was happening. After one showing, my dad arranged for me to go up to the projection booth. The stairway to the booth seemed almost endless, like something from a fantasy movie. When I finally got all the way up the stairs and opened the door, I found myself in this dingy, overheated cavern with two big projectors. Standing there was a middle-aged guy wearing a gray lab coat who turned out to be both the owner of the theater and the projectionist. It felt like the ending of *The Wizard of Oz* (1939), where I pulled back the curtain only to find that the wizard was in fact just a man. It was my first realization that the magic that happens on

RIGHT Steven Spielberg frames a shot while filming his science fiction epic *A.I. Artificial Intelligence* (2001).

OPPOSITE Spielberg behind the camera on *Close Encounters of the Third Kind.*

ABOVE Laurent Bouzereau's grandmother Hélène Van Den Haute at the Éclair Studios, August 1962.

the movie screen is very different from what happens behind the scenes. I was fascinated nonetheless, particularly when he explained that every fifteen minutes or so a dot would flash up on the screen—known as a cue mark—which indicated that he needed to change film reels. I felt like he had shared some great secret with me, and I think that was the moment I started to find my calling behind the scenes. I wanted to know how you created that seamless on-screen magic.

Soon I was given my first silent movie projector, which I used to project *King Kong* (1933) and cartoons in my bedroom, using a white sheet provided by my mom and held up by a long plastic tube provided by my dad. I hung up the sheet behind my bedroom curtains, which I would open dramatically as if my room was a real movie theater, and I'd force my family to watch those films over and over again. Because the films didn't have soundtracks, I created sound effects using movie-score LPs, like composer John Williams's soundtrack for *Earthquake* (1974), which included actual earthquake sounds. Not long after that, I got my first Super 8 movie camera and started making short films with my younger sister.

Movies were always an incredibly important part of my childhood, and it felt natural that I would pursue a career in film. My family didn't really have connections to the movie industry, but my maternal grandmother had worked at Éclair Studios, the number-one processing lab for feature films in France, which was located north of Paris in Épinay-sur-Seine.

By 1978, my grandmother had retired, but that year she managed to arrange for me to work at the color timing department during my summer holiday. I jumped at the chance and found the experience fascinating. Every day we would receive footage—known as dailies—from all the great movies that were being shot in France. Then the technician would work on the color timing, balancing all the shots and building what would eventually become the overall look of the film. It was my first small step toward a career in film, and my grandmother always liked to say that she worked all those years in the darkness of the lab so that she could help me step into the light and realize my ambition as a filmmaker.

As excited as I was about my time in the lab, it paled in comparison to my next piece of film-industry experience. In 1978, the latest James Bond movie, *Moonraker* (1979), was shooting in France. This was unusual, as normally the 007 films were shot at Pinewood Studios in the UK. For tax reasons, however, they had decided to relocate *Moonraker* to France. My dad was a counselor of the Bank of France, as was the gentleman who ran one of the studios where *Moonraker* was being shot, Les Studios d'Epinay. My dad persuaded him to let me spend some time at the studio, so I called in sick to school for a week and found myself on the set of *Moonraker*.

Here I was, at the age of fifteen, inside Hugo Drax's space station! It was an enormous construction conceived by Ken Adam, one of the greatest production designers of all time. I got to see Roger Moore; Richard Kiel, the actor who played Drax's henchman Jaws; and Lois Chiles, the Bond girl Holly Goodhead, plus all the extras running around. I was placed with the sound mixer and his team, but they were annoyed at me because I kept walking around during filming and making noise. I was just so fascinated by everything, thinking, *Oh my god, this is so much fun.* But to them it was a job. I'd get to the studio super early in the morning before the set was even lit. On my first or second day, I saw director Lewis Gilbert—who had also helmed the Bond movies *You Only Live Twice* (1967) and *The Spy Who Loved Me* (1977)—just standing there staring at this set. Years later, I wrote a book on James Bond, and I interviewed Lewis at his home in England. I told him about this moment, and he said, "I was just thinking, *How the hell am I going to film this thing?*"

Being on the set of *Moonraker* was another important step in my understanding of how movie magic springs from the most mundane things. I watched the scene being filmed in which Drax asks Jaws to expel Bond and Holly into space. Two crew guys were lifting the doors to the airlock, and the red emergency lighting was literally a light bulb with a piece of red gel stuck over it. Also, all these Drax minions were at workstations looking like they were typing important information into computers, turning knobs, and so on. But there was nothing there for them to switch on and off—it was all illusion.

It seems very naïve now, but I had never been on a movie set before. This was all a discovery for me. From then on, I would pay closer attention to the way films were made. After seeing a movie, I would come out and look at the lobby cards exhibited outside theaters and think, "Huh, that scene is not in the movie. I don't remember that." That made me realize that not all the scenes make it into the final cut of a movie. Nowadays, you have Blu-ray special features with deleted scenes, gag reels, and so on, but back then we had none of those things. There was a real magic to discovering that there were extra scenes cut out of your favorite film, and that really fed my curiosity about the mysteries of the filmmaking process.

At the time, Paris had more movie theaters than any other city in the world. I went from one theater to the next watching everything, including silent films. But I was always more attracted to American movies than the kinds of films that were made in Europe.

Disaster movies were one of the big mainstays of American cinema at the time. Despite being traumatized by *Airport '75* (1974) and *The Towering Inferno* (1974), I immediately connected to the spectacle in these movies. I've always felt that cinema should be artifice, but a lot of European films at the time were about presenting a slice of life. I wasn't interested in that—I wanted to be transported. I loved the fantasy and escapism that Hollywood filmmaking offered. Big American movies always felt like an event.

Back then, there was often a six-month delay between the US release and the French release of a movie, but interestingly, movie soundtracks were frequently released in France way in advance of the films themselves. Because of this, I would often hear a movie before I saw it. In fact, my first introduction to Steven Spielberg's work came not through seeing his films but through listening to composer John Williams's soundtracks for Steven's first few blockbusters: *Jaws* (1975), *Close Encounters of the Third Kind* (1977), *1941* (1979), and *Raiders of the Lost Ark* (1981).

By the time I discovered Steven's work I was already starting to follow certain directors. I loved Alfred Hitchcock, and when he died in 1980, they rereleased most of his movies. I watched almost his

LES DENTS DE LA MER

LEFT A French lobby card from Laurent Bouzereau's personal collection features Roy Scheider taking on the shark in *Les Dents de la Mer*, aka *Jaws*. The film's French title translates to "The Teeth of the Sea."

entire filmography in the space of a month. François Truffaut was also big for me—not just because he was an acclaimed French director but because he had written a book on Hitchcock and appeared in *Close Encounters*. I was a big collector of film memorabilia, and every Saturday I would go to a movie store in Paris that sold posters and lobby cards, looking for new treasures. One Saturday morning in 1980, I was in the store when Truffaut walked in. I was discussing his new film *The Last Metro* (which was coming out that Wednesday) with the store's owner, and I was stunned to see Truffaut suddenly appear. It was an "open sesame" moment. Here he was in my favorite movie store.

He bought two books (one was by his mentor in film, critic André Bazin), and while he was at the cash register, I started talking to him. We chatted about Hitchcock, his role in *Close Encounters*, and working with Steven Spielberg. I said, "I'm so excited about your new movie, *The Last Metro*," and he

said something I've never forgotten: "I'm so scared about it." At the time I met him, Truffaut's last film, *The Green Room* (1978), had been a financial failure, despite receiving a positive critical reaction. It was so interesting to me that this idol of mine could be so worried about failure; that experience really altered my outlook. I realized that it didn't matter how successful you were as an artist—each time you released a new project into the world, you were still very vulnerable. It was a real lesson in humility. The irony is that *The Last Metro* put Truffaut back on the map as a director. It was a gigantic success worldwide. Sadly, I never saw Truffaut again. He died just a few years later, in 1984, at the age of fifty-two—and that encounter always stayed with me.

My fascination with Steven Spielberg's work began when I was in high school. Under teacher supervision, students ran a cinema club that would show all kinds of movies, including some that were not suitable for kids, like *Deliverance* (1972)! Then one day in

1976, they showed Steven Spielberg's first film, *Duel* (1971), and I was blown away. It was so amazing in its simplicity, and yet it felt huge. I immediately connected with its vivid cinematic language. I was, of course, aware that Spielberg was the director of *Jaws*, a big hit in France that I had not been able to see yet because my parents felt I was too young.

Although I couldn't go to see *Jaws*, I was very aware of the whole mythology around the film and found other ways to experience it. I collected all the *Jaws* photos and posters I could find and covered my bedroom with them wall-to-wall. I finally got to see *Jaws* when it was rereleased a couple of years later and it changed my life completely. I was so fascinated by it and went to see it again and again. I wasn't just enjoying the story; I was looking beyond the frame to understand how the film was made—looking at the continuity and noticing, for instance, how the sky would change from one shot to the next. It wasn't about finding weaknesses in the movie—I wanted to know every single frame of the film and be a true appreciator of it. I wanted to enter that world and understand the camera as a tool, learning how to use it to tell stories and evoke emotions.

> " When *Close Encounters* came along in 1977, I was completely fascinated by the way it first appears to be a scary movie and slowly reveals itself to be something wondrous."

Steven Spielberg was doing this in a spectacular way in the seventies, and I really felt a connection to his sensibilities. When *Close Encounters* came along in 1977, I was completely fascinated by the way it first appears to be a scary movie and slowly reveals itself to be something wondrous. Following *Close Encounters*, he directed *1941*, a World War II spoof that was savaged by critics. But I absolutely loved the film! I was not interested in judging *1941* as a critic—I was interested in how it fit into Spielberg's oeuvre. I was amazed at how this movie emerged from Steven's brain alongside *Jaws* and *Close Encounters*, and wanted to understand how it related to the other films he had made up until then and how it would

relate to everything that came after. I respected him as an artist. All artists, whether they're painters, sculptors, or filmmakers, go through different phases, and these phases need to be understood rather than dismissed. I was falling in love with Steven's cinematic language, and I wanted to really understand it.

Coming to America

In 1977, I made my first trip to the United States, and it opened up a whole new world for me. I went to stay with a family in Athens, Georgia, and the daughter of that family came to stay with the Bouzereau sisters in France. It was an incredible experience for me. My dad said to me, "When you are over there, I want you to write down everything new that you've never seen before." I made this huge list—which I still have to this day—that had everything from marshmallows to twenty-four-hour supermarkets to drive-in theaters. I was getting hooked on American culture, not to mention American movies. That summer saw the release of so many great films, including *Star Wars* (1977), which I saw before all my friends in France—where it wasn't released until October. I knew nothing about *Star Wars* at all, and I was totally astonished. The summer of 1977 also included *The Deep*, *The Spy Who Loved Me*, *The Other Side of Midnight*, and *Orca: The Killer Whale*, which was a *Jaws* knockoff. There was also

ABOVE Bouzereau in Athens, Georgia, in 1977. Photo by Martha Wyllie.

COLUMBIA/EMI présentent

RENCONTRES
DU TROISIEME TYPE

Distribué par WARNER-COLUMBIA FILM
Visa ministériel n° 7.598

the disaster thriller *Rollercoaster* with Sensurround sound. It was like frigging movie heaven!

The whole experience left me with a calling for America—I started to get this feeling that perhaps I'd been born in the wrong country! I loved the huge cars, the gigantic food: I just thought, *I want to live like this.* After returning to France, I finished high school and managed to get a clerical job working for Europex, an export company that sold film rights around the world, including, at the time, *Superman: The Movie* (1978).

Around this time, by pure coincidence, my dad was doing quite a lot of business in America. On one trip to the US via the Concorde, he happened to be seated next to Sally Faile, a rich heiress. They got talking, and it turned out that she had started to produce movies. My dad told her that I wanted to pursue a career in film and would love to be in America, and she said, "Great. Send him over." So, in 1982, I went to New York to work for her. She had just made a little horror film called *The Returning* (1983), starring Susan Strasberg, daughter of legendary actor and acting coach Lee Strasberg. I worked for Gabriel Walsh, Sally's partner at her production company, Willow Productions. I basically did a little bit of everything as they edited and tried to sell their new film—from getting lunch to watching

ABOVE A French *Close Encounters* lobby card from Laurent Bouzereau's collection featuring François Truffaut as UFO expert Claude Lacombe.

RIGHT Indiana Jones (Harrison Ford, *right*) dukes it out with a Nazi stooge (Pat Roach) on a French *Raiders of the Lost Ark* (1981) lobby card.

LES AVENTURIERS de L'ARCHE PERDUE

Visa N° 9172

UN FILM PARAMOUNT Distribué PAR CINEMA INTERNATIONAL CORPORATION
Droits d'auteur Lucasfilm Ltd. (LFL) MCMLXXXI. Tous droits réservés.

cuts to the creation of a promotional poster. I really fell in love with New York in the process.

That summer had huge significance for me because it saw the release of not just Steven Spielberg's masterpiece *E.T. The Extra-Terrestrial* (1982) but also *Poltergeist* (1982), which he produced and co-wrote. Once I saw those films, there was no turning back, and I started making plans to live in the US permanently. Sally decided to leave the movie business and move to Paris, of all places, but she let me live in her apartment in a historical building at 740 Park Avenue while she tried to sell it. It was insane. The walk-in closet was the size of any future apartment I'd have. Needless to say, it was all downhill after that, at least for a while.

Upon settling down in New York, I tried to get work anywhere I could. I ended up working as a publicist for a company called Spectrafilm, which specialized in distributing foreign films in the US. When I joined, they had *Confidentially Yours* (1983), which was actually Truffaut's last movie, and *The 4th Man* (1983), one of director Paul Verhoeven's first features (before *RoboCop*, 1987). I worked there from 1985 through 1988 and got to take some of the films to the Cannes Film Festival, which was exciting. They later closed, like a lot of distribution companies, and I went on to work as a director of future development for Stanley

Buchthal, who had just produced *Hairspray* (1988), directed by John Waters. But by this time, I had grown tired of New York. The city itself had become depressing, and I was struggling financially. My parents suggested I move back to France, but Los Angeles was calling me. I didn't want to bring my US journey to an end without first experiencing the home of Hollywood and the movies I loved so much.

So, in December 1989, I moved out to LA, and within three months, I got a job as story editor for Bette Midler, whose company, All Girl Productions, was on Dopey Drive at Disney Studios. It was a

ABOVE Laurent Bouzereau reads a François Truffaut biography in 1996. Photo by Géraldine Bouzereau.

LEFT A French *E.T. The Extra-Terrestrial* (1982) lobby card featuring Henry Thomas as the film's young protagonist, Elliott.

OFFICE OF
LARRY PALMBERG
(AKA LAURENT BOUZEREAU)
RESIDENT
FRENCH FILM MAKER

Back then, home-entertainment documentaries and other special features weren't as popular as they would eventually become, so I was able to basically walk in off the street and get a job directing and producing a LaserDisc for Amblin and Universal! I was just turned loose to do my own research, with nobody really looking over my shoulder. I remember at one point when I was looking for material on one of Steven's projects, someone at Universal said to me, "We have a dumpster in the back lot. Just go in there and start looking. But wear gloves because it's the summer and there may be rattlesnakes in there." I ended up finding some real treasures, including a concept painting for a *Duel* theatrical poster.

Amblin was happy with my work on *1941*, and after it was released, the fever for special features really started to catch on. The next thing I knew, Universal Pictures Home Entertainment approached me and said, "Hey, why don't we do *Jaws*?" And next came *E.T.* Then Columbia got in touch and said, "Do you want to do *Close Encounters*?" Suddenly I was directing and producing a whole bunch of retrospective documentaries for Steven's films, and for other directors like Brian De Palma and Martin Scorsese. It just became complete madness.

> " Amblin was happy with my work on *1941*, and after it was released, the fever for special features really started to catch on."

I felt Steven and I hit it off when I interviewed him for the *1941* documentary because he could tell that I had such a deep appreciation for a film that has often been maligned. That relationship grew as we worked on the various home-entertainment projects together. Then, in 2000, when Steven was directing *A.I. Artificial Intelligence*, I was hired to join him on set to document the making of the film. Prior to that I had only been producing retrospective documentaries on his older films, but now Steven had invited me to capture his filmmaking process as it was happening, which opened a whole new world for me. Ever since *A.I.*, I've had the privilege of being on set, documenting every one of Steven's films.

Steven has always been extremely generous and kind about my work. I remember in 2005 I won the

hard job because I had to review bad scripts all day long, but I was making progress in other parts of my career. Not only had I written a book on one of my favorite directors, Brian De Palma—*The De Palma Cut* (1988)—I had recorded an audio commentary for the Criterion LaserDisc of one of his most famous films, *Carrie* (1976).

During the nineties, new technology revolutionized home entertainment. The market was then dominated by VHS, but LaserDiscs, which launched in 1978, were becoming increasingly popular with movie enthusiasts despite their higher prices, because of their picture and audio quality and the fact they came with extra features, including documentaries, deleted scenes, and commentaries. Of course, DVDs arrived in the midnineties and soon supplanted LaserDiscs, but before that happened, I regularly visited a store on Ventura Boulevard, Dave's Laser Place, to check out the latest LaserDisc releases. Once, during an event held at the store, I met an executive from Universal Pictures Home Entertainment, Colleen Benn. I told her that I'd love to be involved in some way with producing the extra features on LaserDiscs, and eventually, this contact and another connection led to a meeting with Martin Cohen, the head of postproduction at Amblin Entertainment, Steven Spielberg's production company.

Marty was an incredible force. He had started off in the cutting room, working on Spielberg's adaptation of the Alice Walker novel *The Color Purple* (1985). From there he'd risen to become head of postproduction. When we met in 1993, Marty had just worked on *Jurassic Park* (1993) and *Schindler's List* (1993). Marty said, "I heard you like *1941*. We're doing a new cut of the film, and we should do a documentary. Do you want to do it?" It was crazy. Of course, I said yes, and that's how I first met Steven Spielberg.

ABOVE A plaque created by Amblin to welcome Laurent Bouzereau back to the office after his American citizenship ceremony in 1998.

OPPOSITE TOP An ad placed by Lucasfilm to congratulate Bouzereau on receiving the Pioneer Award in *Variety*'s 2005 DVD Exclusive Awards.

OPPOSITE BOTTOM Steven Spielberg (*left*) and Bouzereau celebrate the release of the Netflix/Amblin Television 2017 documentary series, *Five Came Back*. Spielberg served as executive producer in addition to being interviewed for the series.

Pioneer Award at the DVD Exclusive Awards. For the ceremony, Steven kindly recorded a congratulatory speech, which was so incredibly gracious. Steven's movies forged my taste and, frankly, gave me a career. Never in a million years did I think I was going to be part of that world, even in my own modest way.

That's the thing I love about America. It was such a tough, ten-year climb to get to the point where I was given a career-making opportunity at Amblin. Even though there were times when I didn't know where my next job was coming from, I never thought I was going to fail. I always thought, *Well, I'll be doing something in film.* I didn't set out to become a documentary filmmaker. My dream was, and still is, to direct narrative features. But this was part of the dream.

In 1998, I became an American citizen. After the naturalization ceremony, I came back to the Amblin building on the Universal lot to discover they had fitted a plaque to my door that said "The office of Larry Palmberg." Before that, I had joked that when I became an American, I was going to change my first name to Larry and my surname to Palmberg, a portmanteau of my two favorite directors, Brian De Palma and Steven Spielberg. Amblin and Universal threw a dinner party for me and presented me with an American flag. This great moment was symbolic of my whole journey—my love of American movies leading me to become an American myself. I couldn't be more appreciative of the journey that I've been able to have.

Working with Steven Spielberg over the last three decades, my fascination with his filmmaking has only grown. Observing him at work on so many different films, energetically conjuring up new scenes on the fly, always in the thick of the action on set, has further fueled my appreciation of his unique gift.

As much as I am fascinated by every stage of Steven's career, the first ten years of his filmmaking will always hold a special place in my heart. This book is my love letter to that formative period in his career that gave the world, and me, so much inspiration. Having interviewed Steven at length about every film from that era and having become something of an expert on these movies through the process of making documentaries on many of them, I felt it was time to share my personal love and appreciation for them with other fans around the world.

Although my career with Amblin and Steven began with *1941*, I decided to start at the beginning with the movie that first announced to the world that Steven Spielberg was a filmmaker of rare talent, *Duel.*

I

DUEL

(1971)

" I'd like to report a truck driver that's been endangering my life."

—David Mann (Dennis Weaver)

The premise of *Duel* is simple: During a business trip, salesman David Mann (Dennis Weaver) gets on the wrong side of the driver of a Peterbilt truck who pursues him mercilessly through the highways and byways of Southern California. Richard Matheson wrote the script based on his own short story. Matheson was the brilliant author of *I Am Legend* (1954), *Hell House* (1971), and many other genre classics. He was very much part of the generation that reinvented science fiction and horror during that period. Steven read *Duel*, loved it, and soon found out that Matheson was already in the process of writing the screenplay adaptation. Although Matheson's adaptation was masterful, Steven ultimately elevated his script to become something even more cinematic, going beyond what was on the page.

When Steven made *Duel*, he was under contract at Universal as a TV director. He started out directing shows like *Night Gallery*, an anthology series very much in the spirit of *The Twilight Zone*—both were created by the legendary Rod Serling. These shows presented dark fables, often stories where the protagonist gets something they desire only to find that it ultimately destroys them. That sensibility is apparent in *Duel*—perhaps unsurprisingly, since Matheson also wrote for *The Twilight Zone*—and it would later surface in Steven's own anthology series, *Amazing Stories*, which debuted in the mideighties.

Steven got his TV contract at Universal after Sidney Sheinberg, the head of the studio, saw his short film *Amblin'* (1968), the story of two hitchhikers making their way through the Mojave Desert. The film is only twenty-six minutes long, but it was so striking that Sheinberg gave Steven a seven-year contract. In the 1970s, the whole mentality of Hollywood was changing. A new wave of younger

directors was coming in to replace the old guard. This revolution led to the rise of what became known as the Movie Brats, a group of firebrand young filmmakers who would transform the industry. Along with Steven there was George Lucas (*Star Wars*, 1977), Francis Ford Coppola (*The Godfather*, 1972), Brian De Palma (*Carrie*, 1976), Martin Scorsese (*Taxi Driver*, 1976), and John Milius (*Big Wednesday*, 1978). They all knew each other and were facing the same sorts of struggles dealing with outdated studio systems and attitudes. It was a very special period in cinema history, with the Movie Brats taking on Old Hollywood and ushering in a new era.

In just a few years, Steven would make *Jaws* and completely change the face of cinema. But before that, like all the other filmmakers of his generation, he was striving to get his own feature films made and working in TV just to get his foot in the door. Despite this, when you watch Steven's early TV work, his cinematic language is readily apparent. Steven's first job at Universal was directing a segment of the *Night Gallery* pilot (1969)—which was split into three different stories, each helmed by a different director. Steven's story, "Eyes," stars Joan Crawford, an absolute legend of cinema any young filmmaker would be intimidated to direct. The story revolves around Crawford's character, a rich, self-obsessed blind woman who pays a luckless gambler (Tom Bosley) for his eyes, undergoing a surgical procedure that replaces her own eyeballs with his, giving her sight for a period of just twelve hours. It's a simple one-act play, but the way Steven approaches it is incredibly visual. When the doctor (Barry Sullivan) first visits Crawford's character, we see him upside down, and then the camera pulls back and we realize it's shot through the crystal of a chandelier, which is causing the reorientation of the image. It's a great touch but not the kind of thing that was often

PAGES 22–23 David Mann (Dennis Weaver) is threatened by a monster truck in *Duel*.

OPPOSITE The cover of the script for the pilot episode of *Night Gallery*, Steven Spielberg's first television assignment for Universal.

NIGHT GALLERY

No. 26562

January 3, 1969

UNIVERSAL CITY STUDIOS
UNIVERSAL CITY, CALIFORNIA

seen in television at the time, and it immediately communicates to the viewer that there's something twisted about the transaction taking place between the two characters. When Crawford's character finally removes the bandages, there's an electrical blackout, and Steven films her distress in a near-surrealistic way, against black, taking us directly into her own mindset: She is experiencing darkness both figuratively and literally. He was reinventing the language of television and bringing an additional layer to what would have been a typical TV episode in another director's hands.

Through little moments like this, you get a sense of his desire to break away from the regular studio way of shooting a TV show.

Duel was produced as a TV movie, but it was executed so well that Universal decided to give it an international theatrical release. In fact, they had Steven go back and shoot a few more scenes to lengthen the run time. This longer version was exclusively created for the international market and wasn't released in the US until much later. TV movies at the time were often seen as very disposable,

FULL FACE OF MISS MENLO
ZOOM BACK

TO FULL FIGURE — SHE TURNS 3 TIMES
IN BEWILDERMENT

SHE CROSSES RIGHT DISSOLVE INTO
MED. SHOT — STATE OF PANIC —

BACK OF HEAD ARMS EXTENDED

BACK OF HEAD WITH DOWN SHOT
OF MISS MENLO

SHE DESCENDS STAIRCASE

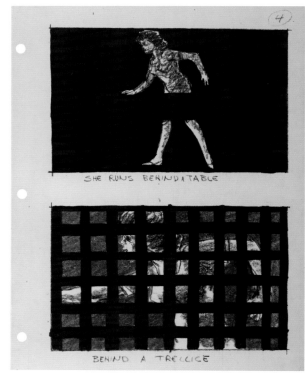

SHE RUNS BEHIND A TABLE

BEHIND A TRELLICE

❝ *Something Evil* follows a young couple that moves into a house with their young boy who becomes possessed. It's interesting because it has shades of *Poltergeist* (1982)."

so it was unusual for a studio to spend money on converting one into a theatrical release. It turned out to be very popular in Europe. The film was selected for the Avoriaz International Fantastic Film Festival in France, which was essentially like the Cannes Film Festival for horror and science-fiction movies. I first heard of *Duel* because it won the grand prize at Avoriaz in 1973, the year the festival began.

Interestingly, Steven also directed other TV movies, including *Something Evil* (1972), a supernatural thriller. This came out right after

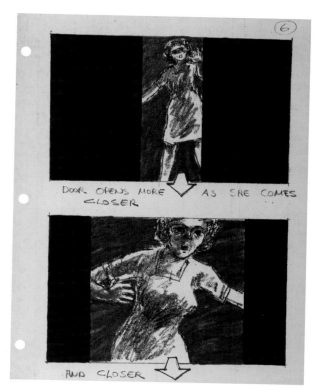

DOOR OPENS MORE AS SHE COMES CLOSER

AND CLOSER

SHE PRESSES AGAINST WALLS AS SHE MOVES AWAY FROM CAMERA

SHE GETS SMALLER AS SHE MOVES AWAY FROM CAMERA

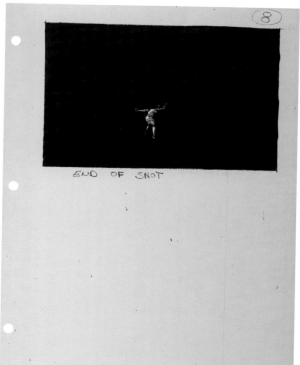

END OF SHOT

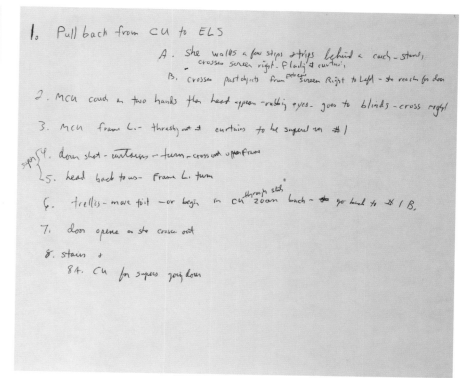

William Peter Blatty's book *The Exorcist* became a huge hit in 1971—and two years later, William Friedkin released his film adaptation to huge acclaim. *Something Evil* follows a young couple that moves into a house with their young boy who becomes possessed. It's interesting because it has shades of *Poltergeist* (1982)—the boy is a conduit to some kind of supernatural force, which is the crux of that film as well. *Something Evil* doesn't quite have the same impact as *Duel*, which is timeless, but it's certainly very creepy.

After that, Steven directed another TV movie called *Savage* (1973), which stars Martin Landau, Barbara Bain, and Carl Gottlieb, who had appeared in *Something Evil* in a tiny part and would go on to co-write *Jaws* and appear in a small role in the film. *Savage* was written by Richard Levinson and William Link, the guys who created *Columbo*— Steven directed the first episode of *Columbo* season one, "Murder by the Book" (1971), so he had a prior working relationship with them. *Savage* is a very convoluted political story about a reporter

PRODUCERS: William Link
Richard Levinson

PROD. #33302
May 7, 1971 (F.R.)
Rev. 5/12/71 (F.R.)
Rev. 5/18/71 (F.R.)

[handwritten annotations:] casting call Jo Scully at Warners — Hoke Howell — Sargeant — Joanna Barnes — Dina ~~Hyatt~~ Merril — Janet Lee — Carolyn Jones — John Aston — ferris — Anne Jackson — Hope Lang — David Wayne — ferris

COLUMBO

MURDER BY THE BOOK

by

Steven Bochco

[handwritten annotations:] retakes — Scene 50 — entryway — ferris show Columbo Franklin (CU franklin + 2 tight shot franklin) — NOW I've really got you — Columbo coming anyway — ① Drive up — ② Lobby — ③ Police outside office door — ④ Mess up office + fill with CU for registration dissolve — ⑤ Insert typing typewriter 1st paragraph — ⑥ Peters nifty stuff — ⑦ Columbo 1st entrance by drink fountain

— PLEASE NOTE —

investigating compromising photography of a Supreme Court nominee. It's a film that Steven didn't really want to direct at that stage of his career; following the international success of *Duel*, he was looking forward to directing feature films full time.

Primal Fear

Duel is absolutely bursting with ideas and layered with themes that continue to surface in Steven's films to this day. It's no surprise that the world of television was so limiting for a director eager to move into features and further develop his cinematic language. At the heart of *Duel* is a sense of primal fear that is very relatable. We've all been in situations where we get into some kind of disagreement or altercation with a stranger, perhaps through a road rage incident, and fear it could escalate into something we can't control. In *Duel*,

bad things happen to good people without reason, which is such a fundamental concept.

The thing that Steven really understood when directing *Duel* is that, while the story appears to be a thriller on the surface, it's actually a horror film. The truck is driven by a person, but we never see his face, just his arms and feet operating the vehicle. The truck itself is presented as the antagonist and has the feel of a gunslinger—it looks like something from another more savage era and is decorated with the license plates of its apparent kills. The truck feels almost paranormal, even though the film does not outwardly have the trappings of the genre. I consider *Duel* a supernatural film, and the fact that we never see the truck driver's face is not just a convention of suspense; the truck driver's anonymity hints at something much darker and more irrational. *Duel* is much like *Jaws* in that regard. In *Jaws*, the people of Amity Island are terrorized by a

OPPOSITE Steven Spielberg's personal copy of the script for "Murder by the Book," the first episode of *Columbo's* first season, which was one of the young filmmaker's early directing assignments at Universal.

ABOVE Dennis Weaver as the everyday "Mann" in *Duel*.

killer shark, an idea taken from real-world headlines. Around the world, shark attacks are an everyday threat, but Steven portrays the shark in *Jaws* as a devilish monster out to kill innocent victims. Like *Duel*, this speaks to the randomness of evil and our primal fear of attack. *Jaws* is widely perceived as, in part, a horror film, and *Duel* comes from that same stable. To me, *Duel* has much in common with more traditional horror movies like John Carpenter's *Halloween* (1978), particularly the way in which the face of the killer, Michael Myers, is obscured by a mask. It's an incredibly unsettling trope, a killer without a face, and it fires the audience's imagination to new levels of tension and fear.

One of the most terrifying aspects of *Duel* is the way in which David Mann struggles to get help from regular folks as he attempts to escape the truck. Even though it's clear to the viewer that he's being ruthlessly pursued by the driver, Mann's pleas are ignored by bystanders. No one really believes him, except perhaps the character played by Lucille Benson (owner of a snake farm/gas station where the truck tries to kill Mann) and an elderly couple he stops on the road. Mann even struggles to articulate what's going on. He's like someone waking from a bad dream and trying to explain what scared them while they

> ❝ Is it possible that Mann is delusional, tormented by the demons of his failing marriage to the point where he believes he's being persecuted by a demonic truck?❞

were asleep.

In the theatrical release, new scenes were added in which we learn that Mann's marriage is under pressure, and his wife (Jacqueline Scott) thinks that he's not strong enough to stand up for her. Is it possible that Mann is delusional, tormented by the demons of his failing marriage to the point where he believes he's being persecuted by a demonic truck? Is the truck a symbol of his impending divorce and how he feels about his wife? Is it a rite of passage, the ultimate test that will force him into a new way of life—if he survives?

RIGHT A lobby card for *Duel* from France.

OPPOSITE Dennis Weaver as David Mann. Steven Spielberg cast the actor based on his performance in Orson Welles's masterpiece *Touch of Evil* (1958).

A Cinematic Approach

Duel also shows Spielberg's appreciation for the cinematic legacy of Alfred Hitchcock, particularly the sequence at a roadside diner, Chuck's Café, which truly belongs alongside the paranoid aspect of the crop-duster sequence from Hitchcock's *North by Northwest* (1959). The suspense starts after Mann slams into a fence when dodging the truck, which continues past him and seems to almost magically disappear. In one long shot, we follow Mann from his car to the café, and then to the bathroom and back to the main dining room, passing a pool table—until this long shot is interrupted by the shock of Mann seeing the truck parked right outside. To underline the reveal, Steven cuts to balls hitting on the pool table. Not only does this create a jump, but it thematically tells us: This is a game—and Mann's death is the goal. Mann then sits down and orders—with the waitress oddly framed to the right so the shot can include the truck, with the reverse shot on Mann including the shadow of the neon sign on the wall. What follows is a descent into Mann's paranoia as he tries to guess who among the patrons in the café might be the truck driver. The suspense is masterfully devised to trigger our emotions, but the scene also shows that Mann is on his own. It is so brilliantly distracting that we forget that Mann could call the cops, or drive in another direction, or escape out the back door of the café. Like Hitchcock at his best, Spielberg focuses his energy on pure cinema and on making us believe that logic is of no importance.

BELOW The Peterbilt truck that Spielberg picked to serve as the antagonist in *Duel*.

OPPOSITE David Mann (Dennis Weaver) becomes increasingly panicked by the truck's relentless pursuit.

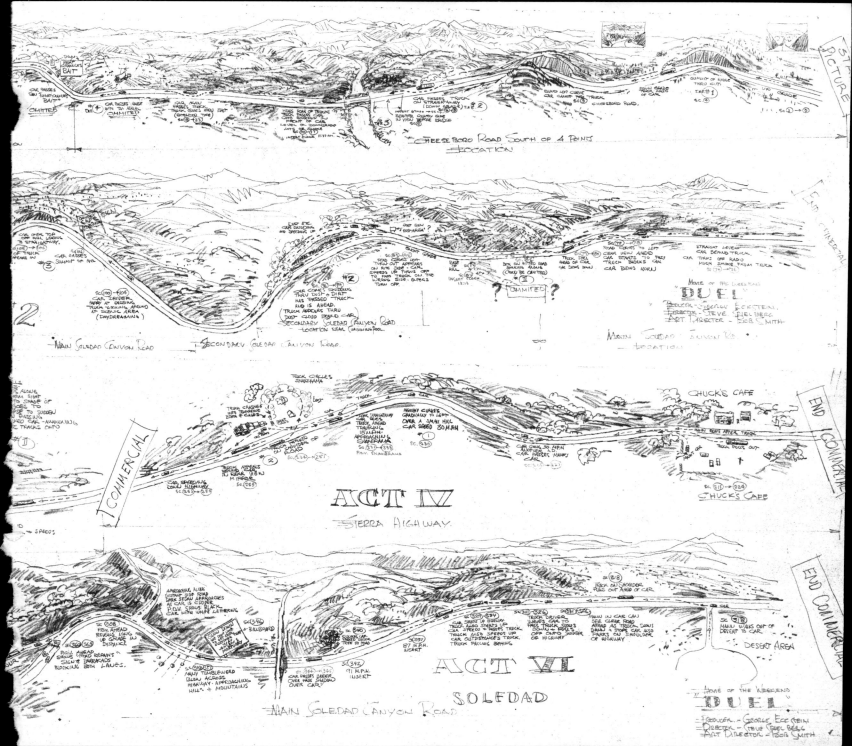

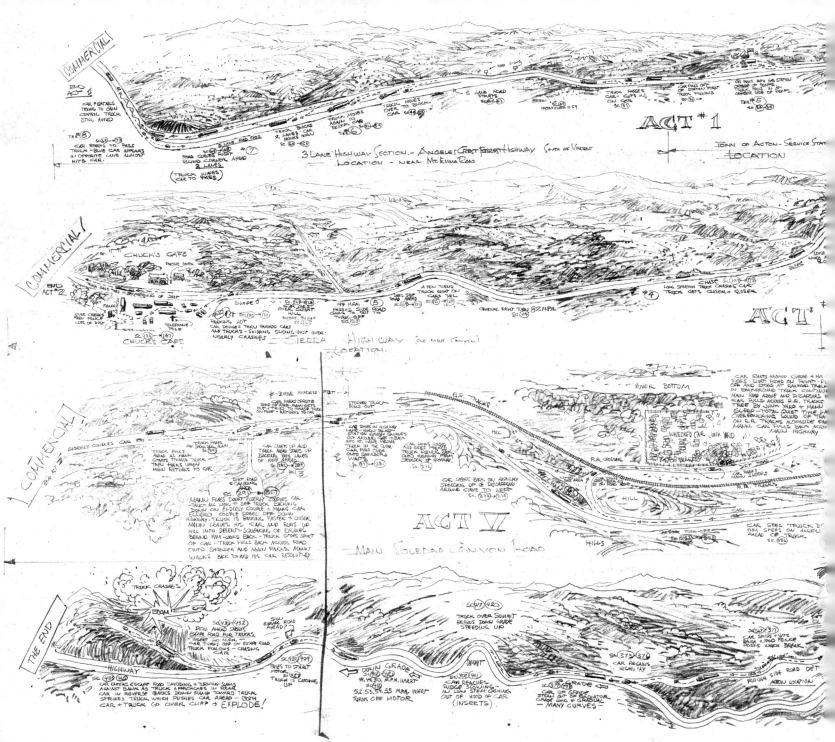

The Real Thing

Obviously, *Duel* was filmed before the advent of digital effects. It was also made on a shoestring budget; the original shoot lasted around twelve to thirteen days, and so Steven really had to think on his feet. One technique he employed was using the same stretches of road multiple times, but shooting them from different angles, so it seemed like a completely different area each time. He's always displayed an exceptional understanding of editing and instinctively knows when he has what is needed for a scene.

I remember being on set with him during the shooting of *War Horse* (2011). He wasn't quite getting what he needed from the real horse that

BELOW Two French lobby cards for *Duel* show the stricken truck after Mann taunts it over a cliff in the film's finale.

OPPOSITE A film still captures the wreckage of the Peterbilt truck following the successful cliff drop stunt.

day, and at one point he just said, "If the next take doesn't work out, I know how to cut this." Like all great filmmakers, he can edit in his head. He's worked with some incredible editors over the years, including his mainstay editor Michael Kahn, who has edited most of his movies, along with Verna Fields on *The Sugarland Express* (1974) and *Jaws* and Carol Littleton on *E.T.* But from the very start, Steven had an intrinsic understanding of how the footage he was capturing in the moment would translate into a final cut, even on his first feature.

Some directors need to have ten different cameras to make sure they are getting a huge amount of coverage, so they have options in the cutting room.

Steven is not like that: He knows exactly what he wants, and he knows how to get it. Alfred Hitchcock was similar. He would have his art department build the exact part of a set he was going to show in a frame because his vision of what was going to be in each shot was so absolute. Steven is the same, but that's not to say that he isn't spontaneous when he shoots—he's one of the most energetic, innovative, in-the-moment filmmakers I've ever met. But you can only improvise if you're mega prepared, since at that point you know the context in which you're working, and that gives you the freedom to explore.

Another brilliant thing about *Duel* is that it all takes place during the daytime. Directors often use darkness to create a sense of foreboding, which isn't possible with a film that takes place in daylight. But in *Duel*, Steven evokes the loneliness of these deserted highways and everyday settings and really finds suspense in them. It's scary because it's unexpected—there's no creature hiding in the dark, and it's all out in the open.

Of course, one of the key aspects of *Duel*'s success is the performance of Dennis Weaver, who has to carry much of the film on his own. Weaver was best known for his television work at the time, but he had also appeared in Orson Welles's *Touch of Evil* (1958), a film that Steven loves. While Steven is often associated with big, special-effects-heavy blockbusters, at heart he really is an actor's director. Actors just love working with him because he knows how to get the best performance from them. Sometimes a director has a vision for a performance in their own head, but they struggle to communicate it to an actor. That's never the case with Steven. I can't count the number of times I've heard actors on his sets say, "He just said one word to me, and I got what he wanted." That comes from confidence. When you feel comfortable with someone, you open up. And Steven is very good at putting his actors at ease.

Duel at Home

There are a lot of interesting themes in *Duel* that give Matheson's simple story great depth. Like all the films from this era of Steven's work, home plays an important thematic role. The threat of never being able to return home is what drives Mann's actions. We only get a small glimpse into his home life through the added scene in which he calls his wife from the road. He makes the call from a laundromat, the camera framing part of the conversation through the open door of a washing machine as a woman loads her clothes. It's that type of detail that immediately tells the viewer to pay attention: It's almost like looking through a peephole, as if you are witnessing something you should not be seeing. It's a very domestic scene filled with subtext that informs the audience that not only is Mann's marriage in trouble, but his masculinity is in question, and he is perhaps also failing to recognize his spouse as anything other than a housewife. Of course, the theme of threatened manhood at the center of the film is also reinforced by the name of the character, David Mann. His name also helps position him as someone we can root for and relate to—he is literally an everyman.

The idea that Weaver's character is somehow

UNIVERSAL présente
DUEL
avec **DENNIS WEAVER**

Scénario de **RICHARD MATHESON** d'après son histoire   Réalisé par **STEVEN SPIELBERG**   Produit par **GEORGE ECKSTEIN**

TECHNICOLOR · UN FILM UNIVERSAL DISTRIBUE PAR CINEMA INTERNATIONAL CORPORATION

UNIVERSAL présente **DUEL** avec **DENNIS WEAVER**
Scénario de RICHARD MATHESON d'après son histoire
Réalisé par STEVEN SPIELBERG
Produit par GEORGE ECKSTEIN
TECHNICOLOR - UN FILM UNIVERSAL DISTRIBUE PAR CINEMA INTERNATIONAL CORPORATION

" The film includes many shots of Weaver in the rearview and side mirrors of his car, which only show part of his face and imply that he is somehow only part man."

lacking as a man is reinforced by Steven's framing. The film includes many shots of Weaver in the rearview and side mirrors of his car, which only show part of his face and imply that he is somehow only part man. Only by confronting the truck can he become whole again and put his crumbling personal life behind him.

I love how Steven uses Mann's attaché case. It symbolizes Mann's work and livelihood, and it's ultimately what saves his life when he uses it to jam down the accelerator on his car, crashing it into the truck, and luring it over the edge of a cliff. Steven often uses everyday objects to represent something

much more meaningful. The most notable example might be in *E.T. The Extra-Terrestrial*: The humble phone becomes a symbol of intergalactic communication. Whether Steven is evoking fear or wonder, he gives the audience something they can relate to that helps bring the story home.

After luring the truck over the cliff to its "death," Mann becomes hysterical, jumping and laughing with joy. Interestingly, Roy Scheider's Chief Brody reacts in a very similar way when he finally kills the shark in *Jaws*. The ending of *Duel* is also very sad— following the truck's symbolic death, Mann settles into quiet contemplation, almost as if his reason for being has died along with the truck. The sense is that Mann has just been through this terrifying experience and conquered his foe, emerging triumphant, but now he must go home and tackle his personal life. The ending holds a real sense of dread, and it's an approach Steven would reprise to some extent on *The Sugarland Express*, which has a similarly contemplative ending.

Because the truck does not explode at the end of *Duel*, there is something restrained about the scene. It doesn't vanish in a ball of flame as it might in a typical Hollywood film, and this makes the sequence even more fascinating and unpredictable.

ABOVE A very rare behind-the-scenes image from *Duel* on a French lobby card shows the crew during shooting at the gas station/ snake farm location.

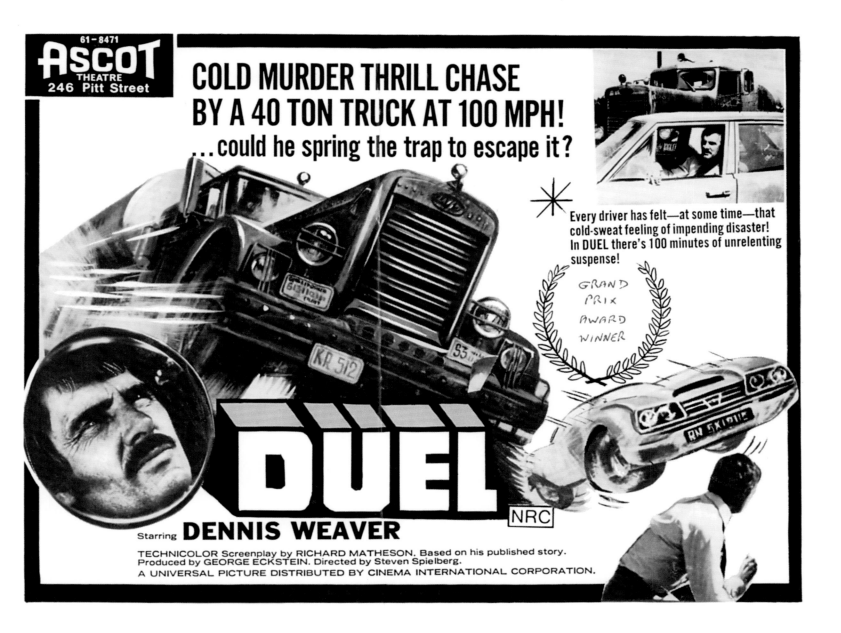

In *Duel*, Steven often seems to buck conventions in a very deliberate way that really elevates the film way above standard TV-movie fare. What is also fascinating is the way Steven treats the truck like a living, breathing creature: When it goes over the cliff and crashes to the bottom, we feel as if this manmade object is actually dying. The *Duel* score, composed by Billy Goldenberg, plays a key part in selling that idea. Goldenberg's use of percussion is very primal and gives the sense that the truck is some kind of organic creature.

By the way, I have always thought that the driver of the truck doesn't die. If you watch the film closely, the cabin door is open when the truck goes over the cliff, which I interpret to mean he could have jumped out.

The Road to *Sugarland*

Duel was an incredible debut for Steven, and its success overseas really opened the world for him—

in a literal sense, since the first time he ever traveled to Europe was on a promotional tour for the film. Finally seeing Europe, where he met people like Italian filmmaker Federico Fellini, had a huge impact on him. It's no coincidence that his next film, *The Sugarland Express*, his first official feature, is his most European movie in terms of its themes and style. It's an American movie in the sense that it takes place in America and features a great deal of Americana, but its sensibilities are heavily influenced by the kinds of films that the French, British, and Italians were making. The so-called heroes are two outlaws on the run—a couple trying to reach their infant son who has been put into protective care. Ultimately, the ending is tragic and there's no neat resolution.

The so-called Movie Brats were really obsessed with French New Wave directors like François Truffaut—European filmmakers who would shoot in the street or on the road, which is essentially what Steven did on both *Duel* and *The Sugarland Express*.

ABOVE An ad for the Australian release of *Duel*.

SPIELBERG ON *DUEL*

Can you tell me about your relationship to television and filmmaking before you made *Duel*?

When I first started out directing, I had no interest in television. In fact, I was really a snob about TV. I wanted to direct movies. But when I was twenty-one years old, going on twenty-two, I was offered a contract by Sid Sheinberg who ran Universal—and I was faced with the reality that there wasn't a movie producer in the world who was going to give me a feature just because I wanted to direct film. And there were probably very few TV producers anxious to hire me. So, I quickly decided that I would fight very hard to start in television, use it as a training ground, and if I did good there, maybe somebody would give me a movie.

The first thing I did, of course, was the Joan Crawford *Night Gallery* episode, which Sid Sheinberg kind of muscled me through. The producers weren't so sure they wanted to hire me because I was so young—it was crazy. And then after that, I didn't work for about a year. I took off a year from my contract and just did some writing. I came back and did another episode of *Night Gallery* called "Make Me Laugh" [and] a feature-length episode of *The Name of the Game* titled "L.A. 2017," and then a friend of mine, Jerrold Freedman, was producing a series called *The Psychiatrist*, starring Roy Thinnes, and asked me if I wanted to direct a couple of episodes. I directed the first one and the middle one. And that was a great experience, it was fantastic. I realized, "Wow, you can be creative in television—even though the time pressure is enormous!" In the early seventies, you had five days for an hour episode. And yet, you could get a lot done in a day's work. Of course, it wasn't an eight-hour or ten-hour day; we were shooting fourteen-, fifteen-hour days, just to get all the shots in. But it was a great experience for me to start out in that way. The Joan Crawford experience wasn't so pleasant because

it had a lot of interference from everybody you can possibly imagine trying to save my ass. I didn't think it needed saving, but they did, and I went along with the ride. Then I realized, well, maybe it does need saving, maybe I'm not doing a very good job. I had a lot of people giving me advice—I didn't want to come across as a maverick, independent filmmaker, screaming: "I'm off to New York to make underground films." So, I just pretty much played by their rules. In contrast, when Jerry Freedman came to me to direct *The Psychiatrist*, he had no restrictions and just said, "Hey, do whatever you want. Make it into a little art film. You can be New Wave, you can be avant-garde, or as esoteric as you want." That was a wonderful sign of friendship—I took his advice and made a very strange show out of the first hour. And it proved to me that television was fun, and that it was a nice place to start working.

I love your *Columbo* episode, "Murder by the Book." I first saw it as a kid in France. I remember noticing all those great visual ideas. It just felt creative and cinematic.

What I tried to bring to TV was a lesser emphasis on the close-up—movies are about master shots and letting the audience look at the overview. Orson Welles, certainly, John Ford, and Howard Hawks shot wide—and when they went in for the close-up, it was to tell a story—to drum home a point. They used a close-up as a powerful tool of narrative storytelling. Television seemed to use the close-up because screens were so small. They wanted people to see what the actors were saying; they wanted to get mouth movement. So, when I came to television, I used wider shots, and it got me, in a strange way, noticed, simply because I was shooting differently than most television directors.

But I wasn't doing a lot of TV work. I was trying to pick and choose. But most television producers

OPPOSITE A *Duel* poster created by artist Michel Landi for the French theatrical rerelease.

40　SPIELBERG THE FIRST TEN YEARS

MOVIE OF THE WEEKEND

D U E L

ACT ONE

FADE IN

1   EXT. OPEN COUNTRY - HELICOPTER SHOT - DAY   1

Behind titles, we see Mann's car (a low-power, economy model)
being driven along a two-lane, rural highway. No music; only
the faint sounds of his car motor and those of two widely
separated vehicles he passes which are going in the opposite
direction. Titles end.

2   MOVING SHOT - MANN'S CAR   2

Camera drawing straight ahead of the car as it is driven along
the curving back country highway. Camera starts to slow down
after several moments and the car moves closer until we see
Mann more clearly.

3   INT. CAR - ANGLE ON MANN   3

His suit coat off, his tie removed and shirt collar opened, his
sleeve cuffs folded back twice, a harness strap diagonal across
his chest. There is sunlight on his left arm and on part of
his lap. His hair is ruffled by the wind from the open window
at his left. He is humming softly with the music on the car
radio, the fingers of his right hand tapping idly on the steer-
ing wheel. Camera draws around him slowly, revealing a curving grade ahead between two high hills. Just visible, climbing
the grade, is a truck pulling a tank trailer. Camera moves down
to the speedometer, Mann is holding his speed at a steady 55
miles per hour. After several moments, camera pans to the
dashboard clock and holds. It is 11:31.

4   HELICOPTER SHOT - MANN'S CAR   4

Camera shooting from the left and at a shallow downward angle.
Now the camera starts to pull ahead, drawing around so that
Mann's car remains in sight. After a while, the truck is revealed foot by foot; a gigantic gasoline tanker truck pulling
a tank trailer, each of them having six wheels. It is not a
new rig but dented and in need of renovation, its tanks painted
a cheap looking silver color. We hear the grinding strain of
the truck's motor. The vertical pipe to the left of the cab
is spewing dark smoke which clouds back across the trailer.
Mann's car starts to close in on the truck and trailer.

K films
présente

STEVEN SPIELBERG

avec DENNIS WEAVER / scénario RICHARD MATHESON d'après son histoire / réalisé par STEVEN SPIELBERG / produit par GEORGE ECKSTEIN

ABOVE David Mann (Dennis Weaver) runs for the refuge of his car during one of the truck attacks.

OPPOSITE TOP Is this all a bad dream? David Mann (Weaver) questions his own sanity.

❝❝ Bottom line, I was grateful when anybody gave me a job in television— I was always able to do a couple of shots that I was proud of . . .❞

weren't interested in working with "this kid." They were much more interested in Abner Biberman or Virgil Vogel—who was a friend of mine and helped me a lot when I first got started—or Richard Benedict, an actor turned TV director, a wonderful director. These were fine directors who had proven themselves again and again. Producers went to them before ever going to me. And the few shows I was offered I didn't care for. But after starving [laughs] and needing to make a little money, I went back to Sid Sheinberg and said, "Okay, Sid, I'll work for my dinner." And, he replied, "Well, we need journeymen." I agreed and he got me episodes of *Marcus Welby, M.D.* and *Owen Marshall: Counselor at Law*. Both were great situations for me, but in the case of *Marcus Welby*, you couldn't have asked for a greater movie star to work with than Robert Young. I was able to talk to him. He had his

character down, and I wasn't going to inform him or give him revisionist directions about Marcus Welby. He was very gracious to me and not resentful of my age— which was such a problem in those days, especially in television, where the average age of a crew member was fifty-five years old. Bottom line, I was grateful when anybody gave me a job in television—I was always able to do a couple of shots that I was proud of and would tell myself, "I got away with that. Nobody fired me, that's great."

And then, when I met William Link and Richard Levinson, who were the creators and producers of *Columbo*, and Steven Bochco, who was writing for them at the time, they asked me if I would do the first show of the season after the success of the pilot episode with Gene Barry and Peter Falk. It was a great honor to be invited to do that, and when I read the script, I thought, *Man, this is the best script anybody has ever given me, ever, to direct*. The writer was Steven Bochco.

So, I treated that like a little mini-movie and made it with the psychology of a film director, not a TV director. I thought, *They're giving me $130,000 for this hour, but I'm going to make it look like a million bucks*. Russell Metty was my director of photography [he shot Stanley Kubrick's *Spartacus* (1960), John Huston's *The Misfits* (1961), and Orson Welles's *Touch of Evil*].

How did you connect with *Duel*?

Columbo was a great experience for me and was as close as I had ever come to making a movie. I was sitting around the office one day, looking through scripts, continuing to write, trying to get my little feature ideas off the ground, trying to get somebody to hire me to do a first film. Nona Tyson, my assistant, found *Duel*. I was very fond of her. She said, "I read this short story by Richard Matheson in *Playboy* magazine. . . ." I was surprised: "What do you mean, *Playboy* magazine?" She explained there were great fiction stories published in *Playboy*, and she pointed to *Duel*. I read it and felt it was terrifying. I thought, *This is like a Hitchcock movie. It's like* Psycho *or* The Birds, *only it's on wheels. A truck chasing a salesman through the desert!*

Nona also found out that Richard Matheson was in the process of writing a screenplay and that it was going to be done as a "Movie of the Week," produced by George Eckstein. I called up George Eckstein, who I'd never met, but he knew of me because I was often mentioned as "Sheinberg's folly"—basically, the youngest person under a term contract in Universal's history. I was regarded as this young filmmaker who loved lenses and dolly shots but didn't know anything about acting—that was the

reputation I had then. In any case, George invited me over to his office and asked me to bring the work I was proudest of. So, I brought over the rough cut of *Columbo*, which hadn't even aired yet. He saw the cut, then he called me back to his office and said, "Okay, give me your ideas and how you'd like to make this into a movie," and he handed me the script of *Duel*. I read it and returned with all my ideas, and he said he'd get back to me. A day went by, two days went by—I didn't hear a thing. On the third day I got a call from George, who said, "Okay, I'd like you to direct this." It was the second greatest phone call I ever had, the first being when Sheinberg got me out of college to be a director. And that's how it all began.

What was your impression of Richard Matheson? He was already a cult figure with his episodes of *The Twilight Zone*, the movie *The Incredible Shrinking Man* [1957], based on his book, and his novels *I Am Legend* and *Hell House*.

I was intimately familiar with the work of Richard Matheson because I was a complete, obsessive, compulsive *Twilight Zone* follower. Certainly, I'm a big fan of *The Incredible Shrinking Man*. At the same time I met him, I also met Ray Bradbury for the first time, so it was a banner week for me.

> **What took time was getting complicated shots moving in and out of the truck, pulling ahead of the truck with the car coming into the shot . . ."**

One of the great aspects of _Duel_ is that you never see the driver, which makes it almost a horror movie.

My attraction to the project wasn't because it was a kind of horror movie, but I thought it was just a complete cat-and-mouse game with classic suspense. And, to give credit where credit is due, it's Richard Matheson—it was very clear in his teleplay that you didn't see the driver. You might see a hand or his boots, but you never saw his identity. That notion attracted me more than anything else because the unseen is always more frightening than what you throw in the audience's face.

How did you visually approach the movie?

First, I didn't quite know how I was going to achieve this film in ten days. I had ten days to shoot a seventy-three-minute film. They assigned me a very venerable and highly regarded production manager named Wallace Worsley. He was kind of gruff—he was a pussycat on the inside, but on the outside, he was a tough person who looked at me and often gave these derisive snorts of, "Yeah, prove it. Prove you can make this into a movie. Because if you can't, you're history, son, and we'll bring somebody else in who can." I really respected that. He took a hardline position with me.

I explained how I was going to shoot _Duel_ entirely on location. Worsley said to me, "You cannot shoot a movie of this scale on location in ten days. You need to send somebody else out to shoot background plates and do the film on a soundstage using rear projection." He let me call him Wally, and I went: "Wally, it will look fake. It will never work." So, we made a deal—Wally said we would spend a day and a half filming background plates, have those in our back pocket, and should I get behind schedule, I agreed I would complete the film on a soundstage.

I had to prove that I could stay on schedule, so I didn't have to go back inside to make a fake-looking movie on a soundstage. And I did stay on schedule, enough to earn me the right to shoot the whole film outside, and when I did fall behind schedule in the last three or four days, Wally concluded that no one could have done that film in ten days. We wound up shooting it in twelve, maybe thirteen.

The studio was not very happy, but I was getting good stuff. Now, the other thing is, in planning the movie and to stay on schedule, I couldn't just do single setups, and I knew I had to use multiple cameras. But there're only so many cameras you can hang off a car before it starts to look like you shot the film on a soundstage—exactly what I was trying to avoid by filming on location.

So, we got Pat Eustis to bring this camera car he had invented and designed for the movie _Bullitt_ [1968]. That's how I was able to get some cool low-angle shots of the truck and the car.

What also helped was that when you shot from either side of the road, you got a completely different look. That way, I was able to quickly get ample coverage for the chase and give the illusion we were at different locations, where in fact we had just reversed our position.

What took time was getting complicated shots moving in and out of the truck, pulling ahead of the truck with the car coming into the shot, and getting

UNIVERSAL présente **DUEL** avec **DENNIS WEAVER**
Scénario de **RICHARD MATHESON** d'après son histoire Réalisé par **STEVEN SPIELBERG** Produit par **GEORGE ECKSTEIN**
TECHNICOLOR · UN FILM UNIVERSAL DISTRIBUE PAR CINEMA INTERNATIONAL CORPORATION

details of the dead bugs I'd put on the grille of the truck and across the windshield. But that created the suspense.

Robert Smith was my production designer, or art director, as they were called in those days, and he did this map of the entire movie. I said, "Let's plot the entire film on an overhead map, so I can figure out my shots." It was like an architect's drawing, with all the highways in Pearblossom, Soledad Canyon, and Sand Canyon, out in Palmdale, where I shot the film. We included all the incidents and set pieces that happen in the story: the cafe, the phone booth, the snake farm, and so on. . . . It was a huge mural. It wrapped around the entire motel room where I was staying during production. But I was able to, every single day, make notes on the map and plot what the menu was going to be for the day. On this film, that bird's-eye view map is really what helped me understand the geography of the film. I always knew exactly where I was.

Let's talk about the casting. I know you went to Gregory Peck, Dustin Hoffman, David Janssen, and they all passed on the project. How did you come to Dennis Weaver?

Dennis Weaver was suggested by the studio because he had huge ratings from earlier TV films he had done. I loved Dennis Weaver, and when I was brought into the casting circle and Dennis's name came up, I immediately went nuts. I said, "It's got to be Dennis Weaver." George asked me why I was so hot on him, and I immediately replied *Touch of Evil*, the Orson Welles classic film, in which he played the Mirador Motel night manager. I remember George saying Dennis was also pretty good as Chester in *Gunsmoke*. I agreed, but I was a big fan of his from that one film, *Touch of Evil*. Weaver reached a level of anxiety, panic, and paranoia in *Touch of Evil* that I envisioned David Mann arriving at in the last act of the story. Where I wanted him to get to was that character he played

ABOVE The *Duel* crew films the climactic ending in another rare behind-the-scenes still from a French lobby card.

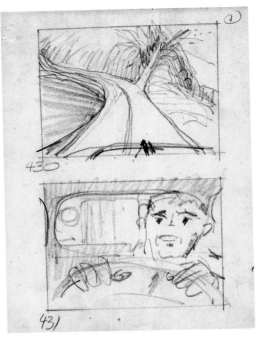
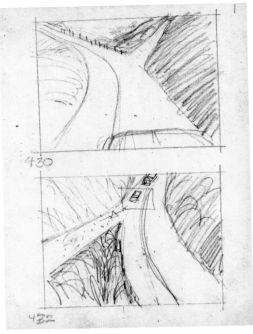
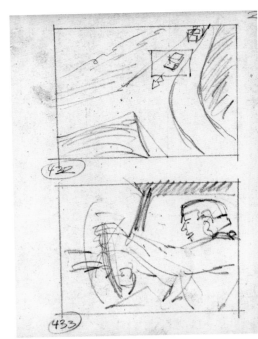
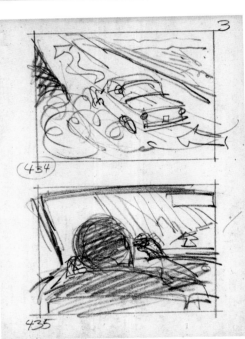
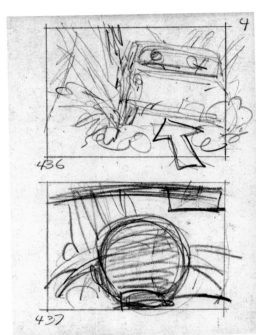

in *Touch of Evil*. When Dennis Weaver said yes it was one of the happiest days of my life.

Jumping to Carey Loftin, who had been the stuntman on *Bullitt*, why did you want him for the truck driver?
Carey, who liked to be called Old Vapor Lock, was a guy I knew of because I'm a big fan of all the old westerns. Carey Loftin and Dale Van Sickel, who also worked on *Duel*, were two of the most famous stuntmen in the annals of Hollywood history. It was Carey's idea to bring in Dale—and Dale drove the car for stunt scenes, while Carey drove the truck.

Carey was a brilliant truck driver. I couldn't have gotten any of the shots I wanted if it weren't for how safely Carey drove that truck and yet made it look dangerous, frightening, and deadly. Carey was a very, very safe driver. On certain scenes we couldn't

get the truck to go fast, and I had to use tricks like having the camera lower to the ground to create the illusion of speed. As long as we didn't show the road, it still looked like the truck was going very fast. I did have to use the old-fashioned technique of speeding up the film in a couple of shots, but for the most part, I was able to cheat by using geography moving by very quickly, like placing the truck against cliff walls which made going 40 mph look like 70 mph.

Another piece of inspired casting was the truck itself and how you modified it to make it almost look like a monster.
Our art director literally had a casting call for trucks and got in about seven semis for me to choose from. The Peterbilt that I selected was a little more retro; it was an older truck. It had a face. I could very easily anthropomorphize it by simply standing back and

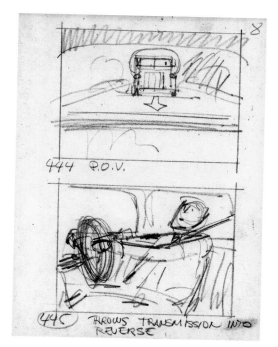

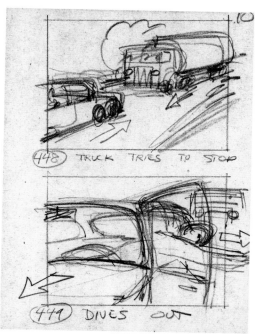

saying: Well, the windows are the eyes, and it has a huge protruding snout, the grill and the bumper are the mouth—it had a face. The other trucks were more flat-nosed and had less of a personality. But my eye went right to the one truck, and I said, "You got the part."

It may be my interpretation, but the license plates on the truck remind me of a gunslinger showing off his exploits and past victims.

That was the intention. He was basically a marauder, and all those license plates were the states where he had driven motorists into the ground or off cliffs. Those were the notches in his Colt .45.

The truck was the antagonist in the story. It had to have a personality. It couldn't just be a sparkling new, freshly minted truck. So, the idea was to make the truck look like a veteran of these road crimes. This was "Murder, Incorporated" on wheels. As I said,

there were fake dead bugs over the grill and on the windshield. The truck was dirty and streaked with oil coming out of every single possible vent. The truck was put into makeup every day. While Dennis Weaver was in his hair and makeup chair, a crew with large brushes and mops would be spattering the truck and making it look grisly and horrible. It was no different than Frankenstein's Monster, the Wolf Man, or the Phantom of the Opera.

David Mann's reddish orange car—how did you select it?

I knew I wanted the car to be red because, in looking at the locations, the desert was pretty much beige and brown, basically earth colors. I needed the car to stand out and to be able to pop in all the wide shots.

THESE PAGES Storyboards for *Duel*'s all-action finale sequence.

Aside from the amazing chase, you have a great handheld shot of David Mann going inside the café. This is before the Steadicam existed.

It was a handheld Arriflex camera. I really wanted to get the audience to have a first-person experience through the Dennis Weaver character. To that end, we follow him coming out of the car, after he's almost been killed, and walking into the café, going into the bathroom to throw water on his face, then walking back into the cafe, sitting down, and looking out the window at the parked truck, all in one shot. And when he turns and looks at everyone in the café, that's our first cut—and everyone there is a potential suspect. So yes, I used a handheld

Arriflex, and we had to ADR [use automated dialogue replacement for] everything in that scene—all the sound effects and voices—because the camera was noisy.

Duel seems to owe a lot to Hitchcock and your appreciation of the way he staged suspense.

What I learned from Hitchcock was, don't ever let the audience off the hook. Keep viewers at the edge of their seat as long as possible before giving them a clue or relief. If Hitchcock was ever whispering over my shoulder during the making of Duel, it was simply that: "Take your time and draw out the suspense as long as possible."

```
Country:        FRANCE

Name of paper:  NOUVEL OBSERVATEUR

Circulation:    200.000

Date:           April 9th 1973

Film:           D U E L


Frightful




                            PHILIPPE SELZ
```

```
Country:        FRANCE

Name of paper:  PARIS MATCH

Circulation:    1.000.000

Date:           April 10th 1973

Film:           D U E L

A fantastic DUEL. The anguish of all the
drivers expressed in an implacable film.
A film you must absolutely see.




                            PHILIPPE SELZ
```

```
Country:        FRANCE

Name of paper:  L'EXPRESS

Circulation:    600.000

Date:           April 9th 1973

Film:           D U E L



In a few minutes, with the simplest
resources, "DUEL" obtrudes as a strong
film, a film that will not be forgotten.




                            PHILIPPE SELZ
```

```
Country:        FRANCE

Name of paper:  VALEURS ACTUELLES

Circulation:    100.000

Date:           April 9th 1973

Film:           D U E L

One hour and a half of suspense.
Remarkably filmed, this cinematographic
allegory is also a dramatic exercise with
an extreme intensity.




                            PHILIPPE SELZ
```

RIGHT Original memos featuring glowing Duel reviews from France.

UNIVERSAL présente **DUEL** avec **DENNIS WEAVER**
Scénario de **RICHARD MATHESON** d'après son histoire
Réalisé par **STEVEN SPIELBERG**
Produit par **GEORGE ECKSTEIN**
TECHNICOLOR - UN FILM UNIVERSAL DISTRIBUE PAR CINEMA INTERNATIONAL CORPORATION

One of the great moments in the film is with Lucille Benson and her snake farm. The truck runs into the cages, and snakes are everywhere. I see this as a precursor to *Raiders of the Lost Ark*!

Yes, and don't forget the tarantula that climbs on Dennis's leg! It was fun to use reptiles to add to the chaos and anxiety. Not only was the truck against him but all the forces of nature were against this character as well. You mention Lucille Benson—I asked her to come back in a similar role in *1941*.

Did you use a stuntman for Dennis in the phone booth as the truck drives toward it?

There was no stuntman at all in that scene. We shot from two different angles, perhaps even three, but that was all Dennis. He did it himself, and he was very insistent on driving the car, except for certain things where we literally had to say, "Dennis, you're not doing this next shot." But Dennis was very proud of the fact that he was in that phone booth when the truck was coming. Now, he had plenty of time to get out, and it was practiced and rehearsed repeatedly. There were all sorts of fail-safe points if we needed to abort. But Dennis did it just at the right time, and we only did it once. I didn't want to tempt fate and do it a second time.

I love how you use voiceover during the drive up the hill before the final face-to-face duel between Mann and the truck. I read that you recorded his voiceover prior to filming the scene and played it for Dennis so he could get more intensely into the moment.

Yes, it helped him react to his own thoughts. He was able to use those playbacks to be able to physicalize and emote what he was feeling. We would record in the morning and work on the lines, and just play them back on a small speaker.

You do have a little cameo appearance in the movie during that final climb.

Yes, accidentally. In fact, I have a couple of appearances in the movie. For one thing, I needed to be in the car sometimes with Dennis. So, I sat in the backseat way over to the left, and you can see me in the rearview mirror. You can also see me reflected in the glass of the phone booth when Dennis Weaver goes in to make the call to report the truck, trying to call the police. There I am with the script in my hands looking up and down making sure that all the lines are right. There was no coverage. Since I was not looking at dailies, I didn't have the luxury of coming back and filming the scene over again. It was one

ABOVE A French lobby card featuring Lucille Benson as the gas station/snake farm proprietor and Dennis Weaver as David Mann.

of those unfortunate errors. And I think there're a couple of moments where the boom mic appears. But that's what happens when you don't have all the time you need to make your movie.

Let's talk about the last scene of the movie, which is, to this day, an iconic movie moment. How did you manage to have the truck go over the cliff?
I don't know how they really did it. I was busy on the cliffside figuring out seven camera positions, making sure I got the shots because that was the only truck we had. No take two. I was obsessively focused on that while Carey and the physical special effects team were figuring out how to have the truck drive over the cliff. I ended up just using footage from one of the seven cameras, which was placed all the way down because the shot was so extraordinary. The operator behind that camera deserves a medal; he followed the truck and the car all the way down, including the large cloud of dust and the tanker part of the truck reemerging from that cloud and continuing its journey down the cliff. It was just an extraordinary shot, and that's the only one I used.

> ❝ Sound design is like a glove to the camera. It has to be a partner to everything you see and everything you sense.❞

And because of the insane schedule, you kept shooting and never watched dailies.
I was living out on location the entire time I was shooting, and there was no setup to watch dailies. I was just relying on lab reports to say that there was no hair in the gate and no negative scratches and that the film was exposed properly. I was relying on my director of photography Jack Marta to tell me if he thought it was going to be okay. I relied on his expertise and his years of wisdom spent on so many shows. When the movie was over, I went into the editing room and was faced with something uglier than not being able to see my own dailies: I was faced with the fact that I had three and a half weeks to an air date on ABC from the day I wrapped the principal photography. So, I couldn't just do it with one editor. A total of five editors worked on *Duel*,

with me bicycling from one editing room to another, for three and a half weeks. [Frank Morriss was the main editor.] Yet it was an amazing time; I was going room to room trying to provide as much input as I could. We were able to create several sequences that weren't even in the script or weren't even in the way I shot the film, by stealing footage from other scenes if we didn't have enough coverage. I was just blown away.

Sound design has always been part of the fabric of your films, and *Duel* is an early example of using sound as a character.
Sound design is like a glove to the camera. It has to be a partner to everything you see and everything you sense. In this case, sound was going to make everything scarier—sound was going to make everything more suspenseful. *Duel* was a haunted truck movie almost, and some of the scares come through sound design.

At the very end, when the truck "dies," I thought of Godzilla, and I put in a dinosaur roar when it goes over the cliff. I used the very same sound effect when the shark is blown up in *Jaws* and the big carcass is sinking to the bottom of the ocean. I placed the groan where the fin of the shark comes out of the cloud of blood, to mimic where that sound landed in *Duel*, when the truck came out of the cloud of dirt. It was my way of saying, "Thank you, *Duel*, for putting me on the map. Thanks for giving me a career." Because without *Duel*, I wouldn't have gotten the green light to make *The Sugarland Express*, which led to *Jaws*.

I loved that when the truck goes over, there's one last horn blast with an echo; it is literally like the scream of a person falling over. There's also Billy Goldenberg's score. Some of it was very reminiscent of Bernard Herrmann's for *Psycho* [1960], but there was also something very tribal to his approach.
His contribution to *Duel* was very important because he didn't do a conventional score. He used African instruments and drums, and he did something like "Tubular Bells" [used in *The Exorcist*]. It was so experimental and so courageous to have a score like that, especially on an ABC "Movie of the Week." Billy's score for *Duel* is one of the best he ever did. I think he was very inspired by the story, and he wanted the score to be atmospheric rather than melodic. He added so many layers of creepiness with his music that it really brought *Duel* up even further.

How was *Duel* received?

It had huge ratings, and then I went out and shot some extra footage to expand the film so it could have a theatrical release overseas. I shot a new opening for the film—we start over black, and the car pulls out of the garage, and from Mann's POV, you travel through LA, the freeway, and eventually the deserted highway, which is where the television version started. I expanded the scene when Dennis stops at the gas station—he calls his wife, which clearly establishes that their marriage is on the rocks. I created a sequence with him stopping as a train is passing; the truck suddenly appears behind him and starts pushing him toward the moving freight train. And lastly, there is a new scene with a stranded school bus where you think the truck is going to attack, but it instead helps the bus get back on the road.

I love how you can credit *Duel* for getting you to Europe for the first time!

Yes, *Duel* unlocked for me the gateways to the continent of Europe. I had never been to Europe before, and it was amazing. Rome was the first stop. I got to visit the city and met Federico Fellini, who had just seen *Duel*. I'm very proud of a picture I have that was taken the day after he saw the film with his arm around me, standing in front of the Grand Hotel. I'm as skinny as a rail, and we became acquaintances from that moment on. We had infrequent encounters but still stayed in touch from time to time.

I visited a total of five countries in three weeks to do press. I walked on the beaches of Normandy for the first time. I wanted to go there, and I was there on a very blustery day, under very similar conditions to the actual June 6 invasion. And yes, I went to the Avoriaz International Fantastic Film Festival. That was a thrill for me.

The film became an instant classic. Europeans were reading a lot of symbolism into it. But basically, you were instantly labeled an "auteur," which must have been thrilling.

I had made a version of *High Noon* [1952] on wheels. They were reading all these esoteric abstract symbolism in it—you know, class warfare in America. And I proved their point because my next film, *The Sugarland Express*, was also about cars, and the same European critics said, "Spielberg is revisiting those themes and carrying them even further." It taught me to think a little bit more in the abstract, but nobody ever sees the same picture the same way.

You know, I haven't seen *Duel* in a long time. But

my memory is that I was proud of it. I still wonder how I got all those shots done in such a short amount of time. To this day, I don't think I could do it again! But I was so hungry back then, I was so ambitious, I was so excited about having been given this chance. I would also not approach that same story in the same spontaneous way. I would be the European intellectual mind, analyzing the script of *Duel* and putting all those different levels of interpretation into it. I think I'd be too headstrong about telling that story again. Sometimes you have to look back and say, those early films are a mark and a measure of who I was back then. I'm not the same person today as I was back then. Once you grow up and you have children, you have a family, and you learn more about the world you live in, and you make new friends and you lose some old friends, you change. I could never go back and make those early films as well as I made them when I was of the appropriate age and had the naïveté to be working on subjects like that. But on the other hand, I couldn't have made *Schindler's List* or *Saving Private Ryan* [1998] when I was in my early twenties either. So, it is a fair trade off.

UNIVERSAL CITY STUDIOS, INC. AN MCA INC. COMPANY

You and a guest are cordially invited
to attend a special screening of

D U E L

A theatrical film version, which
is being released this month in
theatres throughout Europe.

Thursday, November 9, 1972
Universal Studios Screening Rm. 3
8:00 p.m.

R.S.V.P.

George Eckstein
985-4321, ext. 1838

100 UNIVERSAL CITY PLAZA · UNIVERSAL CITY, CALIFORNIA 91608 · 985-4321

ABOVE An invitation to a screening of *Duel* from producer George Eckstein.

II

THE SUGARLAND EXPRESS

(1974)

> **"That's what I've come to tell ya. Welfare has come and taken baby Langston forever. They're going to keep him in that foster home."**
> —Lou Jean (Goldie Hawn) to her husband Clovis (William Atherton)

PAGES 52–53 Goldie Hawn as Lou Jean Poplin in *The Sugarland Express*, Steven Spielberg's first official feature film.

BELOW LEFT Spielberg during shooting of *The Sugarland Express*.

BELOW RIGHT The cover of the original *Sugarland Express* screenplay.

OPPOSITE A page from a promotional press brochure for *The Sugarland Express*.

It's interesting that Steven's first official theatrical film, *The Sugarland Express*, is based on a true story, given that the first decade of his career is so closely associated with fantasy entertainment. It's an adaptation of a real-life 1969 incident in which twenty-two-year-old Robert "Bobby" Dent, who had recently been released from prison, took police officer James Kenneth Crone hostage with the help of his wife, Ila Fae Dent. Commandeering Crone's police cruiser, the Dents hit the road with the police officer held captive, as dozens of law enforcement vehicles pursued them in an enormous slow-moving caravan.

Steven's adaptation of the story, written by Hal Barwood and Matthew Robbins, would focus on fictionalized versions of the Dents, Lou Jean Poplin (Goldie Hawn) and Clovis Poplin (William Atherton), with Michael Sacks playing patrolman Maxwell Slide, the film's analog for Crone, and Ben Johnson as Captain Harlin Tanner, the lawman overseeing the pursuit. Although *The Sugarland Express* took a realistic approach, the fictionalized story centers on the Poplins' attempt to get back their baby, who has been placed in foster care, giving the film an emotional core that is perhaps more typical of Steven's work as a whole.

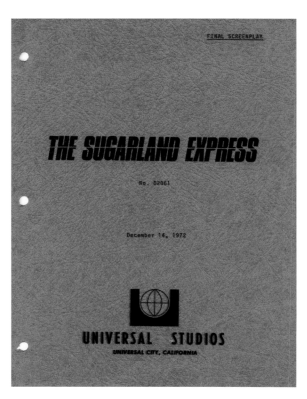

FINAL SCREENPLAY

THE SUGARLAND EXPRESS

No. 02061

December 14, 1972

UNIVERSAL STUDIOS
UNIVERSAL CITY, CALIFORNIA

192   CONTINUED

CLOVIS' RADIO VOICE
That's it, Captain. ~~Got your man~~
here and I'm ready to shoot the
sucker. ~~Now you hear me.~~ It's him
for the baby, that's the deal.

stands on car to see over fence

→ *Frame within screen at drive-in.*

Tanner ~~pulls the cord taut and stands up on the doorsill. By~~
craning his neck he can make out 2311 in the middle of the lot,
lights flashing, and three heads inside, a gun up to one of
them! *binocular shot!!*

TANNER
Okay, I see you. Now what kind of
deal are you talking about?

Someone stands hands him a bullhorn.

CLOVIS' RADIO VOICE
We keep on to Sugarland. ~~No road~~
blocks, no snipers, no nothin'.
Once we get the baby, we let the
man go. Now you listen -- he's →
gonna tell you something. → *expecting the best*

Angles of Slide wanting to talk— "my turn" c'mon my turn!

There is a rustle and Slide's voice is heard, faint and choking.

~~SLIDE'S RADIO VOICE~~
~~They're pretty wired up, Captain,~~
~~he means business....~~

① 2 cops listen
② 5 cops listen
③ 10 cops listen

193   INSIDE A HIGHWAY PATROL UNIT   ← *several angles*

A highway patrolman from Region 5 and his hollow-eyed partner
listen grimly to their brother officer.

SLIDE'S RADIO VOICE
~~...It's been a long haul, and I~~
suppose you might want to end it
right here and now....

CAPTAIN TANNER This is Maxwell Slide.

194   INSIDE THE KION NEWSWAGON   *④ Dietz & Berry Listening*

~~Dietz and Berry are listening in, cameras and tape recorders~~
~~forgotten. Alongside are the big network news trucks.~~

SLIDE'S ~~RADIO VOICE~~
...If that's your thinkin', I want
you to know I understand. I know
what I'm saying. You can come on
in. Tell everyone I told you that.

Cops parked everywhere
around Dybala's chicken
LouJean can hang
out her car &
bridge up her body into
take out window

* Criss-cross cop search
Long RD FM Right to
Left - passes but L-R
another combs - follow &
stop at cross street → then
DPS must put on breaks

Magic Hour
montage of caravan
going over freeway
overpass silhouette -
& other shots too -
inside 2311 sort

Buck Rogers Station
w/ 20 pumps &
10 queen stamp
dispensers - one of the
other funny

It is so imperative
to emphasize the connection
between Baby & parents.
great bubbly loving shots
of Baby Langston -
maybe match cut to
laugh of LouJean or
Clovis so we can say
to ourselves - he's his
fathers own image or
he has his mothers
laugh.

Baby Langston
running baby-circles
around camera
slow zoom in to face
from cute to frenzy.

for majic hour
montage of cars on RD
also a montage of
police dispatcher sounds
first one, then two,
then local, then
city, then car to car
until it & the music
is unintelligible.... &
leads right into
Schooner 4 corners &
TAUNER on Mike -
almost a yellow Rose of
Texas musical number

Yellow Rose of Texas

THIS PAGE Steven Spielberg's personal notes from the production of *The Sugarland Express.*

Something I find fascinating about *The Sugarland Express* is its varied tone. On the one hand, it's an action film: It's *Duel* on steroids, with massive chase sequences involving dozens of cars. It also has a lot of comedy and is super energetic and fun. But then, in the final act, it takes a very tragic turn when Clovis is shot and killed by the police. What starts off as a madcap escape comedy ends in real tragedy, and that's quite a leap for a filmmaker to pull off successfully, but Steven does just that.

There's also a lot of important firsts in *Sugarland* that would become significant in Steven's career. It marks his first collaboration with legendary director of photography Vilmos Zsigmond, who would go on to win an Oscar for his work on *Close Encounters*. Crucially, it's also the first film Steven made with composer John Williams, who would create timeless scores for almost every movie in Steven's filmography and become one of his most important collaborators.

It's also particularly significant as the film that made *Sugarland* producers Richard D. Zanuck and

David Brown realize that Steven would be the perfect director for their next movie, *Jaws*. *Sugarland* was not a big box office success, but it was very well reviewed. It became an incredible calling card for his talents, confirming that he understood framing, action, and how to get great performances from his actors. And the performances are exceptional, particularly from William Atherton and Goldie Hawn as the Poplins. For a feature debut, it feels incredibly elevated. The fact that Steven shot *Sugarland* on location in Texas probably fed into the decision to hire him for *Jaws*, which was also a very physical production.

In the late sixties and early seventies, Hollywood was producing a lot of crime thrillers featuring outlaws and car chases. There was *Bullitt* (1968) starring Steven McQueen; Sam Peckinpah's *The Getaway* (1972), which also starred McQueen and Ali MacGraw; and William Friedkin's *The French Connection* (1971), starring future *Jaws* star Roy Scheider and Gene Hackman, among others.

ABOVE Spielberg blocks out a shot with star Goldie Hawn.

Perhaps most significantly, there was Arthur Penn's *Bonnie and Clyde* (1967), with Warren Beatty and Faye Dunaway as the infamous true-life outlaws. The tone of *The Sugarland Express* is not unlike *Bonnie and Clyde* in terms of the mixture of irony and action, all leading to a tragic outcome. Both films also tell the story of an outlaw couple lionized by the media and embraced by the public, so Steven was certainly working in a genre very much of the time.

Sugarland tackles head-on the media's role in whipping up a frenzy around the Poplins. There's a remarkable scene in which the couple passes through a small town where there are crowds of people who've come out to support them, handing them gifts. The way Steven frames the story is

by fans and gifted with a large teddy bear also introduces another key Spielberg motif. Toys are heavily featured throughout the film—as they are in key sequences in *Close Encounters* and *E.T.*—and serve as a constant reminder of the couple's quest for their child. There's a toy tiger on the back window of the car the Poplins use to escape; the introduction of their baby at the foster home starts with a shot of a toy riding horse; and the teddy bear falling out of the car in the film's third act presages the tragic end to the Poplins' quest.

> " The way Steven frames the story is an indictment of how the media, in concert with the public, can really build people up while also destroying them."

an indictment of how the media, in concert with the public, can really build people up while also destroying them. It's extremely timely and really speaks to the cult of celebrity. *Sugarland* is also about the misuse of power, in this instance by law enforcement. Many of Steven's early films feature untrustworthy government agencies or other authority figures who are out of their depth—whether it's the mayor in *Jaws* who wants to keep the beaches open despite the presence of a killer shark, or the US military's attempt to cover up the presence of aliens in *Close Encounters*.

The scene in which the Poplins are mobbed

The *Sugarland* Aesthetic

The Sugarland Express used the Panaflex 35mm camera, which was an exciting breakthrough at the time created by Panavision. It allowed Steven to get some very ambitious shots from inside the Poplins' police cruiser that wouldn't have been possible without it. Even back then Steven was at the cutting edge of technology and always excited about new tools of the trade.

No rear-projection effects were used in the film—everything was shot on location and inside real vehicles. This brought an intimacy to the scenes inside the police cruiser that helps establish the car

OPPOSITE Two behind-the-scenes images from *The Sugarland Express* show Steven Spielberg in the thick of the action.

ABOVE A French *Sugarland* lobby card featuring (*left to right*) Clovis Poplin (William Atherton), Lou Jean Poplin (Goldie Hawn), and patrolman Maxwell Slide (Michael Sacks).

PAGES 60–61 Spielberg with the Panaflex 35mm camera that revolutionized shooting on *The Sugarland Express*.

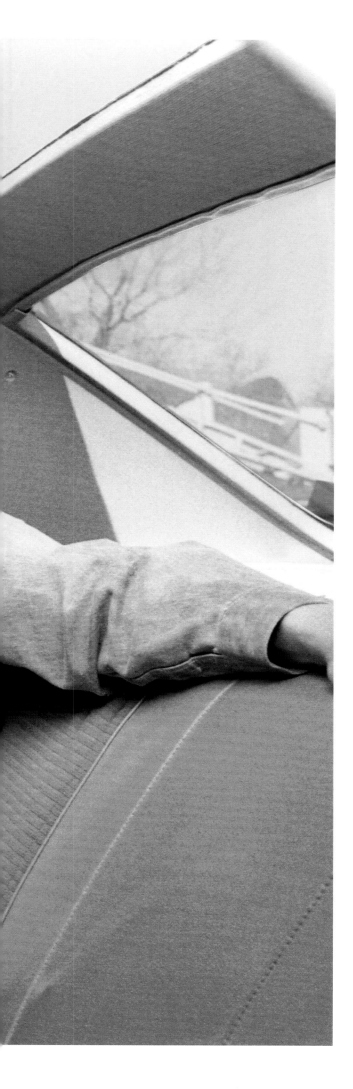

interior as a transitional home for the Poplins during the extended high-speed pursuit. It gives the viewer the sense that they are also imprisoned inside the car—it feels incredibly claustrophobic, the audience becoming almost like a fourth character within that space.

But the use of the Panaflex camera was not gratuitous—it wasn't a clever trick for the sake of it. It's all in the service of this story. Opting to use rear projection would have given the scene an artificial feel, and I think subconsciously the viewer always senses those kinds of tricks. It was a deliberate choice by Steven to anchor the story in reality. While *The Sugarland Express* has a very real, almost gritty feel, Steven's overall visual approach, and the large canvas that the widescreen format provided him, shows his commitment to creating something cinematically exciting.

Using the widescreen format, Steven showcased a perfect understanding of composition—on several occasions, he composed his shots with two characters on either side of the screen while the space between them is out of focus, brilliantly utilizing the space of the frame. The most potent example is during a tender moment when Lou Jean and Clovis are hiding out in an RV on a car lot that has a view of a drive-in movie theater. As Lou Jean and Clovis speak, smack in the middle of the frame is a Road Runner cartoon. Later, they watch and laugh as Road Runner takes on Wile E. Coyote. This moment is framed with a reflection of the cartoon playing over Clovis—a near-surrealistic shot that shows him growing somber as the coyote falls and smashes into the ground below. It's a premonition of things to come for Clovis and his wife, and one of the most powerful moments in the film.

Even though *Sugarland* is a road movie with multiple characters often separated by geography, Steven used some interesting visual techniques to connect these people in interesting ways. For example, in one scene, a Texas cop is chewing gum, and then the film cuts to a scene in Louisiana, where there is also a cop chewing gum. Another example is when Lou Jean goes into a portable toilet, and when she closes the door, the screen goes completely dark and the film cuts to the foster parents opening a door and coming out of darkness. These clever juxtapositions of elements that are visually similar help connect those two worlds and make them feel like they are part of the same story.

There's a lot of subtle foreshadowing built into

Sugarland, as if Steven is preparing the audience for the worst. In fact, the film opens with a sequence in which Goldie Hawn's Lou Jean steps off a visitor bus at the jail where Clovis is imprisoned. As she walks toward the jail, she passes a car on the side of the road that seems to have bullet holes in the windshield. With this, Steven provides a premonition of what will ultimately happen to these characters, setting up from the beginning the demise of Clovis and the capture of Lou Jean.

Heading Home

The home theme in *Duel* also comes through very powerfully in *Sugarland*. Ultimately, the film is about a couple trying to get home to be reunited with their baby, but in this case the home is decidedly broken. Steven communicates this through his shot choices—the first time you see the Poplins' child, Baby Langston, he's in his foster parents' garden, playing on his own. With Baby Langston in the foreground, you see the police arriving in the background to speak to the foster parents, but the camera stays on the child. Then the mother, played by Louise Latham, comes out and grabs the kid. There's a feeling of isolation and separation suggested by Steven's choice of shots. The broken home theme is also very prevalent in Steven's early films, particularly *Close Encounters* and *E.T.*, and it became an important aspect of Steven's oeuvre.

The Road to *Jaws*

There are several elements of *The Sugarland Express* that foreshadow aspects of Steven's next film, *Jaws*. Most notably, as the Poplins' notoriety grows, groups of vigilantes set out to take them down, similar to

> ❝ The broken home theme is also very prevalent in Steven's early films, particularly *Close Encounters* and *E.T.*, and it became an important aspect of Steven's oeuvre."

how in *Jaws* a group of locals head out to kill the shark. One of the snipers in *Sugarland* wears a similar outfit to the one worn by the character Ben Gardner (played by Craig Kingsbury) in *Jaws*, including an Elmer Fudd hunting cap. There are lots of interesting little connections between the films from the first ten years of Steven's career—it's almost like they exist in a beautiful shared universe connected by recurring motifs, themes, visuals, and ideas.

Another example of shared visual language can be observed in the scene at the end of *Sugarland* in which the Poplins arrive at Baby Langston's foster home. Unaware that the cops are waiting for them inside, Clovis is shot and fatally wounded. To capture the moment, Steven used a dolly zoom shot that's similar to an iconic Hitchcock shot from *Vertigo* (1958), in which the foreground image stays in the same position while the background either grows or shrinks, giving the impression of dizziness.

It's a technique Steven would reprise in *Jaws* for one of the film's most famous shots: the moment when Roy Scheider's character realizes that the shark is attacking its second victim, a young boy, Alex Kintner. In both instances, Steven's use of the technique creates a disorienting effect.

The ending of *The Sugarland Express* also has many parallels with the *Duel* finale. In *Sugarland*, text revealing the fate of the main characters plays over a subdued scene in which Michael Sacks's character is

ABOVE The *Sugarland Express* sound effects and dubbing crew plus Steven Spielberg (*center right behind sign*) and writers Matthew Robbins (*sitting at left of sign*) and Hal Barwood (*kneeling at right of sign*).

" Although *Sugarland*'s protagonists are outlaws, viewers come to identify with them throughout the course of the film."

released from his handcuffs by another officer, while the sun sets over a river that fills the background of the frame. There's a mournful, contemplative quality to it that echoes *Duel*, although in this case the ending is much darker. It's a notably downbeat climax, one that Steven debated with the producers at the time. Although *Sugarland*'s protagonists are outlaws, viewers come to identify with them throughout the course of the film. The Poplins just want to go home, and that's a very primal and relatable theme. But the ending snaps the audience back to a very harsh reality in a way that is both moving and somewhat unsettling.

Interestingly, if you juxtapose the final shot of *The Sugarland Express* and the first sequence of

Jaws, the two films almost lead into each other. *Jaws* begins at night as a woman, Chrissie Watkins, goes for a swim in the ocean and comes to a grisly end. Looking at the films this way, the calm waters at the end of *Sugarland* seem to foreshadow the much less calm waters of *Jaws*.

So, while it's true that *The Sugarland Express* is one of Steven's less well-known films, there's much in it that's profound and worthy of analysis. And, in terms of Steven's work and career, his first official theatrical movie became an essential step on his journey.

A Tribute to Dick Zanuck

I've never made a documentary for *Sugarland*, but in 2013, I did create one on producer Dick Zanuck for Turner Classic Movies, which Amblin Television and Steven executive produced. Steven loved the idea of honoring Dick's work and was happy to be interviewed. Of course, I ended up asking him a lot of questions about *The Sugarland Express*, which are reproduced in this book. Overall, though, the interview was focused on the way in which Dick protected Steven during the early part of his career and provided him with the tools he needed to make his movies. He was such a huge figure in Steven's early success.

After Dick watched the documentary, he immediately called me and said, "I don't have any notes. I'm blown away." And I said, "Great. Could you send a letter to Steven and my producers at Amblin Television because it would be great if they could hear that directly from you?" So Dick sent them a beautiful letter about the film, and then he said, "Let's have lunch on Thursday." I had to push it to Friday because I had another commitment. Then, on Friday morning, I got a call that he had died. He'd had a heart attack in the shower and passed away at the age of seventy-seven. Ultimately, we ended the documentary with the incredibly generous letter Dick had sent us. Later, we screened the film as part of a celebration of Dick's life. Everybody in Hollywood was there, and it was such a gift to be able to tell Dick's story to all these leading lights in the industry.

LEFT A promotional poster for Laurent Bouzereau's film *Don't Say No Until I Finish Talking: The Story of Richard D. Zanuck*. Steven Spielberg served as executive producer on the film.

BELOW "The start of a great relationship." A photograph of Zanuck and his *Sugarland* director, inscribed by the producer for Spielberg.

SPIELBERG ON *THE SUGARLAND EXPRESS*

With *The Sugarland Express*, your first feature film, you connected with the legendary producers Richard Zanuck and David Brown. That encounter would change the course of your career. Can you talk about the rich history, particularly with Dick Zanuck, son of the great Darryl F. Zanuck, who created 20th Century Fox?

The first time I ever heard the name Dick Zanuck was in association with his presidency at 20th Century Fox. There was a tremendous dynasty in the Zanuck name that represented risk, challenges, quality. It represented audacious decision making. It represented, always, for me, supporting directors like John Ford. And so, it wasn't surprising when Dick Zanuck became the new head of 20th Century Fox. The name Zanuck symbolized a legacy. Everybody knew that Fox was synonymous with Zanuck. I never thought I'd ever have a chance to some day not only meet but work with Richard.

Describe your first meeting with Dick Zanuck, when he was running Fox.

I had written a story and then collaborated on the writing of a screenplay called *Ace Eli and Rodger of the Skies* [1973], with a friend of mine from college, Claudia Salter, and of course, this was written for me to direct. Studios became very interested in buying

the project, and I was very interested in getting them to also "buy" me, although I knew that the chances of my being given a shot at directing a big Hollywood movie were nil.

But I got through a door when Robert Friar, who was one of the producers on the movie and had bought the script, brought me into a meeting with Dick Zanuck and David Brown at 20th Century Fox. And that must've been 1970 or '71.

What are your immediate memories of that first encounter with Dick?

The thing that really impressed me more than anything else was that we had a conversation. There had been a lot of producers up to that point who were just very happy to get me out of their office as fast as possible. But Zanuck took the meeting seriously.

I had been in many meetings where I was not taken seriously. So, I knew what it felt like to have somebody looking through you, not at you. Richard had a wonderful conversation with me, and he was very honest: He came out and said that he felt that I was too young in experience. They really were excited about the script, wanted to make it, and hoped that I would continue my involvement in the project with some writing services, but that he probably would not be hiring me to direct the movie. Dick put me in a position where I had to honestly question my own experience and whether I was ready to direct a feature film, and I wasn't. I honestly can tell you right now, I wasn't then, but it was a fair meeting. I walked out of that office feeling better than I did before I walked in, even though I knew I didn't have the job. Dick made me feel that I had won something in that meeting. This was my first introduction to a man who was soon going to change my career.

> " The name Zanuck symbolized a legacy. Everybody knew that Fox was synonymous with Zanuck."

Shootout Shots

CLOUIS & SLIDE

1. CLO looking → down each row of cars
2. SLIDE L-R scramble between cars
3. CLO down one row jumps out at him
   Low dolly up
4. Surprise shot CLO jumps out & points gun
5. Slide surprised starts to run →
6. over clo shoulder as he aims to miss & we see
   where all 3 shots go
7. turn for Slide for run & dolly Low & ahead until he is stopped
8. area around them erupts as hunters are attracted to shots

*(9) Peek-a-boo cuts - Low dolly past CLO seeing SLIDE hopping between cars

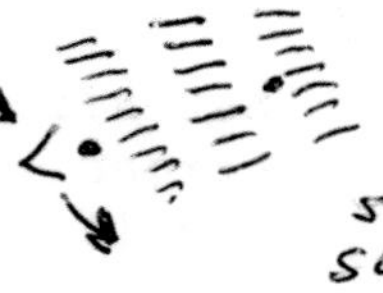

reverse on CLO & SLIDE

seeing SLIDE subliminally between cars.

Lou Jean inside trailer

1. erupts
2. back window a shot goes in Hunter curtains fly
3. Lou fires at back window it goes out & sparks fly around hunter
   who retreats

T - (4) Lou Jean runs out of home w/ gold stamps →
   everything erupts around her as she runs
   (2) POV hunters → past them to Lou - she fires
   gun once & hunters recoil & hide

INT 2311

she hits button & yells → finds CLO & SLIDE
huddling when she opens door → (~~door opens~~) to reveal

identical position looking up - scared Twins in fear!!

talking to each other

"I guess that's them!"

*(4) Shoot camera (left) ALSO!!

hunters -
1. Lou fires back & hunters duck
2. Kid falls in puddle "[illegible]"
3. hunters discuss shells ~~exchange~~ guns - Standby #1 takes out Luger.
4. Kid hesitates shoots at Big John sign
5. other position for Hunters - Lou violent him away gas tank
6. explode a car
7. Shells falling at feet of hunter hands into box that Kid brings from car.

car blows up the talk - astonished hunters "was that your hit or mine!!?"

*Kid's been his Big John hits

OT
1. Insert - cars turning into Swiss cheese
2. Sign
3. Crowd forms
4. Car hit spins [illegible]

How was David Brown? How did he compare to Dick?

David was avuncular and very scholarly. David was the college professor you always wanted to get and never could be admitted into his class because it was always filled up. Both David and Dick were very friendly, but of the two, David just looked more like a literary individual, while Dick was much more of the fighter. He was much more of the lineman, the quarterback, the guy who was going to be busting his balls to protect his directors, protect his movies, and get the movies made. Dick had a forceful way about him, whereas David was much more laid back and much calmer. Yet they were both very warm and friendly to me, and treated me as if I were the adult in the room, which I didn't expect.

What happened with *Ace Eli*?

The movie was made eventually, and it turned out that I was the only one who wasn't told that the director,

the writer, and the producer were taking their names off the project and changing their names on the credits. I had my name under "Story by." Regardless, it was nice to be on the screen in a film with Cliff Robertson, whom I had gotten to know while I was doing rewrites for him in Fort Lauderdale, Florida.

Was it tough for you to transition from TV to film?

There was no transition from TV to film for me since I had treated all my TV shows like films. I shot them as if I was making a movie; the setups were unconventional. That's the reason I wasn't given a lot of TV work after my first few television shows came out. Television producers felt that I was not going to cooperate with their style guides. Every show like *Marcus Welby* and *Owen Marshall* had kind of a safe look. I would always find a quirky angle or a way to shoot something without cutaways or coverage, and I soon became persona non grata on the lot. People

just stopped hiring me to do episodic television for that reason.

I'm curious—why did you choose *The Sugarland Express* as your first movie?

It was a story that I read in the *Citizen News*, a paper that was delivered to the door stoop of my apartment in North Hollywood. I had read this story that was called "A Modern-Day Bonnie and Clyde," about these two people who went on a kind of barnstorming tour of Texas with twenty police cars following behind. It was an interesting story that captured my imagination. I never really wanted to base the entire movie on the factual account of Bobby Dent. But I did want to use it as a springboard to fashion a completely fictitious story about a husband and wife who were evading the law to get their child back from child services in Texas. So, I approached two writer friends of mine, Hal Barwood and Matthew Robbins,

and asked them if they wanted to do this with me, and they jumped at the chance.

I know that you first went to Universal with it and they passed on it, and then you went to another studio and they passed. Then you ended up at Universal anyway. Was it a big journey to get the film financed?

It was just an unconventional story, and we got a lot of rejections for financing. But eventually I took it back to Jennings Lang at Universal, who was running motion pictures at the time—Sid Sheinberg was running television and about to take over motion pictures. Jennings liked the script and simply said, if you really are that passionate about it, you need to insure our investment by putting a movie star in one of these parts, if not all these parts. So, I went on a kind of learning journey to find movie stars. And I was turned down by the best of them.

ABOVE Richard D. Zanuck and Steven Spielberg confer between takes on *Sugarland*.

PAGES 72–73 A set of *Sugarland Express* storyboards outline a key action sequence from the film's finale.

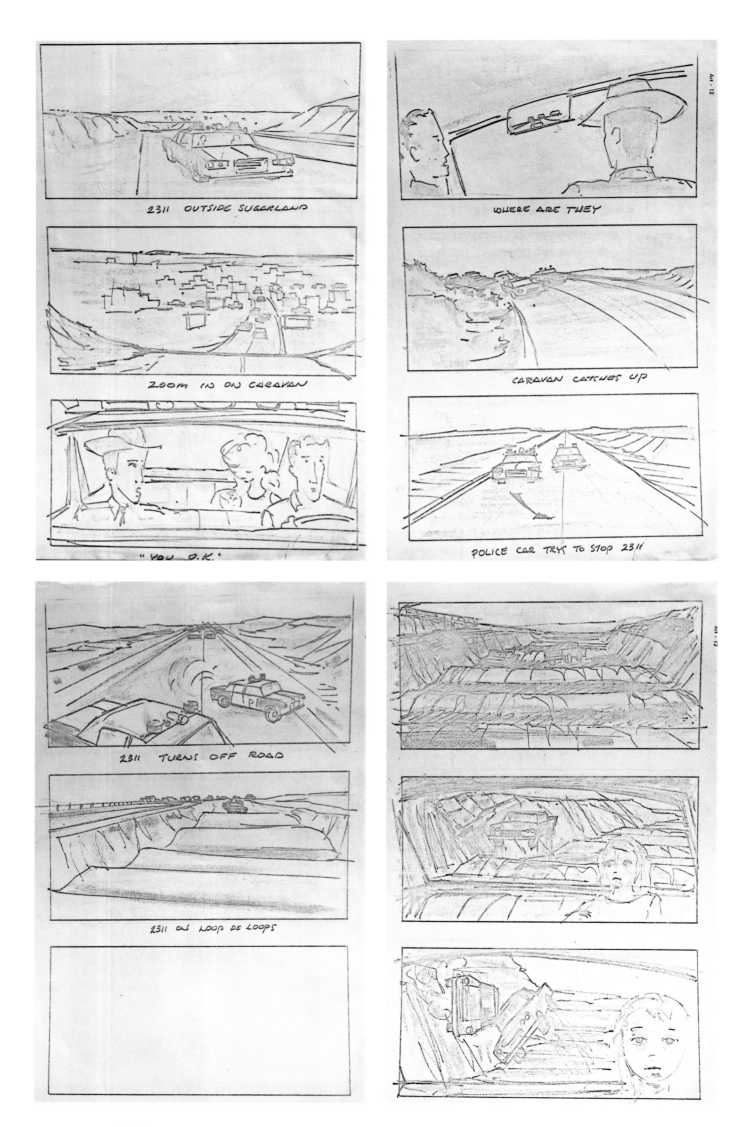

2311 OUTSIDE SUGARLAND

WHERE ARE THEY

ZOOM IN ON CARAVAN

CARAVAN CATCHES UP

"YOU O.K."

POLICE CAR TRYS TO STOP 2311

2311 TURNS OFF ROAD

2311 ON LOOP DE LOOPS

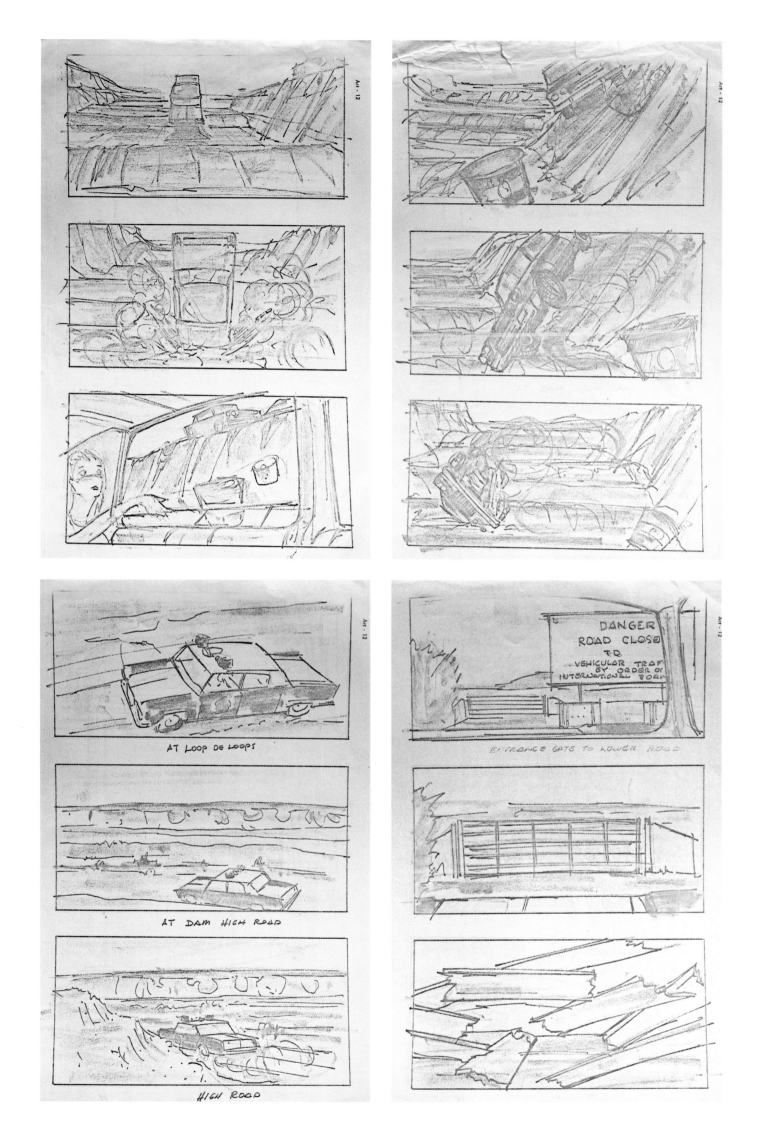

AT LOOP DE LOOPS

AT DAM HIGH ROAD

HIGH ROAD

ENTRANCE GATE TO LOWER ROAD

DANGER
ROAD CLOSE
FD
VEHICULAR TRAF
BY ORDER O
INTERNATIONAL BORD

I didn't see Dick and David again until I had turned in the script of *The Sugarland Express* to Jennings Lang at Universal. The studio wanted producers that could protect both their own investment but also be good stewards and custodians of the director, especially a first-time feature director like myself. They gave the script to Dick Zanuck and David Brown to see if they wanted to produce it. So, the second time I saw Dick and David was for a meeting about a screenplay they quite liked: *The Sugarland Express.*

Were they very different in their approach now that they were independent producers? In Dick's case, he was no longer a studio chief.

I had no savvy about what it meant to be the head of a studio and suddenly be producing movies. As far as I was concerned, Dick Zanuck was doing the same thing he'd always done. Whether he was sitting behind a desk or on set, he was making movies, and that's how I viewed him. I didn't even think of questioning why he and David were now in independent production.

I saw *The Sugarland Express* as a kid and underappreciated it at the time but, watching it today, I am blown away by your sense of composition, and your usage of the anamorphic format is extraordinary. I particularly like the shot where Goldie and Bill are on either side of the screen and a Road Runner cartoon is in the middle, subtly foreshadowing their demise.

I had never imagined shooting any movie in anamorphic because I was so comfortable with the 1:85 aspect ratio. But because there were going to be so many police cars in *The Sugarland Express*, and so many of those police cars would be going across the frame, not just into the frame, my director of photography, Vilmos Zsigmond, convinced me that the right aspect ratio would be 2:35. So we shot it in Panavision.

You did that amazing 360-degree shot inside the police car.

I was having fun with that aspect ratio, which was completely new to me. One time, when I was very young and making 8mm movies, there was an anamorphic lens you could purchase at a camera store that would squeeze the image. Then if you took the anamorphic lens off your film camera

ABOVE A French *Sugarland Express* lobby card shows the caravan of police cars trailing the fugitive Poplins.

RIGHT Steven Spielberg gets a good vantage point on the action during the shooting of *Sugarland*.

OPPOSITE TOP Steven Spielberg prepares to shoot a scene inside the Poplins' car.

OPPOSITE BOTTOM Goldie Hawn as Lou Jean Poplin on a French lobby card.

74

From: CHUCK JONES

LATER TO SEE THEM PLAYING A PART IN YOUR FILM.

GIVING BIRTH TO A COYOTE IS SELDOM AN UNALLOYED PLEASURE BUT TO SEE HIM GROW UP TO APPEAR IN A CAMEO PART IN SUCH A PICTURE ADDS A NOTE OF DIGNITY I NEVER EXPECTED

THANK'YOU

Chuck Jones

ROAD-RUNNER DUST

+ WILE E. COYOTE

From: CHUCK JONES
Chuck Jones Enterprises
6290 Sunset Blvd.
Hollywood 90028

JUNE 7, 1974.

DEAR STEVEN SPIELBERG,

"SUGARLAND EXPRESS" IS SUCH A
DELIGHTFUL FILM THAT ONLY LATER
DID I REALIZE HOW TECHNICALLY EX-
CELLENT IT WAS TOO — IT BEARS OUT
THE LITTLE UNDERSTOOD OR PRACTISED
MAXIM THAT "IN CREATIVE WORK THERE
ARE ONLY TWO FACTORS; WORK AND
LOVE — AND ONLY THE LOVE SHOULD
SHOW"

THE ROAD-RUNNER AND COYOTE WERE
BORN IN 1948 — WHICH MUST BE
ABOUT THE YEAR YOU WERE BORN—
COINCIDENCES SELDOM MEAN ANY—
THING AND I'M SURE THIS ONE IS
NO EXCEPTION BUT IT GIVES ME
REAL PLEASURE TWENTY-SIX YEARS

From: CHUCK JONES

OCT - 1974

DEAR STEVE:

"DUEL" - OF COURSE! I KNEW I'D WRITTEN SOMETHING TO SOMEBODY ABOUT THAT FILM - MY DAUGHTER WENT TO SCHOOL AT THE V RANCH SCHOOL UP AT MAYER - AND BUD BROWN WHO RAISES PERUVIAN PASSOS IN SCOTTSDALE AND RUNS THE FRIENDLY PINES CAMP IN PRESCOTT IS AN OLD AND VALUED FRIEND.. I MIGHT HAVE KNOWN YOU WERE RAISED ON SAGE-BRUSH AND DESERT PERSPECTIVE, NO CITY BOY HAS A NICTATING LENS ON HIS EYE-BALL. COME AND JOIN ME AND RAY BRADBURY SOME AFTERNOON IN ONE OF OUR MARTINI DIALOGUES. MAY I SNEAK INTO A PRESS SHOWING OF "JAWS" WHEN READY? I EXPECT TO BE GOING DOWN TO TOWNSVILLE IN JANUARY TO LOOK AT PLANKTON AND MAKOS SO I'D LIKE TO KNOW WHAT TO EXPECT.

BEST - CHUCK

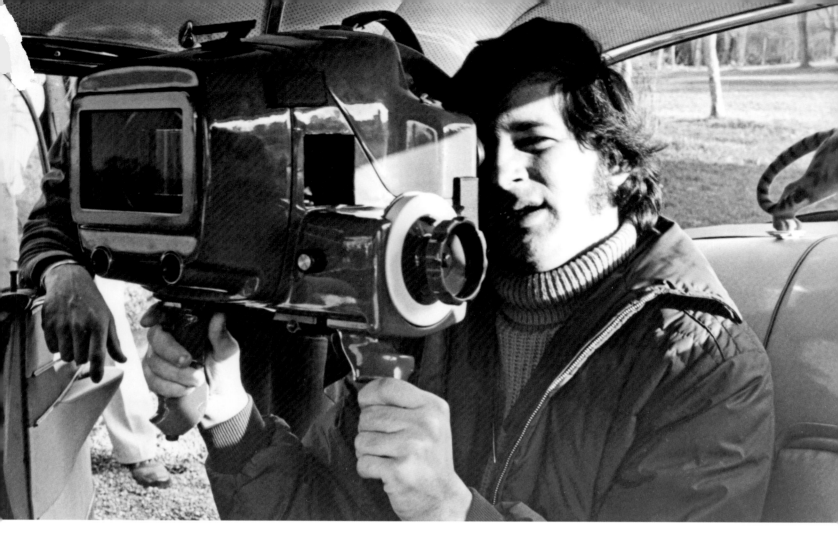

and put it on your 8mm film projector, that would then stretch the image out. So, I made one film in widescreen when I was a kid, maybe fifteen years old. But I didn't like it. It was just too hard to compose for it and find compositional balance. So, I was reluctant to use 2:35 when I was making *Sugarland*. But Vilmos convinced me, and I kind of went to anamorphic school and learned on one movie everything that I then used on subsequent feature films.

We were scheduled to be the first feature film to have the Panaflex camera from Panavision. This camera was going to really allow me complete fluidity and independence with my shots. And Dick Zanuck really, really worked hard to get that camera to me on time. Not only that, but he insisted that the head of Panavision, Bob Gottschalk, personally deliver the camera to our production in San Antonio, Texas, which he did.

How did you cast Goldie Hawn?
My first choice and only choice for Lou Jean Poplin was Goldie Hawn. Even though I was turned down by several actors to play Officer Slide and Clovis Poplin, Goldie agreed to meet with me after reading and liking the script. After our meeting, she committed to starring in our movie. That's what gave Universal

financial cover that they had a genuine, Academy Award–winning movie star in the lead. Jennings sent me a gift-wrapped box and when I opened it there was a single green lightbulb inside. That's how he let me know I was greenlit for actual production.

And Bill Atherton was so amazing in the movie, along with Ben Johnson and Michael Sacks.
Oh yeah, Bill was great in the movie, Ben was great, and Michael Sacks was fantastic. I had loved Michael Sacks in *Slaughterhouse-Five* [1972], which is why I went to him. Bill Atherton, I didn't know very well, but he came in and read for me and he was subtle and internal and so honest.

You had so many interesting stunts in the film. You once said your favorite stunt involved stuntman Teddy Grossman. He played one of the news reporters whose van is hit, and he jumps off into a ditch.
That stunt was incredible. Teddy was on top of a red news van, and before it hit a puddle and flipped over, *he* flipped off the top of it and perfectly hit his mark in the puddle, exactly where the camera was.

It gave the shot a kind of awesome dynamic effect. I learned a lot about stunt work on *Sugarland* because I had never done that much of it on any television show before.

I know you had bad weather during the shoot in Texas and that you all got sick at some point.
I got the flu. I've gotten sick on several movies. I just would pick up a cold or catch a virus. I've always worked through it. I had one insurance day in my entire life—on *Sugarland*, my first feature film. I couldn't get out of bed I was so sick. I had a 103 temperature, and I was just very ill. Dick Zanuck called an insurance day. I think that is the first and last insurance day I ever used.

Dick was famous for being on set all the time and an incredible support to his directors. The stories on *Jaws* are legendary. How was that first experience for you once production started?
Dick was really a fantastic support system for me in that he never made me feel like he knew more about the script than I did, that he knew more about directing than I did. He never once got into

INTEROFFICE MEMORANDUM •

FORM 2022

DATE ▶ April 5, 1973

TO ▶ JIM FARGO

FROM ▶ STEVEN SPIELBERG

SUBJECT ▶

COPIES ▶

Dear Jim:

Little did I learn the true meaning of what a good assistant director is until I worked with you on SUGARLAND EXPRESS.

(1) He must have a very loud voice.

(2) If looks can kill, he must always be happy.

(3) He must be dedicated to the director's ideal for a minimum of six takes.

(4) He must have ideas of his own, while disguising his own ideas about directing.

(5) He must have patience with cameramen of foreign origin -- and never attempt to change his own accent when trying to get through to him.

(6) He must be a crack shot with rocks and beer cans.

(7) He must be able to tell the production manager he is mistaken and still keep his post.

(8) He must know what his director is thinking at all times so he can stop him before it is too late.

(9) He must be kind and considerate of the leading lady the whole day through.

(10) He must be a diplomat, a scholar, a mender of hurt feelings, and a man of many hats.

He must be Jim Fargo.

Best,

Steve Spielberg

SS:nt

a conversation about how I was going to direct the picture. Never once. All he basically did was to show up and be there all the time, every day. On the set. During early production meetings, he never interrupted me when I was speaking. He never overruled me on an idea that he thought was better than what I was suggesting. All he did was back me up and say, "Yeah. That's a great idea. Let's do that." I had never been supported that way in my life. Not in television, not in making independent movies, and I had never had anybody who had my back, and in a way had my front, too. Because he was not only protecting me, he was also refreshing my confidence on a daily basis. Yet even though this was my first film, he gave me complete autonomy as director.

How challenging was the making of the film?

Sugarland was my first feature, so everything about it was difficult. Everything about it was new. I'd done a lot of television, but just the fact that this was my first motion picture put a lot of pressure on me. I cannot even describe, except to other people who have made a first film, what that feeling is really like.

Every day feels like it could be your last day. But Dick Zanuck always knew, could always sense, when I was troubled or when I was preoccupied with something. All my life, I've chewed on the inside of my finger when I'm a little bit stressed. If he saw me do this, Dick would put an arm around me and ask, "How are you feeling? Can I help you with anything? What do you need?" At that very early stage in my career, I had never been shown that kind of support.

It's amazing to see how much Dick liked to be part of the crew.

I would look at my director of photography, Vilmos Zsigmond, I would look at the electricians, the gaffer, and the sound crew, and there was Dick! He was part of the envelope that we shot our movies within. And so, after a while, I just took his presence for granted. He was always there.

The film has a dark ending, and Dick Zanuck told me you almost had a change of heart over it.

Yeah, the dark ending with the death of Clovis was always intended—which by the way came from the original true story, which did end tragically. But I was

ABOVE Goldie Hawn and Steven Spielberg on location in Texas for *The Sugarland Express.*

a bit confused making my first film, and the balance between making a commercial picture and a brutally honest one. I started to flirt with making it a happier ending. Of course, the people I was listening to in those days talked me out of it.

I'm sure it was quite stressful when you got to the point of showing Dick and David the film.
I'll never forget when I showed them my cut of it. I was terrified. We were in a screening room at Universal. It was David, Dick, and I—I think that was it. And when the film was over, Dick tore a piece of paper out of a notebook, and he said, "Here are my notes." And he handed me this piece of paper. I took it and saw that there was nothing written on it. I looked up and both Dick and David were smiling. Dick said again, "Those are my notes."

> ❝ At the time, when I was writing a screenplay, I would often put on soundtrack albums to inspire me; one of them was *The Reivers*. ❞

Music is such an important aspect of your cinema, and *Sugarland* marked your first collaboration with John Williams, who went on to write scores for so many of your films. Before discussing John, how would you describe your relationship to music, particularly growing up?
I played the clarinet in elementary school, from the fourth grade through junior high school. Played a little bit in high school—I was never good, so I never pursued it. But I love music. I had classical music in my life since I was a child. My mother played classical concert piano, and she brought that musical culture into my life and into our family. I was raised on Schumann, Beethoven, Brahms, Chopin, and Shostakovich, and then I discovered motion picture soundtracks, which I started collecting when I was just about ten or eleven years old. In a sense, a film score is a form of classical music. It follows a narrative and can be very dramatic, almost like opera.

When did you become aware of the function of the score in film?
I think I became very aware of the importance of music

watching Disney cartoons and animated features. Both musical scores and songs were very much part of the fabric of a Disney film. But the one that hit me the most was Miklós Rózsa's score for William Wyler's *Ben-Hur* [1959]. I was only thirteen but I remember having an extraordinary reaction to the music. By the time I was making *The Sugarland Express*, I might have had a collection of over five hundred soundtrack albums. I was a motion picture score junkie!

Who did you like among the great composers?
I liked Erich Wolfgang Korngold, Dimitri Tiomkin, Franz Waxman, Max Steiner, and Bernard Herrmann. They had done big films—big scores. Later, in the sixties, I liked Elmer Bernstein and his work for DeMille's *The Ten Commandments* [1956], Jerry Goldsmith, and of course John Williams. I first discovered John Williams through the score he did for *The Reivers* [1969], directed by Mark Rydell and starring Steve McQueen.

At the time, when I was writing a screenplay, I would often put on soundtrack albums to inspire me; one of them was *The Reivers*. I didn't know who John Williams was, but I had seen the movie and remembered how much I loved that score. So I made a promise to myself that if I ever had the luck of getting a first feature, I would go and ask this guy, John Williams, to write the score for it. When *The Sugarland Express* got underway, he was the first and only composer I went to.

How did you connect with John? What was that first meeting like?
Zanuck and Brown knew him. Of course, John had done *The Poseidon Adventure* [1972], and the same year as *Sugarland*, he also did *The Towering Inferno* and *Earthquake* [1974]. But I was most enamored with *The Reivers* and *The Cowboys* [1972], also directed by Mark Rydell, and wanted that kind of music for my first movie.

I remember the first time I met John. We had lunch together—he was an elegant man, always has been, and very friendly, very warm, but he looked a bit like how I imagine William Shakespeare, with the red hair and beard. He seemed British without the accent, milk white skin and beautiful hands. And to prove how much I loved film music, I hummed the Alex North theme from *Spartacus* [1960] and told him how much I loved his scores for *The Reivers* and *The Cowboys*. John was either impressed by that or acted like he was [laughs], perhaps thinking I was nuts.

Whatever you said, it worked!

Sugarland Express was just the beginning of what John has done with all the films we did together—he rewrote the narrative musically and lifted the entire picture to a level I could not have anticipated, nor could I have even imagined. He inserted so many beautiful emotions to the performances; they were already there, but the music took them to another level. I was not surprised as much as I was grateful that John's music could do that and could turn the movie into something better than what it would have been without his music.

I know and have witnessed how much you love being on the scoring stage. You talk to the musicians, you film them. You use your phone now, but you used your Super 8 camera back then. How was the experience of being on the scoring stage with John for the first time?

It was extraordinary. I had sat on scoring stages before for my television work, and when Billy Goldenberg scored *Duel*. I was there every day with Billy, so I knew the power of being at a scoring session. But when Johnny came with a full orchestra for *Sugarland*, and with Toots Thielemans, the famous harmonica player, John had done something I never thought the movie could achieve. Specifically, he created an intimacy with the harmonica that really brought the film to a focused and intimate place.

So, like Louis and Rick at the end of *Casablanca* [1942] and the famous line "This is the beginning of a beautiful friendship," the second we finished scoring *Sugarland*, I simply intended to hire John on every movie I ever would make.

ABOVE Goldie Hawn as Lou Jean.

| | |

JAWS

(1975)

"You're gonna need a bigger boat."
—Police Chief Martin Brody (Roy Scheider)

It is impossible to imagine cinema without *Jaws*. As much as Steven had already made an impact with *Duel* and *Sugarland*, nothing could have prepared audiences and filmmaker alike for the phenomenon that *Jaws* became. The preceding films were important steps that paved the way, but the Steven Spielberg that we know and love arrived with this movie. I've seen *Jaws* so many times over the years, and to this day, I still love to rewatch it. Even though it's a scary story, it always feels comfortable to me, like an old friend.

Jaws has always been such an important film to me and such a huge inspiration. When I was asked to

246A/ BRODY CLIMBS OUT OF WINDOW

get GAFF

sideways wall

247a/ BRODY MOVING UP ON FLYING BRIDGE

Shark rolls sideways for bites - not straight kut

great cloudy dark eye

BRODY GAFFS shark - draws blood

247b/ BRODY SLIDING ON WET DECK - SHARK SURFACES WITH TANK IN HIS MOUTH

PAGES 80–81 In this scene from the *Jaws* finale, Chief Brody (Roy Scheider) gets into position to take a shot at the shark.

RIGHT Storyboards for the *Jaws* finale as Brody clambers to the top of the sinking boat to take a shot at the gas tank lodged in the shark's mouth.

OPPOSITE Steven Spielberg on board Quint's boat, the *Orca*, during the *Jaws* shoot.

create a LaserDisc documentary for Universal's 1995 home entertainment release, it was a dream come true. It was super exciting for me because nothing had been done on the movie since it had come out twenty years earlier and the cast and crew had not talked about it in years.

But as I started work on the documentary, it was like a blank slate that begged the question, where do I even begin? I started by going through Steven's archives at Amblin and reading all the different versions of the script. I also visited the archives at Universal, a *Raiders of the Lost Ark*–like warehouse filled with boxes of materials. I was amazed that all this stuff from the making of this iconic film had just been filed away. I found a bunch of memos from studio head Lew Wasserman, as well as Dick Zanuck and Steven, plus casting lists and all sorts of other stuff. I even found the original *Jaws* letterhead that had been used during the production. Of course, I borrowed it and used it for all my correspondence on the project. I created a whole little universe for myself.

Looking through the unit photography was a fascinating experience, as it retraced the order in which scenes were filmed. The Universal photo department would give me contact sheets featuring multiple images, and I would go through and choose the pictures I wanted to use. But I discovered that all the photos of the shark had been crossed out with magic marker! There was a memo from Dick Zanuck requesting that these pictures not be used in the film's publicity campaign. I got some nail polish remover and used that to erase the big black lines so that I could see the shark pictures. Fortunately, the matching negative to each photo I had selected was intact and I was able to print some revealing behind-the-scenes photos that had not been seen before.

TOP Steven Spielberg during shooting of the scene in which Amity Island locals mistakenly believe they have caught the killer shark.

ABOVE *Jaws* producers David Brown and Richard D. Zanuck on location on Martha's Vineyard.

In parallel to my research work, I also interviewed as many people in the cast and crew as I could, including stars Roy Scheider (who played Chief Martin Brody), Richard Dreyfuss (shark expert Matt Hooper), Lorraine Gary (Brody's wife, Ellen), and Susan Backlinie (Chrissie Watkins, the shark's first victim). Unfortunately, two of the film's most notable actors had by then passed away: Robert Shaw, who

played seadog shark hunter Quint had died in 1978, just three years after the film was released, and one of my favorite actors in the film, Murray Hamilton, who played Amity's mayor, Larry Vaughn, had passed away in 1986. But we managed to pay tribute to their performances through film clips and photos from the set. I also contacted co-writer and actor Carl Gottlieb, production designer Joe Alves, stuntman Ted Grossman, and cinematographer Bill Butler, who was working on the friendly dolphin movie *Flipper* (1996) at the time—quite a departure from *Jaws*! I even found Australian underwater photographers Ron and Valerie Taylor, who sent me behind-the-scenes footage from their live shark-filming expeditions for *Jaws*.

Then, Jeff Cava, who was working at Universal in editorial, said, "Hey, I found this little 16mm film." It turned out to be a huge find for the documentary: footage of special effects legend Robert A. Mattey (*20,000 Leagues Under the Sea*, 1954) and his team testing the mechanical shark, but not in water. Of course, when they took the shark to Martha's Vineyard, where the film was shot on location, it

LEFT On the beach at Martha's Vineyard, (left to right) Steven Spielberg, Roy Scheider, Richard D. Zanuck, and Valerie and Ron Taylor, who filmed the real-life shark footage used in *Jaws*.

BELOW Spielberg with a prize catch during some much-needed downtime on Martha's Vineyard.

stopped working and sunk as soon as they put it in the ocean! Several sharks were built for the film.

Piece by piece, the documentary really started to come together. My archaeological work also unearthed deleted scenes, some of which had been put into a television version of *Jaws* when it was shown on network TV decades before. Back then, studios had a knack of extending their big hits and putting them on TV with deleted scenes. One of the most notable things I discovered was original footage featuring a character who was kind of a sidekick to Quint but had been almost completely removed from the original film. I also found the dailies for the famous "You're gonna need a bigger boat" scene, where Brody first sees the shark out at sea. It's amazing that the final scene is so scary because in the dailies, you can hear all the pneumatic pumps on the shark and, in some shots, literally see the creature sinking into the sea.

Jaws was a famously stressful shoot, primarily because of the problems with the mechanical sharks. Watching the footage really gave me a sense of how difficult it must have been for Steven. Outwardly, he seemed very Zen on set, and there are lots of photos showing him relaxing or asleep while waiting for the shark to be fixed. But it must have been really frustrating. It's hard to imagine what it must have been like to be on a production of this size and caught between the chaos of the sea and a titular monster that wouldn't work.

From Page to Screen

When I was preparing for the *Jaws* documentary, I did a huge amount of research that included a very thorough comparison between Peter Benchley's book and the different drafts of the script. Peter wrote the first draft of the screenplay and reading through his notes on the adaptation process was revelatory. Not being a filmmaker himself, he had a lot of anxiety about the process. One of the big struggles he was facing was maintaining the audience's fear of the shark throughout the entire film while keeping all the other elements from his book. Ultimately, he realized that his script was perhaps too literal a translation of his book.

Tracing the evolution of the film script from the novel was fascinating because the book is a very different kind of story. For instance, the novel features a love affair between Brody's wife and Hooper, and it's hard to imagine that being part of Steven's film. And Steven's ideas for *Jaws* were fantastic. Reading his memos for translating the book into a film is a master class in pacing, structure, and characterization. Each character plays a specific archetypal role that is vital to the story. Perhaps the most extraordinary element that Steven added to the story is the fact that the film's third act is entirely based out at sea, whereas in the novel Brody, Hooper, and Quint return to the mainland on occasion. Steven altered it so that the three men are essentially trapped in the ocean with the shark, which greatly adds to the tension.

TOP A troubled Steven Spielberg at sea during the challenging *Jaws* shoot.

ABOVE Spielberg holds a boom mic while shooting in the cabin of the *Orca*.

RIGHT A photograph signed by *Jaws* novelist and co-screenwriter Peter Benchley to the author: (*left to right*) Roy Scheider, Benchley, and *Jaws* co-screenwriter/actor Carl Gottlieb.

I got to meet Peter Benchley for the first time when making the *Jaws* documentary, and it was one of my favorite encounters on the whole project. Sadly, he died when he was just sixty-five, but it was a privilege to know him. He was an incredible man. I remember him telling me the story of how Steven broke the news to him that he had changed the ending of the book. In the novel, the shark gets worn down by multiple injuries and ultimately just kind of sinks and dies. But Steven had a different ending in mind and shared with Peter that he wanted the shark to be blown up. Peter thought that it would not be believable but when he later saw the movie, he admitted he was wrong. Steven's approach to the ending may not have been realistic, but it was right for the film and brought the audience to their feet.

Peter loved the film. He was a modest, talented, and nice guy who wasn't precious about his novels. After publishing *Jaws* in 1974, he wrote *The Deep* in 1976. This great story about treasure hunters in Bermuda was adapted into a successful 1977 film starring Robert Shaw, Jacqueline Bisset, Nick Nolte, Louis Gossett Jr., and Eli Wallach. And after that he wrote *The Island*, which was turned into a 1980 movie, directed by Michael Ritchie and produced by Zanuck and Brown. Unfortunately, the film was a big flop, and Peter told me that he felt his connection with Hollywood had been damaged. He did continue to write books, though, and successfully turned to advocating for causes related to the preservation of the ocean with his wife Wendy.

> ❝❝ Steven's ideas for *Jaws* were fantastic. Reading his memos for translating the book into a film is a master class in pacing, structure, and characterization."

Amity Island Welcomes You

While there's no denying that the third act of *Jaws* is exciting, I always miss Amity Island when Brody, Hooper, and Quint leave it behind. I just love the town and the people and the way in which Steven really takes his time setting up the world these characters inhabit. You can almost smell *Jaws* because Amity—aka Martha's Vineyard, Massachusetts—is rendered in such a vivid, relatable way. It's a film about a town in crisis, ultimately, and Steven understood the importance of making sure the characters and setting were fully fleshed out and believable before getting to the final showdown. This approach even extends to the supporting players, like Mayor Larry Vaughn. Even though Murray Hamilton's character is often remembered as being a somewhat callous and incompetent individual, he does have a legitimate point of view: He's trying to do the right thing for everybody by

ABOVE LEFT A French lobby card for *Jaws* shows shark panic breaking out on the beach.

ABOVE RIGHT A lobby card featuring the moment that parents Martin (Roy Scheider) and Ellen Brody (Lorraine Gary) attend to their son Sean (Chris Rebello) after he narrowly avoids becoming the shark's next victim.

ABOVE Robert Shaw in the infamous chalkboard sequence that introduces his character, Quint.

minimizing public panic. There are a lot of nuances in these supporting characters, and that really helps differentiate *Jaws* from a typical B-movie.

The way that Steven paces the film also elevates it above any one genre. Early in the film, there are two very impactful shark attack scenes—the killing of Chrissie Watkins at night and the death of young Alex Kintner at a crowded beach.

Following each of these shocking deaths, Steven gives the audience a breather rather than include more shark attacks, which might have made *Jaws* feel like just another monster movie. He pulls back and spends time with his characters—the people whose lives are being impacted by the presence of the shark. I think that's exemplified by the scene in which the townspeople gather to decide what to do about the shark.

Most importantly, the meeting scene introduces us to Quint, who silences the room by scraping his fingernails down a chalkboard. It's such a great character moment because that awful sound lets the audience know that this guy is a disrupter. Also, on the blackboard, there's a drawing of a shark with a victim inside its mouth. This is a relic of early versions

of the script in which Matt Hooper drew the diagram when explaining the size of the shark's jaw. That scene was never filmed, but the idea remains as a background detail that helps make the introduction to Quint so striking. The shark drawing is a clever, almost subliminal visual that keeps the shark in the audience's mind even as Quint takes center stage.

The pressure that Chief Martin Brody feels to solve the shark problem and his guilt over the deaths of Amity's citizens are huge drivers in the narrative of *Jaws*. Brody is a New York cop who has moved to Amity with his family. He's "a fish out of water," so to speak, and he feels like he has something to prove. Following the death of Alex Kintner, Brody is publicly blamed by the child's mother. It puts Brody in this impossible situation, and the guilt he feels becomes a huge motivator that really kicks the story into high gear. There's a powerful moment after the confrontation with the mother when the mayor says to Brody, "I'm sorry, Martin. She's wrong." But Brody disagrees and takes responsibility. It's extremely moving.

The boy's mother, played by Lee Fierro, is a small but hugely important role. In the confrontation

After 4th of July PANIC

ONE MAN remain in
water on a life boey (g wounded
& dies) & he is screaming help—
NOBODY WILL HELP HIM!
cut to reactions faces all
looky — nobody will go in
that water — no way —

3 Attacks at beging
different kinds —

Hoper shows Quint her CO_2 bit stuff
Quint scoffs Hoper Demonstrates
& it goes thru mast head —
Quint impressed, but to prove
a point grabs his trusty harpon
throws it — it goes in save mast
6 inch deeper

little boats are threats — too small
Boat going home fast to avoid shark
repel away a flat boat of shark
danger— scared, pushing home— runs out
of gas — still shark bait— sun going down.

SHARK BEHAVIOR— men who know must say This
particular shark is different, never seen behavior like
this— SAFARI like attacks no good at all

scene, the townsfolk are all celebrating because they think that they've killed the shark, but then suddenly everyone becomes totally silent when Mrs. Kintner arrives. Her emotion is palpable, and the slap she delivers to Brody is a heartbreaking moment: We know that Brody is doing his best, but we also understand that this is a mother who has lost a child in the most brutal way. I think it's especially moving that Steven cast a woman in her midforties for the role. The inference is that Alex was her only son and she likely will not have another. This isn't said in the film, but it's implied in the subtle and brilliant way that Steven sets up the scene.

That's the beauty of Steven's work and of that generation of filmmakers from which he came: They embraced realism and wanted to make films about people. And ultimately, *Jaws is* about people—the shark is just a conduit for discovering who they are. Every single one of the characters, even those in supporting roles, are fully realized and appear to have their own backstory. Early in the film, Quint comes off as a two-dimensional rough-edged seadog character. But as the three leads hunt the shark, he

opens up and the film becomes much more intimate, particularly in the moment in which Quint tells the story of how he survived the sinking of the USS *Indianapolis* during World War II.

When Shaw delivers his speech, it's absolutely riveting; the scene feels almost like an intimate play starring Roy Scheider, Richard Dreyfuss, and Robert Shaw. Invoking this real-life event not only anchors this wild character in reality, but also in history. The speech elevates Quint from being a grumpy old sailor stereotype and makes him a war hero. To accomplish that in this genre of film and at this late stage in the story is a real tour-de-force. It changes the whole mood of the movie and our perception of Quint, and the added pathos makes his later death even more tragic. It's almost as if being killed by a shark is a destiny he cannot escape.

BELOW A French lobby card featuring (*left to right*) Quint (Robert Shaw), Brody (Roy Scheider), and Hooper (Richard Dreyfuss) aboard the *Orca*.

BOTTOM Filming on Martha's Vineyard with the mechanical shark, which Steven Spielberg nicknamed Bruce after his lawyer, Bruce Ramer.

LES DENTS DE LA MER

LES DENTS DE LA MER

UN FILM UNIVERSAL DISTRIBUE PAR CINEMA INTERNATIONAL CORPORATION
INTERDIT AUX MOINS DE 13 ANS

Jaws at Home

Brody struggling to fit in on Amity Island is a further example of the home theme in Steven's early work. Like the characters in *The Sugarland Express*, Brody yearns for a home and is trying to build a new life but is facing resistance from the world around him. Although Peter's novel touches on why Brody left New York, Steven largely leaves it to the audience's imagination.

In addition, the shark poses a very real threat to Brody's family. While the death of Alex Kintner puts him on the road to action, it's when the shark swims into an estuary and almost kills Brody's son that he finally decides to pursue and destroy it. His son is unharmed, but the shark claims another victim, the incident leading to an important progression in Brody's psychology where he goes from feeling guilty and powerless in the face of the first two deaths in the film, to resolving to hunt the creature. This moment is reflected in a single shot from his point of view as he looks out to sea. In this moment, the shark has essentially intruded on Brody's home and that's more than he can take.

Perhaps the most significant example of the home theme is a moment during the hospital scene that follows the shark attack at the estuary. Brody tells

> **❝** Like the characters in *The Sugarland Express*, Brody yearns for a home and is trying to build a new life but is facing resistance from the world around him."

his wife to take their younger son home, and she asks, "New York?" He replies, "No, home here." In this moment, Brody verbalizes his full commitment to make a new life on the island and to protect its people from the shark. Again there's a sense that Steven's characters are always looking for a home, and here, Brody, an exile from New York, is struggling to find his place in this new community. And that plays into the moment where Brody decides to stand his ground, protect his family, and go out to sea to kill the shark. It's a wonderful way to transition into the film's third act, when Brody, Quint, and Hooper are essentially lost in this jungle of water, mano a mano with the beast. While at sea, the home theme

ABOVE A French lobby card featuring the scene in which Hooper is attacked by the shark while in an underwater cage, which was shot in the water tank at MGM Studios.

comes up again when Brody, Hooper, and Quint sing "Show Me the Way to Go Home." That longing to be home and safe is a constant motif.

Jaws of Death

Jaws has, without a doubt, one of the greatest openings and the greatest endings in film history. I always feel that films are remembered most for how they draw you in at the beginning and how they leave you at the end.

I remember as a teenager hearing the underwater sounds playing as the Universal logo appears and feeling like, "Oh my god. It's starting." In a way, the film begins before it begins. The logo is followed by footage from the shark's point of view as it swims through the ocean. It's so evocative and daring because it suddenly places the audience in the position of the killer. That credit sequence, accompanied by the iconic *Jaws* theme by John Williams, is so immersive. Famously, when John played Steven the opening two-note motif—"Da-DUH"—Steven thought it was a joke. Now, it is so recognizable that it instantly conjures up imagery of the film, in particular that opening scene where the shark closes in on its first victim.

ABOVE Steven Spielberg (*right*) directs Chris Rebello and Roy Scheider.

LEFT Mr. and Mrs. Brody: Roy Scheider and Lorraine Gary.

BELOW Spielberg preps a domestic scene starring Scheider and Gary, plus Elmer, the director's real-life dog.

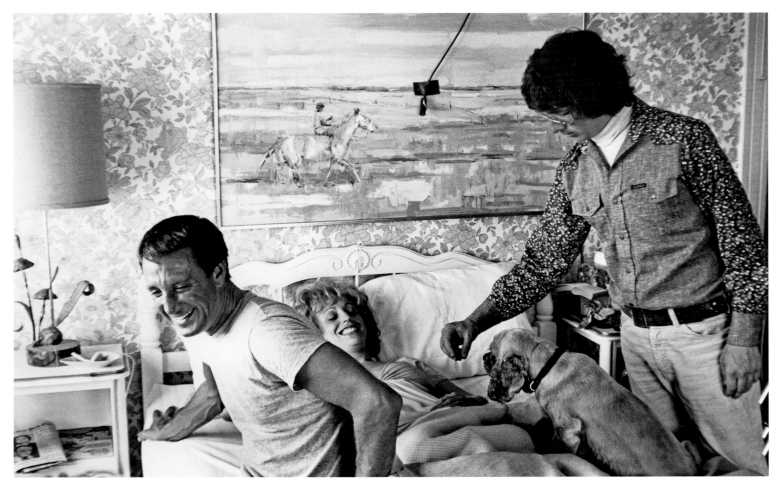

There's a beauty to the sequence that introduces Chrissie. It starts by evoking innocent sexuality as the young woman undresses to swim naked in the sea at night. This taboo element, of course, echoes Hitchcock's *Psycho* (1960), and the iconic scene in which Janet Leigh's character, Marion Crane, is stabbed to death while taking a shower. Both women are unaware of the sudden shocking death that awaits them. There's a vulnerability and primal fear of the unknown in both scenes, especially since both killers are somewhat invisible in both instances:

You don't see the shark, and you only see Marion's murderer in silhouette. There's also a randomness at the heart of the deaths—both Chrissie and Marion are simply in the wrong place at the wrong time, not unlike David Mann in *Duel*. And the way the Chrissie scene is filmed leaves the audience feeling that anything could happen and in a state of constant alert for the rest of the film.

The tone of *Jaws*' third act is very different from that of the first two acts. Once the hunt starts, John Williams's music gives it this very heroic,

RIGHT Steven Spielberg and Richard Dreyfuss examine the dead tiger shark in a photograph signed by Dreyfuss for the author.

swashbuckling feel and turns the movie into a great high-seas adventure. When the three men first harpoon the shark, there's a sense of jubilation. Humor also really comes to the fore, particularly in the banter between Brody, Hooper, and Quint, most notably during the scene in which, within the cabin of the ⏤ Orca, Hooper and Quint compare ⏤ 've received over the years. Most of ⏤ 's were shot on location, even the ⏤ ⏤ ⏤ ⏤ ⏤ the cabin. The sequence in which the ⏤ plodes was also shot in the ocean. A spec. ⏤ rk head was built that was loaded with squibs ⏤ nd all sorts of bits of gore. When the squibs were set off, it caused this huge explosion of flesh and blood. And I love that beautiful shot as the shark's remains fall to the bottom of the ocean. It's an incredible payoff for the audience.

I also appreciate the moment at the end of the film where Brody discovers that Hooper has survived. There's something very poignant about the way that Hooper, surfacing after the shark explosion, asks Brody about Quint—and Brody just shakes his head to indicate that he was killed. It's very subtle. And the last lines of dialogue are delivered full of irony: "You know, I used to hate the water," says Brody, to which Hooper responds, "I can't imagine why." In the space of this simple scene there's tragedy, lightness, and the relief of finally killing the shark all at once. It truly is one of the greatest endings in cinema history, and it's still as powerful today as when the movie was released in 1975.

Talking *Jaws*

When I conducted the interviews for the *Jaws* documentary, producer David Brown mentioned something that really stuck with me: He said, "This is *Rashomon*. You're going to ask every single one of us the same question, and we're all going to have a different version. And if you're not willing to accept this, then you should not be doing this documentary." He was so right. Like in the 1950 Akira Kurosawa film, everyone has their own interpretation of the same event and no one version is ever the full truth.

My approach to interviewing people like Richard

ABOVE A photograph of Susan Backlinie as Chrissie in *Jaws*, signed by the actress to the author.

lived in a comfortable trailer in the San Fernando Valley. Susan was so lovely and appreciative, and when I met her for her interview, I gave her a giant poster of her death scene as a gift.

The release of the *Jaws* LaserDisc on November 19, 1996, was a big deal for me. There were a lot of reviews and positive feedback on the documentary. To have my name somewhat associated with that movie, even in such a small way, was wonderful and kind of brought me full circle. Of course, the success of the documentary was down to the fascination that the film still held with viewers after so many years— *Jaws* had transcended time. But to be the person who got to assemble that documentary was truly an honor, and I really cherish that experience.

Jaws is such a remarkable film, and, as I said, I can't imagine cinema without it. I can't imagine my life without discovering it. *Jaws* informed everything I love about movies. I think that's also true for a lot of people. *Jaws* also changed Steven Spielberg's career forever. He attained a huge level of success with the film, but its creation was so tumultuous that it amounted to a rite of passage: *Jaws* could have just as easily damaged his career as forged it. But despite the difficulties, and perhaps in some ways because of them, Steven absolutely found his voice with *Jaws* and all the elements of his filmmaking that we now think of as Spielbergian are on full display in the movie.

I'll never forget interviewing Steven for the *Jaws* documentary. Bonnie Curtis, his assistant at the time (who later became a producer), said, "Listen, he wants to do the interview, but he is literally slammed. I think he can give you a solid half hour, but then I must pull him out." In my mind I was like, *A half hour? That doesn't seem like anywhere near enough time.* But I said nothing and decided to just go with the flow. So, Steven came in to do his half hour, and once we got talking, he became so excited. I'm sure that over the years, he'd been asked about *Jaws* a bunch of times, but he relished the deep dive I took him on as we discussed the creation of the film and he just loved talking about it. It felt like all my research and preparation had really paid off.

We went beyond the allotted half hour, and eventually Bonnie came in and said, "Steven, you've got to go." He looked at me and said, "Don't leave. I'll come back." I didn't think he would return. But sure enough, he went off, did whatever he had to do, and, in typical Steven fashion, he came back.

> " Steven absolutely found his voice with *Jaws*, and all the elements of his filmmaking that we now think of as Spielbergian are on full display in the movie."

Dreyfuss and Roy Scheider was based on pure enthusiasm. I wasn't interested in doing short soundbite interviews. I wanted to dig deep and go scene by scene. My preparation was meticulous, and I really tried to create a journey in each interview—a story. On *Jaws*, one of my favorite interviewees was Susan Backlinie, who played Chrissie. By then, she had left the film industry, so I had to track her down. She'd been a stuntperson in her heyday, and now

ABOVE Chief Brody (Roy Scheider) in *Jaws'* action-packed finale.

OPPOSITE A list of shark facts created as part of the promotional campaign for *Jaws*.

Sharkfacts:

Provided as a Public Service by the Producers of

JAWS

If you swim in the sea, anywhere in the world, you do not do so without risk. The shark is an ancient, wide-ranging, and ever present threat.

Sharks do not ordinarily feed on human beings. But as volumes will attest, they do attack. How and when and why is still unpredictable.

Therefore, if you must venture into the ocean, at least know your enemy. At present, there is much about the shark's behavior we do not fully comprehend. Some of the important things we do know are enumerated below.

You would be wise to study them.

1 All sharks, no matter what their size, should be treated with respect. There are over 300 species of sharks. Most are predators, born with a full set of teeth and the instinct to use them. Even a shark much smaller than a man has the ability to inflict fatal injuries.

2 The seas off our shore are aprowl with many killers. The proven maneaters include the Blue Shark, the Tiger Shark, the Bull Shark, the Mako, the Hammerhead, and most fearsome of all…the Great White.

3 Fresh water swimmers are not necessarily safe from sharks. A lake in Central America contains some of the most voracious sharks in the world. Experiments have proven that some sharks traverse 100 miles of river to get there. Three of the worst attacks in U.S. history occurred in a brackish New Jersey creek 20 miles from the open sea.

4 The shark is in many respects one of the most successful creatures on the planet. The first sharks appeared over 300 million years ago. They have changed relatively little in the past 60 million years. The sharks prey are many, his enemies few. He is a most efficient killing machine.

5 Shark attacks may be motivated by more than mere hunger. There is evidence that the shark has a "fighting instinct," that he attacks for reasons of true aggression —probably to protect territory, personal space, or status.

6 Some sharks can move in tremendous bursts of speed. The Mako, which can leap twenty feet out of the water has been reported to exceed 30 miles an hour.

7 A shark is a tooth making machine. And the teeth you see in a shark's gaping mouth aren't the half of it. Behind the front row lay at least four to six more rows. Razor sharp cutting and tearing tools, they are often serrated like a steak knife. When a tooth is lost, a new tooth replaces it. In one chomp, a shark can inflict a wound which is massive and almost surgically precise.

8 A major portion of a shark's brain is devoted to the sense of smell. An incredibly small concentration of blood in the water can arouse his feeding desire and bring him running to the source from far away. If you are bleeding, no matter how slightly, get out of the water.

9 A shark's vision is far from poor. Like a panther, his eyes are designed to be efficient in very dim light. In the dark, the shark has a special advantage over you. Never swim at night.

10 Sharks have been known to attack practically anything. Floating barrels. Life rafts. Whirling propellers. And boats. One hooked shark attacked a 35 foot fishing boat, tore planking from the bottom, and sank it.

11 Shark attacks occur in water of every depth. They have killed in the open sea and at the surf line. Some of the worst attacks occurred in water only knee deep.

12 A shark doesn't have to bite you to hurt you. His skin is extremely rough, covered with tiny denticle structures very similar to teeth. Rub him the wrong way, and he can severely abrade your skin.

13 Sharks are superbly equipped to detect low-frequency vibrations—the erratic noises made by wounded fish…and poor swimmers. He can home in on these peculiar sounds from hundreds of yards. Swim smoothly.

14 Of all the sharks in the sea, the Great White (*Carcharodon carcharias*) is unquestionably the most dangerous. The largest yet captured measured 21 feet and weighed over 3½ tons. They undoubtedly grow even larger.

The known food of the Great White Shark includes mackerel, tuna, porpoise, seal, other sharks, and on terrible occasions…man.

for of all large animals found in the sea, man is the easiest prey.

Authenticated by Donald R. Nelson (Ph.D.), Shark Research Specialist, Associate Professor of Biology California State University, Long Beach

SPIELBERG ON *JAWS*

You found out about *Jaws* even before the novel by Peter Benchley was even published, right?

I do remember being in Richard Zanuck's office, working on the postproduction of my first theatrical film *The Sugarland Express*, which both Dick and David Brown had produced, and seeing a galley proof of a book called *Jaws*. I asked the secretary what this was, and she said, "It's a book Dick and David have purchased." This was way before the title entered the national consciousness—it was just a word—JAWS. I asked if I could read the book, still not knowing this was about a great white shark, a predator off the beaches of a town called Amity. I had no idea this was about to become one of the greatest best sellers in the nation. Now, my recollection is that the project had already been offered to another director who was scheduled to meet with Peter Benchley. So, when I read the book over that weekend, it wasn't available for me to direct. But I got through the book. I'm a slow reader. I've always been a slow reader, but I got through it in about two and a half days, which is fast for me. And I immediately thought: *Wow, this is like a TV movie I made about a truck and a hapless driver, called* Duel. And of course, I'm young and I'm stupid and I'm saying, "*Duel* . . . gee . . . that has four letters, and *Jaws* has four letters . . . and they're both about these leviathans preying on innocent people." And I saw such comparison between the two that I thought of *Jaws* as a sequel to *Duel*, only on water. I got very interested in the project, and I went back to Dick and David and said, "I know how to make this into a film. I know what to cut out. I know what to keep. That sea hunt for that shark is extraordinary! I know how to do this." But Dick and David confirmed they were going to meet with another director and Peter Benchley. That was that, until I got a call from Dick asking me to come meet with him and David.

They sat me down and announced, "We want you to direct *Jaws*." I said, "Whatever happened to the director?" And they explained, "We had the meeting with him, but he kept referring to the shark in front of Peter Benchley as 'the white whale.' And Peter became very disinterested in having his shark called a whale." And that's how the project finally came to me.

There were quite a few screenplay drafts written, based on the novel. A few subplots like the ties the mayor has with the mafia, or the romance between Hooper and Brody's wife, among others, were dropped.

The first thing I told Peter Benchley was I didn't see any room in this adventure for the affair between Ellen Brody, the wife of the chief of police, and the ichthyologist. That was like a *Peyton Place* scandal that I didn't feel had any place in the kind of movie I wanted to make. But I was mostly intrigued and swept away by Peter Benchley's enormous storytelling skills in the rest of the novel, with a sea-hunt survivors adventure. That's what I wanted to focus on—and I wanted to get there without having to deal with the nonessential peccadilloes going on in a town without pity. So, the affair never really made it even into the early script that Peter Benchley wrote.

Peter didn't really like working in California; he preferred working in Boston, and he said to me, "Look, I'll give you one good draft, and then you can do whatever you want with it after that." That was fair, and Peter Benchley did a very good adaptation of his own novel. But after he turned it over to me, I didn't quite know what to do because it wasn't the movie I had envisioned. I knew what the first and third acts were, but I didn't have a second act. I remember sitting and writing a script myself, an entire draft from beginning to end, and one I didn't show

JAWS IDEAS

1. Cedar-shingled houses

2. Brody calls rich people the UPPER CRUSTS

3. Fleecing the pilgrims - the townspeople call the tourists pilgrims

4. Dogs being escorted off the Island on ONTIME DOGS

5. Need scene of MAP to orient us as to the swimming places & non-swimming - He used red pencils to show the danger beach closed spots [where the signs must go. & black marks to show [other areas

6. Brody racing to the scene of Boy Scout rescue with the twin forests flying by

7. Karate school kids go to. H school They've been picky on the white picket fences. "Little Karate choppers" Brody must contend with this kind of crime rather than dope or murder

8. 6 kids brought in by deputy - the proof in the pudding is their white scuff marks on their shoes & hand sides. This is the kind of crime busting that is done & the deputy who apprehends kids is pleased as pie. Maybe Brody exults in finding more clues. He reasons that a grown man would kick higher & hit higher on the fence. The splinter-marks show a youngster

9. Brody goes to Library & finds Shark books. takes them home & studies like a student

10. ONE HOUSE has come by - the white pickets are all demolished

11. At end of Vaughan scene with Brody (Boy Scouts in b.g.) Vaughn tries to throw him a bone by requesting that he forget sharks & try to find out who has been picking is his Fences

many people. I don't even think I have a copy of it anymore. A few scenes did survive and wound up in the movie, but this was more of an exercise for me to become familiar with what I wanted *Jaws* to be. It was beneficial because I suddenly had a vision of what the film should be even though I didn't have the skills to write it.

At that point, David Brown and Dick Zanuck both suggested that we go to Howard Sackler, who had written the play and the film adaptation of *The Great White Hope* [1970]. Of course, I'm thinking, "*Duel, Jaws* . . . four letters. . . . And now 'The Great White Hope' and great white shark . . . makes sense. . . . Let's hire him!' I had never seen *The Great White Hope*, but there was some poetic justice in all that. I was courageous and stupid—the privilege of youth!

I met Howard Sackler, who was a dear man. We spent about three weeks at the Hotel Bel-Air, every single day, just pitching out ideas, working on the script for a few hours. Then I'd go home and he would write. At the end of the three weeks, he turned in his draft, which basically is the movie. Sackler really broke the back of the movie and got me saying, "I'm committing." But it wasn't quite there yet, so I asked Carl Gottlieb—a friend of mine who ended up acting in the film as well—to come in, do a polish, and help me with the script. And what we wound up doing was rewriting the script verbally with mainly Richard Dreyfuss and Roy Scheider and sometimes Robert

Shaw, sitting in my rented log cabin on Martha's Vineyard, where I lived during production. The cabin had six bedrooms, and Richard would sometimes stay there during filming. We really had a great time because I'd make up scenes, they'd make up scenes, I'd pitch out an idea, they'd pitch out an idea, Carl would pitch an idea. It was kind of an interesting collaboration between the actors and the director. Carl would write up some of these improvisations, always keeping up with us, writing on his Smith Corona. A rewrite was never distributed until Richard vetted the pages—and sometimes he would call me up and say, "You've got too much comedy here. The guys are acting silly with each other. Do you really want them to be that silly?" And I would either defend it or agree with him. We'd then deliver new pages to the crew and rest of the cast the next day. So, often, I was rewriting the script the night before I was shooting the scenes.

Why didn't Sackler get credit on the film?
He didn't want credit. He said, "I did this as a favor to my good friend David Brown. I made money, and I'm very appreciative." And that was it.

I'm curious about the casting of the three protagonists: Roy Scheider, Richard Dreyfuss, and Robert Shaw. They are fantastic actors, but they weren't big stars, big "marquee" names.

I did go for a big star initially because my first choice for Quint was Lee Marvin, but he wasn't interested. What I heard was that he wanted to go fishing for real! He took his fishing very seriously and didn't want to do it from a "movie" boat. My second choice was Sterling Hayden, whom I thought would make an amazing Quint. He had an Ahab quality about him—he had done a film entitled *Terror in a Texas Town* in 1958, where he played an imposing whaler who walked around with a harpoon. I was a big fan of his, especially from the two films he had done with Stanley Kubrick, *The Killing* [1956] and *Dr. Strangelove* [1964]. I don't remember why, but he wasn't able to do the role. There were other actors who wanted to play Quint, and then Dick Zanuck and David Brown suggested Robert Shaw—they had just worked with him in *The Sting* [1973], which they produced, and loved him. I'd just screened two films with Shaw to refresh my memory, including *A Man for All Seasons* [1966], in which he was spectacular. Based on that, and of course on *From Russia with Love* [1963]— with that great fight on a train where he played the nemesis to 007—I said, "Wow . . . I wish I had thought of him! It's a great idea!" He fortunately said yes.

I'll never forget that one of the first things Shaw said to me was, "I haven't had a drink in two months!" And Dick was always warning me when he sensed that Robert Shaw had been drinking, fearing it would delay filming—but it didn't really matter because

the shark wasn't working anyway. Incidentally, during production, Dick Zanuck and Robert Shaw would play ping-pong together, and one day, when Dick won, Shaw challenged him to a fistfight which was quickly defused by others. If Shaw had gotten a black eye, that would definitely have put us further behind schedule!

Richard Dreyfuss was not my first choice either. I went to Jon Voight first, and he said no. I think we interviewed Timothy Bottoms as well as several other actors, including Jeff Bridges. I was a big fan of *The Last Picture Show* [1971]—I was going after everyone in the cast from that film, including Bottoms and Bridges. We got turned down or they weren't available. These things happen all the time. Richard Dreyfuss got the part because I loved [George Lucas's] *American Graffiti* [1973]. George was the one who told me, "Why don't you cast Ricky Dreyfuss?" I sought a meeting with Richard, who said he was interested in seeing *Jaws*, but he wasn't interested in being in it. I was persistent, and Carl Gottlieb, who knew Richard well, kept saying to him, "Come on, it will be fun." So, Richard accepted another meeting with me, and I talked him into it.

How I cast Roy Scheider is an interesting story. I was going to a whole series of actors, most of them unknown. There was an actor I liked from *Serpico* [1973]—it was not Al Pacino—as well as another one I had seen in an off-Broadway play. But the

ABOVE Steven Spielberg directs Roy Scheider against the backdrop of a defaced Amity Island sign.

TOP Shooting the scene in which Brody and Hooper confront the mayor of Amity, played by Murray Hamilton: (*left to right*) Richard Dreyfuss, Hamilton, Roy Scheider, and Steven Spielberg.

ABOVE Universal's Sid Sheinberg with Richard D. Zanuck and Spielberg during the *Jaws* shoot.

studio, Zanuck, and Brown were pressuring me to get a name for this part. I was having trouble finding someone I liked. Then, I remember going to a party one night, and Roy Scheider, whom I loved from *The French Connection*, came and sat down next to me and said, "You look awfully depressed." I told him, "Oh no, I'm not depressed. I'm just having trouble casting my movie." He asked what the film was—I explained it was based on a novel called *Jaws* and told him the entire plot. At the end of it, Roy said, "Wow, that's a great story! What about me?" I looked at him and said, "Yeah, what about you? You'd make a great Chief Brody!"

What about Lorraine Gary, the wife of Universal's Sid Sheinberg. Why did you choose her for the part of Ellen Brody?
She was the first person I cast for the movie. I had loved her in a TV movie called *The Marcus-Nelson Murders* [1973] with Telly Savalas. I thought she was a very natural actress, almost improvisational in her style. She brought realism to *Jaws* and to that family, which is something I really wanted for the film.

And Murray Hamilton as Amity's mayor?
I had been a big fan of his from *The FBI Story* [1959] with James Stewart to *The Graduate* [1967]. I wanted to work with him, and I saw him instantly as the mayor of Amity. I didn't have to go through many other actors. He was the first choice for the part, and I was lucky to get him.

You hired the famous shark experts and documentary filmmakers Ron and Valerie Taylor to film real-life shark footage back in Australia. How did their contribution inform the story?
I had this idea that we could maybe shoot real shark footage. I was always afraid that the mechanical shark wouldn't look like a real one. Ron and Valerie Taylor were well-known for having escaped the jaws of death and danger to make these outstanding documentaries on great white sharks around the

Great Barrier Reef in Australia. I remember just being knocked out by what they had captured, and I thought they would be great to shoot second-unit footage. However, because the largest shark they could guarantee finding was about seventeen feet long, and the mechanical shark we were busy building was twenty-six feet long, I had this idea of having a miniature cage for the scene where Matt Hooper goes underwater, and to use a little person or a very short man in it. I interviewed several potential candidates, and I remember this tenacious gentleman who came in to see me bleeding, and I said, "What happened to you?" And he replied, "I was afraid I was going to be late for this meeting, and I got into a traffic accident in front of the main gate of the studio." I told him to immediately return to the scene of the accident, but I remember thinking, what a brave guy—he really wants this job! And I was young and courageous and stupid, and I hired him! His name was Carl Rizzo, and he had doubled Elizabeth Taylor during the horse-riding scenes in *National Velvet* [1944]. But there were three

intercuts for the sequence of the shark attack with the cage. Much later, after we wrapped filming on Martha's Vineyard, we shot at the MGM tank with two stuntmen, Dick Warlock and Frank Sparks, subbing for Richard Dreyfuss. Dick is in the wide shots and Sparks was used for Richard's close-ups. As for the Taylors' footage, the real shark got caught in the ropes of the cage, and I rewrote the scene around that piece of existing footage. That's why you have the shark getting entangled in the ropes of the cage, and why it starts pulling the jib down, splintering it.

You decided to film on Martha's Vineyard—what was that experience like?
Martha's Vineyard suited the purpose of the story—everything was perfect. But the main attraction wasn't so much the charm of a whaling town with piers and boats or anything of that nature. It was something you couldn't see with the naked eye; it was the fact that it was the only place on the East Coast where I could go twelve miles out to sea and avoid any sighting of land but still have a sandy ocean bottom only thirty

ABOVE Steven Spielberg studies the *Jaws* script on a Martha's Vineyard beach.

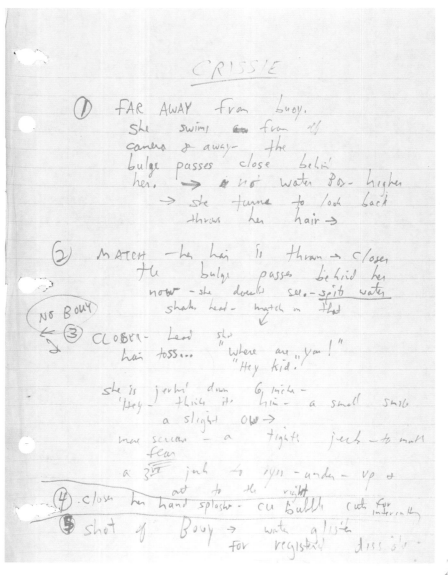

feet below the surface, where we could install our shark sled. That's the depth the mechanical shark apparatus required. Another factor was that once we were at sea on the *Orca*, no matter what direction my cameras turned, you didn't see land. My fear was the minute the audience saw land, they would not feel the danger. I wanted the audience to think the boat couldn't just simply turn around and go back to shore. I literally needed a 360-degree stage at sea. If we had shot the film in a tank without strong tides and without waves and without wind, we would have had an easier time. I kept remembering a movie which I had loved Spencer Tracy in, called *The Old Man and the Sea* [1958], but how it was so stylized and so impressionistic. It looked like a lake, like a studio tank. And the wild sunsets were obvious painted backdrops. I didn't want *Jaws* to look like that. The audience would not have connected with the movie unless it looked real, and that's why I insisted on shooting the picture on open sea in the Atlantic Ocean.

Is it true that, as you prepared the film, you told Joe Alves, your production designer, that you wanted to remove traces of red in the sets, except for the blood?
Yes, for *Jaws*, I didn't want red to be dominant on

any of the sets. I told Joe, "Please . . . when you're designing the picture and finding your colors, don't use too much red, allowing for the blood." And in general, we pretty much stuck to that. The Kintner boy had a red bathing suit, and we did have red wine in the scene with Hooper and Brody at the dinner table, but there was a bit of symbolism and foreshadowing in that.

As you prepared for shooting, did you anticipate it to be as difficult as it turned out to be?
I knew my first film, *The Sugarland Express*, was going to be difficult because so much was riding on it, but *Jaws* was my second movie, and I really had a gut feeling about how to tell the story. I thought that if we could pull the shark off—if we could get the audience to believe in this big, mechanical monstrosity, if it really worked, if it even floated—people would be frightened. But I had no idea, nor did anybody on the production, how difficult it was going to be to float that monstrosity and get it to work in the ocean. And none of us anticipated how long *Jaws* would take. None of us were seamen. None of us understood the water. Freddie Zendar, whom we hired to be our expert in the water, kept warning all of us that it wasn't going to be a walk in the park. And it's not that I didn't believe him, because Freddie was an expert, but I never anticipated what was about to happen to us, and it wasn't just because the shark wasn't working. It was because deciding to go into the Atlantic to make a movie about a great white shark was insane. I didn't see the insanity of it. I saw the authenticity of it. Making *Jaws* really became a fool's mission until the audience proved otherwise.

The storyboards that you conceived with Joe Alves show an alternate opening with the titles through the mouth and teeth of the shark.
One of my bad ideas was to start the movie with the camera inside the gullet of the shark, shooting out toward the teeth with the mouth open. And I shot a sample of that and decided that this was a terrible and gimmicky idea that belonged in a B-movie. I did think it could work for the trailer—I tried it out, and again, it just seemed cheap, and I threw it out.

Was it always the plan not to show the shark in that opening scene?
A lot of things forced me into making certain decisions that did not involve the shark because it was not working for a long time while we were in production on Martha's Vineyard. Regarding the

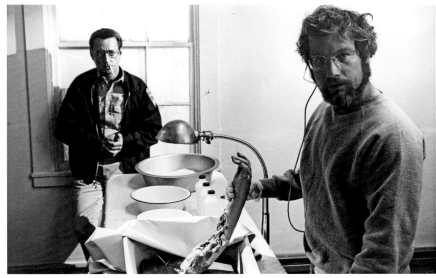

opening scene, the book does describe the shark approaching, but I thought it would be very scary not to show it at all. If the shark had come out of the water, it would have been spectacular but there would have been nothing primal about it—it would have just been another monster moment that all of us had already seen in other films. I wanted the jerking motion of the first victim to trigger our imagination about what was going on below. I felt that was stronger than showing the snout or even a glimpse of fin.

I remember as a kid seeing lobby cards featuring Chrissie's death scene and seeing they were in the daytime. Then, when I saw the film, that scene was at night, and I realized you shot it using the day-for-night technique, by underexposing the image. Why did you make that decision?
I didn't want to shoot at night on the ocean because darkness only extends as far as the arcs will light the

OPPOSITE TOP Steven Spielberg's handwritten notes outline the Chrissie shark attack sequence that opens the film.

OPPOSITE BOTTOM Chrissie actress Susan Backlinie prepares for a take with Spielberg and the camera crew.

TOP (*Left to right*) Richard D. Zanuck and Spielberg confer with production designer Joe Alves.

ABOVE Brody (Roy Scheider) observes as Matt Hooper (Richard Dreyfuss) examines the remains of the first victim.

water, so you'd never see the horizon. I didn't think twice about shooting it during the day using day-for-night and recalled the best day-for-night I had seen was Freddie Young's photography in *Lawrence of Arabia* [1962]. After all, the desert is a sea without water.

And Susan Backlinie, who played Chrissie, the first attack victim, was attached to wires so she could be pulled back and forth to simulate the attack, right?
She had a harness on. There were two eye rings in it, and wires that led to two stakes in the beach. Five crew were on one side, and five crew on the other, and they basically pulled Susan. There was a ribbon hanging from the wire, and when it got to one of the stakes, they had to stop pulling and the other team took over and pulled the other way. What you didn't want to have happen was for both teams to pull at the same time. For extra safety, she had the ability to quick release the wire if something went wrong. It had to be perfectly choreographed to give the impression the shark was pulling her violently to the right and then

immediately violently to the left.

Susan told me you pulled when the shark first attacks her.
Yes, I did it myself, but that was then—I don't go into the water anymore.

How did you cast Susan?
I didn't want an actor to do it. I wanted a stuntperson because I needed somebody who was great in the water, who knew water ballet, and knew how to endure what I imagined was going to be a whole lot of violent shaking. So, I went to stunts to find her, and Susan was up to the challenge.

I understand that you looped her screaming later. You gave her a bassinet of water and did all those sounds during post.
Yes, we went to the looping stage, and she did her own screaming and choking on glasses of water.

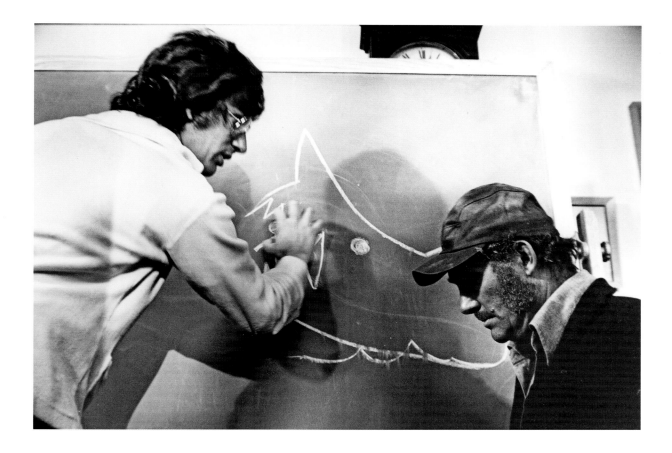

The hand in the sand, Chrissie's remains on the beach—how was that done?
The problem was production brought the hand to me, and it literally looked like shiny plastic and fake. They explained that after a body has been decomposing for a day on the sand with the sun coming down, it apparently takes on that bloated look. A pathologist might appreciate that, but to me, as an audience member, it just looked fake. We tried to put powder on it to get the reflective shine off, but it still didn't work. I turned to a woman from the crew and literally said: "Let me use your arm!" When we're kids, we like to bury our parents or siblings in the sand, and that's what we did. We used some makeup to make the arm look like it had been bitten off and we put live crabs around it to create movement. To this day, when I see *Jaws*, I always have this different vision of ten times as many crabs, moving ten times as fast!

The next victim is the Kintner boy—there's amazing tension and suspense in the way you created that scene.
The death of the Kintner boy on his raft—all the paranoia, tension, and suspense leading up to the actual attack—was something I wanted to do in one sustained shot. It wasn't possible, so instead, I came up with the idea to have bathers with different colored bathing suits walking in front of the camera, creating a wipe that would either reveal Roy Scheider or his

point of view. It wasn't one shot, but it gave a seamless feeling to the scene.

Wasn't there a much more graphic version of the death of the Kintner boy, shot using a dummy?
I don't have a clear memory of that. So much was shot on *Jaws*. I'm happy to have somebody correct me and say, "No, we did do that." What I do remember is asking for a lot of bloody water to go flying up on all sides of the Kintner boy before he's pulled down. That was the one effect I was after.

I always felt that Robert Shaw, who played Quint, has one of the greatest entrances ever in a movie, where he is running his fingernails on a blackboard.
That came from my twisted mind. I wanted him to get everybody's attention by doing something that I can't stand when I hear it done, even by accident, which is fingernails down a blackboard. I wanted to introduce Robert Shaw that way.

I assume he was not doing this for real.
Robert scraped his fingernails down the blackboard, though I think the sound effects designers sweetened it later.

I'm also curious about Ben Gardner's death. Wasn't the discovery of his boat originally shot in the daytime?

ABOVE Steven Spielberg directs Robert Shaw while shooting Quint's introduction scene.

I had an afterthought about the scene. But either way, I always thought the best solution was not to show Ben's death in real time, and to have Hooper discover not only the hole in the boat with the shark's tooth but Ben's head.

Yes, and that was shot later at the MGM tank, while the famous close-up on Ben's head was shot in Verna Field's swimming pool! Did you ever wonder how the shark killed Ben? Did he bite him and spit out his head?
[Laughs] I didn't think that deeply about it. All I know is that he was dead!

In terms of Quint's death, was it very disturbing to film that sequence?
No, it wasn't disturbing because it was toward the end of the movie, and I just couldn't wait to get off the picture. I just couldn't wait to get back to Los Angeles—get on that airplane in Boston at Logan Airport and fly as quickly as a plane could take me back home. So, no, there was nothing scary about it for me. For that sequence, I was following the

storyboards I had been working on for months. I shot the ending of the film and left just before effects pushed the button and blew the shark into shark bait.

As for the portrayal of Quint, I believe a lot of the inspiration came from a local named Craig Kingsbury, right?
Yes, and he plays Ben Gardner in the film. He was a selectman on Martha's Vineyard. I met him in an open casting call—I might even have come close to flirting with the idea of using him to play Quint because he was the purest version of who in my mind that character really was. When I met him, he came up with some great dialogue, and I kept increasing his part. I said to him, "I want you to be in my movie, and you can create your own dialogue." He made up all that stuff when he's on the boat with other islanders, trying to capture the shark, saying, "They'll wish their fathers had never met their mothers, when they start takin' their bottoms out and slammin' into them rocks, boy." It was great! And when Richard Dreyfuss says to him, "Hello," and he replies, "Hello back!" that was also his idea. Very intuitive, colorful, and primal person

ABOVE LEFT A French lobby card featuring Robert Shaw as Quint.
ABOVE RIGHT Steven Spielberg directs Shaw in a scene featuring Quint's truck that would be deleted from the final film.

who just never pursued acting. And what happened is that I sat with Craig with a tape recorder. I was honest and I said to him, "I want you to talk to me because I want to use some of your local color for Quint." Craig gave me some great lines—one of them was in Robert Shaw's speech when he first enters the selectmen town meeting and says, "Bad fish. Not like going down the pond chasin' bluegills and tommycods." That's Craig's line. Carl Gottlieb wrote a lot of that speech based on lines that Craig had given me in one of our conversations.

There's a quick moment where we see Quint on his boat from a distance as the locals think they got the shark. But you had originally conceived an interesting scene for the character involving the John Huston film *Moby Dick* [1956].
That entire script I wrote on my own, after the Benchley draft and before Sackler, had a scene where Quint is in a movie theater on the island watching *Moby Dick*—and laughing at the mechanical whale and Ahab with his harpoon. People get up and leave until he's all alone in the theater. But Gregory Peck, who was in *Moby Dick* and owned the rights to it, just wasn't proud of the film and didn't want us making any fun of it in *Jaws*.

Was there anything else you wanted to include in the film?
There were other scenes in the script that I wrote that I regret not shooting. I had this idea that there was a harbormaster who lived in a small shack— at night, there were all those sailboats with their masts sticking up. The harbormaster is in his shack, watching *Don't Go Near the Water* [1957] starring Glenn Ford, and through the window, behind him, you start seeing the masts moving, one after another, getting closer and closer to the shack. At one point, the harbormaster goes to clean out his coffeepot and is taken by the shark. That was also in my original script, and we just couldn't afford to shoot it. In its place, we have this other scene, with the two fishermen who take the Sunday pot roast, a chain, and a *Texas Chainsaw Massacre*–style hook and toss it out to sea. The shark takes the bait, the pier comes right off, and one of the guys falls in the water. I didn't want to show the shark in that scene, just the pier turning around and coming back toward the guy who is desperately trying to get out of the water, which I thought was a hell of a lot scarier.

Those were things I had written in my own script

before Sackler came on board and that I was hoping would find a way into the final movie, but what's in there turned out to be enough.

There's a great moment in the film between Martin Brody and his younger son, Sean, where the boy imitates his father at the dinner table.
Exploration of human behavior fascinates me. I think we improvised that moment on the day—I wanted Roy to show he was depressed, and his son imitates him. It lightens up the mood, and Brody can see that he does have a life outside his job, that he has children and a family. I remember when I was working on the script of *E.T.*, I wanted a similar scene where E.T. imitates Elliott, which leads to them communicating for the first time. I thought, *Hey, if it worked in* Jaws, *it could work in* E.T.

There was an old couple named the Nockers in *The Sugarland Express*—and I read that you wanted to bring them back in *Jaws*, have them be tourists on the beach.
I wanted them to be passing through Amity, maybe even going out to the beach, spread out a picnic blanket. Mr. Nocker blows up an inner tube, and we get the idea that maybe he and his wife are going

BELOW Steven Spielberg behind the camera for *Jaws*.

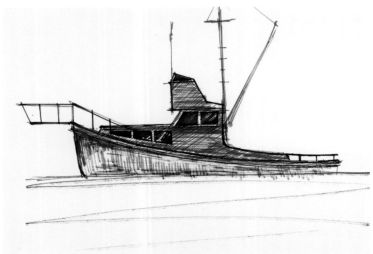

ABOVE Four conceptual designs for Quint's boat, the *Orca*, created by production designer Joe Alves.

to go swimming. But I thought, this movie is already too impossible to make. I've got to stop making it harder on myself!

Following the "fake" attack and panic on the beach, there was the victim in the estuary. That scene changed quite a bit in the cutting room.
I cut the scene down because it was too bloody, too gory. Stuntman Teddy Grossman played the victim—and Teddy is a very funny guy, by the way—but originally, he was riding in the mouth of the shark like a maidenhead of a ship, toward the kid in the water, vomiting blood. That was much more horrible than anything else that came in the first third of the movie, so I took it out.

Ted Grossman is one of the most hilarious people I have ever met.
Dick Zanuck introduced me to Teddy Grossman on *Sugarland Express*. Teddy has made a lot of movies with me. He was one of the best stuntmen in the world. And yes, he has a great sense of humor. Dick and Teddy remained very close through the years.

❝❝ The *Orca* was originally called the *Warlock* before it was purchased by our production designer Joe Alves.❞

I love the moment where the guys are packing up to go out to sea—I read that Robert Shaw improvised some of the dialogue in that scene.
I asked Robert to give Lorraine's character, Ellen Brody, a bit of a hard time by teasing her husband—he is wearing rubber boots and a rubber outfit, so Quint says, "See ya got ya rubbers!" and laughs. Quint is doing this to both Brody and Hooper—and at some point, Robert Shaw recited this little poem, "This is the story of Mary McGee, lived to the age of a hundred and three. For fifteen years she kept her virginity, not a bad record for this vicinity." I said to him, "You got to help me clear this—if that's

from a song, we can't use it without paying for the rights." And he reassured me, "No, I don't think we'll get sued. I got it from a tombstone in Ireland!"

Once we're out to sea, we never leave the *Orca*—Quint's boat.

The *Orca* was originally called the *Warlock* before it was purchased by our production designer Joe Alves. He chose the boat and I liked it a lot, but I felt it didn't have enough character—and Joe agreed. So, he replaced the entire wheelhouse with one of his own design with larger windows, so we could see out. Everywhere you were on the boat, the ocean was breathing down your neck. Joe built a second *Orca* that was essentially designed to sink, with pumps so it could come back up for another take.

A problem we had was when a speedboat pulling the *Orca* went too fast and pulled out the planking from the haul—water rushed in, and the boat sank in about two minutes. I remember vividly the moment where the actors were yelling, "Send boats, get us out, send boats!" Our sound mixer John Carter—who shared an Oscar with his team for *Jaws*—picked up the Nagra recorder, held it over his head, and said, "F--- the actors, save the sound department!" I have this image to this day of John sinking holding

his recorder with water up to his ankles, and then to his knees, while crews on boats were scrambling to pull everybody off the sinking *Orca*. Months later, he was holding an Oscar in those hands!

What happened to the camera equipment?

The camera was on the boat, too, and it went underwater. Our director of photography Bill Butler said: "You know, in a sense, the developing solution we use is saline, and I think the film will be okay if we can rush it to the lab, and as long as we keep it in saltwater." We had big buckets of saltwater and kept the magazines of film in there—they were sent to our lab in New York, and they successfully saved the negative.

Bill Butler was inventive and created equipment just to make *Jaws*. There was the camera platform that could move with the tide and go above or below the surface of the water. He also had a special box where he could put his camera and film in the water, but he reconfigured it so he could still pull focus. I wanted this movie to be at water level and have the camera right down to where the human point of view is most accustomed to being when you're swimming—I'd say 25 percent of the film was shot using that box that Bill Butler reconfigured for us.

ABOVE Off the coast of Martha's Vineyard, Steven Spielberg and his crew prepare to capture a shot featuring Robert Shaw.

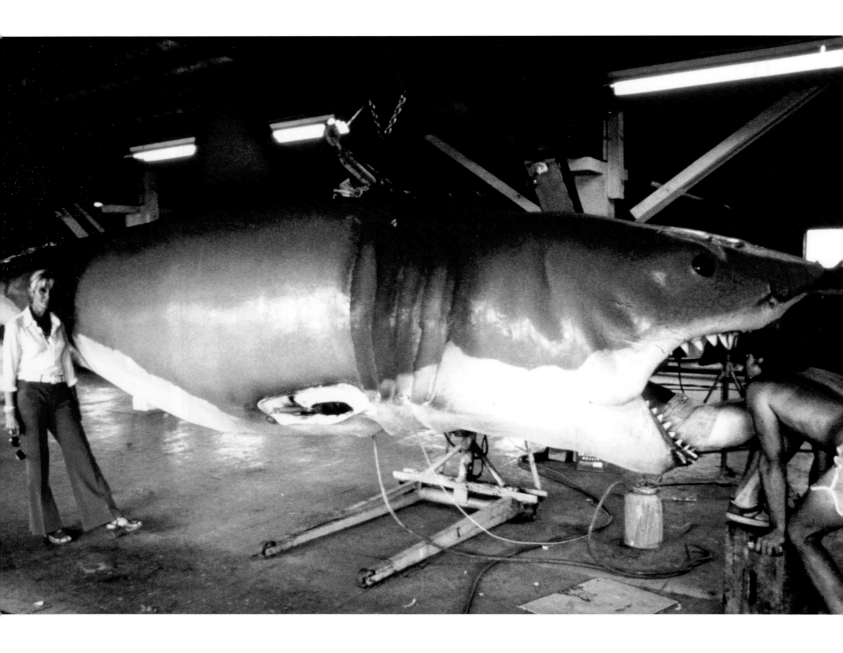

Let's talk about the mechanical sharks, Bruce, who was affectionately nicknamed after your lawyer Bruce Raymer.

That's a much-maligned shark, and I am kind of responsible for creating a lot of bad mouthing about it because the shark was frustrating. It didn't really work all the time—it didn't work hardly at all. I got mad at the shark and at the people who made it, when in fact, Bob Mattey was the best special effects man alive. Nobody else but Bob could have made the shark work as well as it did. So, he did a great job. It was just that we were shooting out on the Atlantic Ocean, and not in a lazy lake—the way Hollywood movies were usually doing it. We had tides to contend with. I would often set up a shot and suddenly the barge holding our electrical generators would start drifting that way, the camera barge would drift in another direction, and the *Orca* would move around its two anchors. Before you knew it, we were completely out of position, and it

would take another hour to reset. When we were finally ready, a bunch of tourists on sailboats would show up, cross the horizon, and ruin our shot. It was just frustrating and tough on all of us—I'd get very angry, and of course, I'd blame the shark. It seldom worked, so it was an easy target. Yet it worked well enough that we, for a while, had the biggest hit of all time. So, in the end, I really owe the shark a lot more than I want to take away from it right now. And I owe Bob Mattey and his team an apology and all my gratitude.

Given all the problems you encountered during production, how did you keep it all going, particularly with your crew?

Jaws was no different than a tour of duty. It was a little bit like in the movie *Mister Roberts* [1955], where I was the captain and wouldn't let the crew have shore leave—the morale dropped lower and lower as we worked six days a week and eventually seven, until someone, usually Roy, Richard, or Robert, would break the tension. I wasn't aware of it, but apparently even the townspeople resented our presence because we were there during the height of their season. I did become acquainted with actress Ruth Gordon and her husband, writer/director Garson Kanin, who lived on the island—I also got to meet James Cagney, famed author Thornton Wilder, and the journalist James Reston. It was amazing for me to get to know those great celebrities who came to Martha's Vineyard during their summer vacation to be on holiday while I was just trying to survive the production. But at night, I usually ate at home and went straight to bed, while the crew would hang out in local restaurants.

I remember one evening we were having a big dinner at the island's historic hotel Kelley House, and there was this tremendous buffet of food. Roy decided to throw a big glob of mashed potatoes and gravy right into my face. And before I could recover to throw something back at him, Richard Dreyfuss took his dessert and threw it in Roy's face. Roy grabbed some cakes and threw them at Richard, who ducked down and it hit someone else behind him. It was like a Three Stooges brawl! I remember Dick

Zanuck and David Brown got up and left right away. Within seconds, we were hurling food at each other. It started with the three of us, but quickly it was a group of ten, literally trashing the dining room. We didn't do property damage, just made a big mess. I remember Richard and Roy, covered in food, running out and jumping in the swimming pool. I said, "What the heck!" and jumped in, too, to wash myself off. That's what happens in the navy when you're not given shore leave! Let that be a lesson.

How supportive were Dick and David during filming, especially as tensions grew?
I needed both there with me because I needed a shoulder to cry on. In fact, I cried on all four shoulders, David's and Dick's. We finished the land portion of the film on schedule. The second we got off to sea, I immediately knew we were going to be out there for months. And that's when Dick and David were always there to reassure me and say, "Keep going. Don't despair, you're getting good stuff." I'd reply, "Good stuff? You saw one shot in dailies." And Dick would say, "But it was a great shot! Get more great shots like that. Tomorrow, try to get five great shots." He was understanding

BELOW Producers Richard D. Zanuck and David Brown on location for *Jaws*.

because he saw what it was like out there. He was out there with us, yet he was nothing but encouraging. Then the studio started to grumble and to question my experience as a director. *The Sugarland Express* had failed at the box office. It garnered great reviews, but Hollywood looked at it as a financial flop. So, I didn't have that to back me up. I did have, however, Dick and David, and they were protecting me from getting fired. A couple of executives at Universal wanted to fire me, and to his credit, Sid Sheinberg, the president of Universal Studios and my mentor, would not let that happen. Sid was our insurance policy. Sid was there to ensure that we finished the movie. Zanuck had hired a very smart man named Bill Gilmore, who oversaw the production. He did a great job coordinating with the crew, especially as we started falling behind schedule. Dick kept that entire group as a very, very tight-knit team.

And you know what else kept us together on *Jaws*? It was the fact that we all felt like we were surviving something big. We all developed a sort of survivor mentality.

How did you kill time while you waited for the shark to work?

I was only getting two shots on some days. We spent a lot of time trying to figure out how to make this movie, sitting around for seven, eight hours, waiting for the shark to work, or waiting for the barrels to sink without coming right back up. I was getting one shot before lunch and one shot before five o'clock in the afternoon. Sometimes, we all just sat around. I had these kind of old-fashioned radio headphones with two antennas. I looked like Ray Walston in *My Favorite Martian*. I wore them all the time. What was very strange was that in 1974, when we shot *Jaws*, the runaway hit song was Abba's "Waterloo"—and it was playing over and over. The title of the song was strangely prophetic given that at that point I felt that *Jaws* would be as great a defeat as Waterloo had been for Napoleon. And I was no Napoleon but could imagine never getting hired again.

There's a famous night shot of the *Orca* with a shooting star in the sky.

There was something so primitive about this battle,

this duel between these three men and nature, that it brought the cosmos into the equation. I wanted to do something that was otherworldly, even if a meteor in the sky is not a supernatural phenomenon. In fact, there're two shooting stars that I added optically to underline the shark becoming almost a mythic character. I also added phosphorescence on the surface of the water when the barrels are moving around the boat at night. That was also an optical effect, and it contributes to the movie reaching a mythical level. It was essential that it happened after Quint's speech about the *Indianapolis*.

I love the scene between the guys comparing injuries. I heard that the bit with Shaw showing his broken front tooth was an improv and a real thing. Yeah, it was real. That was Robert Shaw's idea. I had come up with the guys comparing scars and Robert said, "I got this fake tooth. . . ." He pulled the cap off and asked, "Can I take it off as an addition to the scar-comparing contest?" All the lines in that scene leading up to the *Indianapolis* speech we did right there on set.

And John Milius, your friend, and the great writer/ director, contributed to the writing of that famous speech.
The *Indianapolis* speech about the delivery of the atomic bomb is my favorite part in *Jaws*. It was conceived by Howard Sackler—who only wrote a one-page monologue as Quint starts to talk about one of the reasons he hates sharks. It was a wonderful scene and I kept trying to get Howard Sackler to expand it, but he felt that shorter was better and never would extend it. One day, I was talking to John Milius, and I said, "Could you make this a speech?" And John said, "Sure, it's a great idea. I'll try." So, John sat down and wrote page after page, in long hand I believe, a very, very long speech for Quint. It was essentially too much but pared down I knew it was going to be great. When Robert Shaw, who was himself an accomplished writer, read it, he said, "It's too hard for me to play. There's too much John Huston in some of this monologue. Huston could say this, but I can't do it as well as he would. Let me have a chance at rewriting it." So, Shaw rewrote Milius, who had rewritten Sackler—the final speech in the movie is basically Shaw's version of Milius's version of Sackler's version!

INTEROFFICE MEMORANDUM

FORM 2022

DATE October 4, 1974

TO David Brown

FROM Steve Spielberg

SUBJECT

COPIES

Dear David:

I assume we are in happy agreement over Johnny Williams as composer/conductor of JAWS. Johnny and I have talked and he is convinced it will be his best work sight unseen--and he's very enthusiastic.

Can you take the necessary steps with Harry Garfield to set Johnny, make the deal and do whatever else will lock him into us for the months of December, January and February.

Steve

SS:br

up, my heart beating so fast, I couldn't catch my breath, looking around the room, disoriented. Where am I? I'd calm down, get a glass of water, go back to sleep . . . and the same dream, haunting me all night long for weeks after that.

Jaws was a fun movie to watch but not a fun movie to make. It was made under the worst of conditions. People versus the eternal sea. The sea won the battle—but where we won was with audiences in every country.

Verna Fields was your editor—what can you say about her?
Verna was great. Our affectionate nickname for her was "Mother Cutter" because she was like our mom—she cooked for us, she told great stories of

> **❝ Verna was great. Our affectionate nickname for her was 'Mother Cutter' because she was like our mom . . . ❞**

working with Peter Bogdanovich and the work she'd done with him [such as on *Paper Moon* (1973) and *What's Up, Doc?* (1972)]. She was just a great and charismatic personality. She and Robert Shaw were the most charismatic people on *Jaws*, except she never came out to sea—she stayed in the cutting room. It was frustrating for Verna because she never had much film to cut. Her work really started after we finished shooting. She and I worked together at her house, in her little cutting room by the pool every day, and she did a great job.

Then of course, there's the score by John Williams. Before you had John's score, what temp music did you use?
I temped *Jaws* with Johnny Williams's score from the Robert Altman movie *Images* [1972]. It was a bit of an experimental score, but I thought it was very disturbing, and I thought the shark should be disturbing. But when John saw the movie with that score in, he called me laughing. He said, "No, no, no. It's all wrong for this. You've made a pirate movie with a scary shark. It's got to be primal. It can't be esoteric." Six weeks later, he played for me on the piano the main *Jaws* theme—I expected to hear something weird and melodic, tonal but eerie—

BELOW Production executive William S. Gilmore, Steven Spielberg (*center*), and editor Verna Fields (*right*) on location for *Jaws*.

What are your memories of completing the film?
Being on *Jaws* became a living nightmare, and not
because I didn't know what I was doing or because I
was struggling to find the movie in my head. I knew
the film I wanted to make. I just couldn't get the movie
I had in mind on film as quickly as I wanted. When we
got out to the ocean, a lot of the crew got seasick, and
once that passed, a kind of lethargy set in because we
weren't seemingly getting anything done. The end
never seemed to be in sight, and yet I was the only
person who could reassure the crew that there would
be an end to this some day. I remember on the sixtieth
day of shooting, crewmembers came to me asking,
"When are we going to be done with this movie?" And
I would honestly say, "I don't know. We could finish it
if I get fired, if I'm dragged off the movie and replaced
by someone who could complete it quickly. Or maybe
they'll shut us down. . . ." Whenever I talked about
the possibility of me being fired or the show being
shut down, most of the crew was happy about it—this
wasn't a labor of love for anybody. This was a physically
impossible chore and people wanted to go home. That
song that they sing in the cabin that night—"Show Me
the Way to Go Home"—was my anthem day in and
day out. I remember how we all got tears in our eyes
during the filming of the scene where the three guys
sing, "Show me the way to go home. I'm tired and I
want to go to bed." I looked at my script supervisor,
Charlsie Bryant, and other members of the crew, and
they were all teary eyed—not because this was a sweet
and emotional scene, but because this had become
their mantra too. All they could think about was being
back with their family like in a war.

I never left the island because I knew that, if I
did, I would never come back. Yet I never wanted
to quit. Ever. I had terrible, despairing days where
I could see nobody hiring me again, and I could
imagine *Jaws* being my last studio movie. I thought
I would probably go on to make independent films
if I could get doctors and dentists to put up enough
money to finance a little movie with four people
playing cards in a room. Basically, I didn't have
much hope for any longevity for my career, but I
wanted to finish *Jaws* because I had never stopped
believing in the movie.

When I finally did leave the island, I left just
before the last shot, which was the blowing up of
the shark, because I heard that the crew wanted to
throw me overboard—and I didn't know if they were
going to throw me overboard in cement slippers or
via the poop deck. So, I thought I'd get out of there
quickly.

I got to Boston on the ferry for the night, and the
next day, Richard Dreyfuss and I were scheduled
to fly back to Los Angeles. I vividly recall getting
into my hotel room and having a complete after-
the-fact anxiety attack. I couldn't stop shaking, my
jaw clenching—I couldn't open my mouth. I was
feeling like electrical shocks were going through my
brain—it was like having seizures. I know this sounds
melodramatic, but it's exactly what happened. It
was a full-on panic attack. I don't remember ever
experiencing something similar to that degree. I
called Richard, who was down at the bar, and he
came up to stay with me. I just said to him, "I'm in
really bad shape, Ricky." And he told me, "We'll be
on a plane home tomorrow."

But each time I fell asleep, I dreamt that I was on
the third or fourth day of shooting, and I would wake

OPPOSITE Steven Spielberg jokes
around with the mechanical shark,
a creature he nicknamed "the big
white turd."

TOP Robert Shaw and Richard
Dreyfuss during filming of the
famous USS *Indianapolis* speech
sequence.

ABOVE Shaw relaxes while filming
Quint's death scene.

Terrific idea:
Having scooped a large sonar blip -
Hooper goes to investigate
Gardeners Boat → ~~that~~ looks like
nobody is on it - awash - (he doesn't look
underwater in the boat but goes below
to investigate what sunk bouy, discovers
hole, feels around it, Looks under it
+ his mouthpiece falls out!! there
is Gardner wide eyed death face
staring down at him through hole
~~fell~~ face down dead + pressed
against it!
        The biggest shock so far!

Camera is underwater on Hooper seeing
this, his mouthpiece comes out + he swims for
the surface - camera follows + surfaces right
next to him (sound suddenly from quiet to
~~boat~~ slapping water - his choking - wind.) +
he looks around ocean. scrambles in a
bloody panic for the boat - up + in - camera
is this one shot goes up + in too
+ follows him into awash cabin + +
he pulls body free from underwater → all in
                                            ONE.

A touch - 3rd act ~~aboard~~ ORCA
Brody going below, on his way to hatch door when
a long white stream ~~shoots~~ arcs out from ~~front~~
cabin - Quint comes out with the beer that he opened
throws aluminum cap into sea, belches + passes out of frame
Later Hooper imitates his (by drinking)   Quint drains his beer in one
coffee + crushing paper cup in his bare hand.   gulp → crushes can in hand
                                                  throws it in air - shoots a
                                                  hole in it.

perhaps something to suggest the shark underwater. And what he played me instead with two fingers on the lower keys was 'Dun dun, dun dun, dun, dun, dun. . . .' At first, I began to laugh—I thought he was putting me on. It seemed too simple. He said, "That's the theme for *Jaws*!" I asked him to play it again, and it suddenly seemed right. Sometimes the best ideas are the simple ones, and John had found the signature for the whole movie. Without that score, to this day, I believe the film would have been only half as successful.

During the panic on the beach, the fact that we don't hear the theme immediately tells the audience that there's no shark.
Part of the genius of John Williams is not just being the greatest composer of film music since Max Steiner, but how he spots music, how he places it in a movie. Something never discussed about the art of composition is the placement of music. In *Jaws*, John wanted the music to signal the actual arrival of the shark, not use it as a red herring.

What was the experience of scoring the film, as you started seeing image and music coming together?
After the first scoring session, I was simply blown away. I called George Lucas and I said, "George, this composer John Williams has written a score for me, and you have to come down here and hear it yourself." So, George came to the stages at 20th Century Fox and listened to this amazing music John had created for *Jaws*. Later, he hired him for *Star Wars*.

The impact that the music has had on the art of film scoring but also in pop culture is undeniable.
People remember the theme and they have for generations now. I remember in the summer of 1975 in Los Angeles when *Jaws* had been out for only about three weeks in theaters across the country, I went to 31 Flavors. I was by myself, standing in line, and there were people singing the *Jaws* theme. They were talking about the movie, and they were all going "dun dun, dun dun. . . ." That's when I realized there was a kind of cultural phenomenon that was starting to rise from the depths of that movie and from John's primal musical vision.

The first preview you had for *Jaws* was quite an experience.
We previewed the film at the Medallion Theatre in Dallas, Texas. It was the first time the public ever saw

Jaws. I'd had only one experience prior to this with *The Sugarland Express*, where the preview audience just kept quiet the entire time. But with *Jaws*, it was very, very loud and people went crazy. This preview was the most extraordinary response I could ever have imagined.

At one point, I remember I was standing at the door, and after the death of the Kintner boy, a man got up and started walking out—I thought, *Oh my God. Our first walkout.* Then he began running and I went, *Oh, no, he's not walking out—he's running out.* I could tell he was headed for the bathrooms, but he didn't make it and vomited all over the floor. And I just went, *Oh my God, what have I done? What kind of a movie have I made? A man has just barfed because of my film.* But the great news was, about five minutes later, he went right back to his seat.

And you made changes after the preview . . .
When the shark comes out of the water after Roy Scheider says, "Why don't you come down here and

ABOVE A publicity shot of the three stars from *Jaws*: Robert Shaw, Roy Scheider, and Richard Dreyfuss.

chum some of this shit," I had designed a laugh that would turn into a scream. Back in those days, the word *shit* was an easy laugh, and it instantly got a nervous laughter, and when the shark burst out of the water, it turned into a scream! Popcorn went flying and it was amazing. It was my proudest moment at the whole preview.

But it got me greedy. Earlier, when Hooper goes underwater to explore a half-sunken boat and "encounters" Ben Gardner's severed head, we didn't get any reaction, and I was wondering how to improve on that moment. In the meantime, the numbers were the highest in Universal's history, the executives were happy, the audience loved the movie, we were all happy. But I was greedy, and I said, "There is one more scream we can get in this movie, if I can figure out this thing with Ben Gardner's head." Even though the studio was ecstatic with the film, they wouldn't give me any more money. They said, "It's fine, don't fix something that's not broken. The movie works. Don't mess with it or you'll improve it into a failure." So, I went and spent three thousand bucks of my own money to have the art department build the side of Ben Gardner's boat out of balsa wood, to match the one we had shot before. We cut a hole in it, used the same head, and filmed it using a double for Richard Dreyfuss, in the swimming pool of my editor Verna Fields. Originally, the head was just there, so I shot it coming through the hole about nine different ways. We edited several versions and tested it on my sound effects and music editors and dubbing team, who were still working on the film following our first preview. There was one take where they all said, "Wow, that one surprised me!" We put that cut into the film and took it for another preview in Long Beach at the Lakewood Theatre. That moment got a humongous scream, way bigger than the one with the shark coming out of the water in the Dallas preview. People came out of their seats even higher, and I was thrilled.

Our scores in Long Beach were better than the ones we'd gotten in Dallas. The studio was on cloud nine. On the other hand, audiences had a much lesser reaction to the shark bursting out of the water at the Long Beach preview than at the one in Dallas, and I kept wondering why. But it was obvious: After the new success of the scene with Ben Gardner's head, the audience was on alert, constantly expecting another shocking moment, and their guard was up from there till the end.

I think you had a bit of battle with the MPAA over getting the film a PG rating?

I was very naïve then and didn't know much about the rating board and what it meant to have to lose a few frames from a scene to get a specific certification. But the MPAA informed Universal's Sid Sheinberg and Lew Wasserman, who in turn told Dick Zanuck and David Brown, that I had to trim down the shot of the severed leg coming down and hitting the bottom of the ocean, in the scene in the estuary. I pretty much did as I was told. I didn't fight it. At that point, I was just happy to finish the movie up.

The marketing of the film, specifically the trailer, was very strategically designed not to show the shark.

The trailer was done by Andy Kuehn—he came up with

a great line: "It is as if God created the devil and gave him . . . jaws." It was a great piece of writing because it was also a reference to *The Exorcist* [1973], which had been a gigantic hit two years prior to *Jaws*.

How did the success of *Jaws* change your life and career?

Jaws was the first time I'd made any significant amount of money in my entire life, and it gave me a kind of independence. But that wasn't important to me. I was a director. I was making movies. That's what was important then and still is today. I didn't change my lifestyle, although I just couldn't believe that I was going to be making this kind of money overnight.

The success of *Jaws* gave me final cut on every movie I've made since then. It gave me a chance to make *Close Encounters of the Third Kind*. I had written the story. I was writing the screenplay. No one wanted to touch it until *Jaws* became a phenomenon, and suddenly Columbia said, "Go make your movie."

So, ultimately, *Jaws* was the gift that kept on giving.

In closing, I want to tell you what happens when you watch movies one too many times. I noticed that Ben Gardner in *Jaws* wears a very specific outfit and cap. Later, as I was rewatching *The Sugarland Express*, I noticed that the sniper is wearing a very similar outfit and cap!

Yeah, there is a reason for that. I purposely put Ben Gardner in a similar outfit. I showed the costume designer the sniper from *Sugarland* and said that's how Ben must look. I'm glad you noticed it. Nobody's ever told me they spotted that before. I thought that was just for me. I love that you noticed it!

OPPOSITE TOP Laurent Bouzereau poses with the Ben Gardner's head prop during the making of his *Jaws* documentary.

OPPOSITE BOTTOM The famous *Jaws* one-sheet designed by artist Roger Kastel.

THIS PAGE A vigilante from *The Sugarland Express* (*top, center*) dressed in a costume almost identical to the one worn by Ben Gardner (Craig Kingsbury, *above left*) in *Jaws*.

IV

CLOSE ENCOUNTERS OF THE THIRD KIND

(1977)

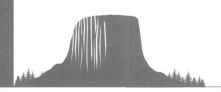

"❝❝ I can't describe it. What I'm feeling. And what I'm thinking. This means something. This is important."

—Roy Neary (Richard Dreyfuss)

When I first saw *Close Encounters of the Third Kind*, what struck me most about the film was how different it was from *Jaws*, even though there are some similarities between the two films. The first section is suspenseful and structured in a way that makes you think that it's going to be *Jaws* again, but this time with aliens in the role of the predator. But as it progresses you come to realize that the film is something else entirely, and the aliens are benevolent. This twist was a tour de force and marked a big transition in Steven's filmmaking. If you watch his movies from this era in chronological order, you come to realize that we're on a journey with him as an artist, and the twist in *Close Encounters* is the point at which he enters another realm. *Duel*, *The Sugarland Express*, and *Jaws* have a certain bleakness to them, while the movies that immediately follow—*1941*, *Raiders of*

PAGES 120–121 The spectacular Mothership from *Close Encounters of the Third Kind*.

RIGHT A French lobby card shows the Mothership landing at Devils Tower.

OPPOSITE Richard Dreyfuss, who plays Roy Neary in *Close Encounters*, on location at Devils Tower, Wyoming.

Encounters and made a cameo in
the film's finale.

OPPOSITE BOTTOM Steven
Spielberg and Richard Dreyfuss
(*both seated*) wait for the
next setup while filming *Close
Encounters* on location.

E.T. The Extra-Terrestrial—are all
nt, adventure, and fantasy. And
gins in *Close Encounters*' last act.
such an air of mystery around
before it was released. During
the film, the aliens were kept
ly any images were released. In
own to watch *Close Encounters*,
cept of what I was about to see. I
views. I was completely devoid
d. I knew it had something to do
hat was it. That kind of mystery
oday. Now, when movie trailers
y get picked apart on the internet,
and spoilers, most fans have an
t a film will feature long before it
hits theaters. But back then, we didn't have those
kinds of resources, so I went into *Close Encounters*
cold. My discovery of the film was completely
genuine and raw.

That's why the change in tone in the film's third
act felt so remarkable. The somewhat sinister

feeling in the first two acts is further underlined
by John Williams's score. The music starts off with
a foreboding, abstract quality, and by the end it
develops into this triumphant symphony.

One of the most memorable aspects of the *Close
Encounters* score is undoubtedly the five-note alien
communication theme created by John Williams.
Through these five notes, the music literally becomes
part of the language of *Close Encounters* and the
bridge between our world and that of the aliens.
Recently, when I was working on the documentary
for Steven's adaptation of *West Side Story* (2021),
composer Leonard Bernstein's son told me, "I have
such incredible memories of going to see *Close
Encounters* with my dad, and him saying, 'How brilliant
is it that this movie is about communication via music?'"

The Man Who Didn't Want to Grow Up

Close Encounters was written by Steven, based on
his original idea. The story focuses on Roy Neary
(Richard Dreyfuss), an everyman blue-collar worker

at a power plant whose life is changed when he has a "close encounter" with a UFO. As Neary becomes increasingly obsessed with the incident, he alienates himself from his wife and children. Driven by visions in his head, he travels to a mountain in Wyoming known as Devils Tower and meets Jillian Guiler (Melinda Dillon) along the way. Jillian's young son, Barry (Cary Guffey), has been abducted by the aliens, and she has come to Wyoming to find him. Together, they manage to breach military security and reach the top of the mountain, where a momentous meeting between humanity and extraterrestrials is about to take place under the supervision of French scientist Claude Lacombe (François Truffaut).

> **"** ... Steven contacted J. Allen Hynek, the UFO expert who coined the term 'close encounter,' and used him as a resource when writing the movie..."

One of the special things about *Close Encounters* is the level of research that Steven undertook for the film. In the course of learning everything he could about its subject matter, Steven contacted J. Allen Hynek, the UFO expert who coined the term "close encounter," and used him as a resource when writing the movie—he even gave Hynek a cameo in the big sequence at the end of the film when the aliens' Mothership arrives. Steven has always been very focused on accuracy, and he wanted this science-fiction story to be as close to science fact as possible. That really paid off because the film feels grounded, despite its focus on these very wonderous events.

Incidentally, a "close encounter of the first kind" is when someone sees a UFO. A "close encounter of the second kind" is when physical evidence is found. And a "close encounter of the third kind" is when direct contact is made, as seen in the climax of this movie.

Steven has often said that Roy Neary was kind of his alter ego at the time—a guy driven by his own imagination and daydreams. Neary's obsession with the images he sees in his head is analogous to a filmmaker's creative process. In that sense, *Close*

ABOVE Steven Spielberg (*right*) directs the train set scene that introduces the Neary family in *Close Encounters*. At far left is Shawn Bishop who plays Roy's son, Brad Neary. Richard Dreyfuss is second from left.

RIGHT Spielberg (*left*) directs Dreyfuss in the scene in which Neary tries to sculpt Devils Tower using mashed potatoes.

Encounters is also a film about cinema: It's about connectivity through images and being obsessed with these visuals. I think one of my favorite things in the movie is the way it opens in absolute silence and darkness. Then, suddenly, the music starts to build as the title appears over black, and it cuts to the bright daylight of the Sonoran Desert. This journey from darkness to light *is* cinema. That opening sums up the arc of the film in a single moment, the thematic movement from darkness to light, where we come to realize that the aliens are not our enemies. As the film progresses, Steven asks his audience to psychologically reexplore their assumptions from earlier in the film and look at these scary moments in a new light. Initially, we are meant to think the aliens are trying to abduct and hurt people, but then we learn that we have misinterpreted their actions, and the aliens have really been trying to make contact and communicate—which, again, is a beautiful metaphor for the role of a film director.

The home theme is also very prevalent in *Close Encounters*. At one point, Neary starts building a massive sculpture of Devils Tower based on the image of the mountain he is seeing in his head. His obsession to re-create it quickly escalates until he has ripped apart his house to make the model—literally destroying his home life to fulfill his vision. Prior to this moment, and before Neary has his encounter of the first kind with the UFO, it's clearly established that he is something of a man-child, struggling to be both a father and a husband dealing with adult responsibilities. When we first meet Neary, he's having an argument with his kids: He wants to take them to see Disney's *Pinocchio* (1940), but they want to go play goofy golf. His kids want to be like grownups, while Neary is chasing after the stars. And at the end of the film, Neary chooses the stars and the sky over his family, leaving Earth on the aliens' Mothership.

Steven has said that if he made *Close Encounters* today, he would not have Neary abandon his family

at the end of the movie. At the time, Steven was in his early thirties and hadn't yet started a family, and Neary's choice made sense to him. As a family man now, however, the concept seems unthinkable. That's another interesting aspect to *Close Encounters*—it embodies who Steven was at a very specific time in his life as well as in his growth as an artist.

Family in *Close Encounters* is depicted in a particularly tempestuous way. Neary's home life is very chaotic. His kids are loud and destructive—one of the first things we see is Roy's young daughter banging a doll against her playpen. In contrast, Neary has his own elaborate toy train set, which he's clearly put together with a lot of love and care—another sign that he's somebody who is not ready to grow up. Toys are important in *Close Encounters*. In the scene when the aliens first visit Jillian and Barry's home, the boy's toys are scattered all over the floor and come to life. Jillian appears to be a single mom raising him alone. As the toys begin to move, and she searches

> **If Neary longs to never grow up, the aliens in *Close Encounters* seem to offer just that possibility."**

for Barry in the house, it's almost as if the boy's playthings become obstacles that keep her from being able to reach him. There's a sense that the world of the child is holding back Jillian, not unlike the way in which Neary's childishness holds him back from being a fully functioning adult.

When Barry is abducted in a later scene, home becomes the enemy. Jillian is essentially attacked by her own home—her vacuum cleaner comes to life, the washing machine switches on, and the phone is

playing the five notes nonstop. Jillian's home is not only under attack but also attacking.

It's also worth noting that, when the house comes alive in the earlier scene and the TV switches on, it shows an episode of the TV show *Police Woman*, featuring Angie Dickinson as an empowered female cop. This is clearly a conscious choice that signals how we are meant to see Jillian, as a heroic single mom raising her kid alone at a time when this was less common. Steven later reprised this idea in *E.T.* with Dee Wallace's character, Mary, who is a single mom raising her kids alone after separating with her husband.

Who Wants to Live Forever?

If Neary longs to never grow up, the aliens in *Close Encounters* seem to offer just that possibility. At the end of the film, when a group of World War II pilots and other characters in period costume walk off the craft having apparently not aged a day since they were abducted, we can only conclude one thing: Somehow the aliens are able to prevent people from aging. Boarding the Mothership seems to freeze people and objects in time. As human beings, we all want to be able to defy time and the aging process. And, as an artist, you always fear becoming old and irrelevant. The timelessness that the aliens offer speaks to an artist's ultimate dream that their work will never age and will always remain relevant.

These themes of longevity are very emblematic of Steven as a filmmaker. The challenge for any director is constantly learning, growing, and even reinventing yourself so that you stay relevant, and Steven is one of the few filmmakers who has been able to do that throughout the years. He once said that *Ready Player*

THIS PAGE Steven Spielberg calls the shots on *Close Encounters of the Third Kind.*

The Mothership

Close Encounters frequently cuts between the micro and the macro, going from the family problems that Neary is experiencing to alien visitation events that are happening all over the world, such as the stunning scene in India featuring thousands of extras chanting and pointing at the sky. The huge scale of the sequence conveys that the film's events are taking place on the world stage, but at the same time, we remain emotionally engaged with *Close Encounters* because it's such a personal drama: there's a woman whose child is abducted; there's a family breaking apart. These events are things that the audience can relate to, and Steven keeps this personal perspective all the way through the film. When the Mothership arrives at the end, we see it mainly through Neary's eyes, and Neary, like David Mann in *Duel*, is very much an everyman character. Yes, this spacecraft is spectacular, but the audience connects with Neary's dream of making contact with the aliens, which is so much bigger than the ship itself. That's what makes the sequence so compelling—Neary, this guy we can all relate to, is getting to live out our dreams.

Another fascinating choice in this scene is that the Mothership does not descend from the sky, instead

TOP Steven Spielberg shoots a major *Close Encounters* crowd scene while on location in India.

ABOVE Spielberg (*center*) directs his cast in India, including Bob Balaban (*second from left*), François Truffaut (*third from left*), and Lance Henriksen (*fourth from left*). Producer Julia Phillips stands next to the director in the foreground.

One (2018) was the hardest film he had made since *Saving Private Ryan* (1998). Much of the film is set in a digital environment known as the Oasis, so Steven had to learn how to work in an entirely digital space and how to match those visuals with live-action footage. Steven is forever a student and always learning. He consistently pushes himself to try to do something different, and that ensures that his work is always surprising and different.

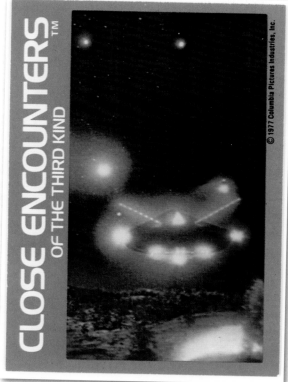

seeming to rise from the Earth. This goes against other UFO movies up to this point—everyone knows that UFOs come from above, right? But Steven has always innately understood that cinema is not about logic—it's about wonder, and the details are not as important as the feeling a scene evokes.

The UFO visual effects shots in *Close Encounters*, created by the legendary Doug Trumbull and Steven, are pitch perfect. These days, using digital effects, filmmakers can render an alien spaceship

ABOVE The Mothership rises from behind Devils Tower in this publicity still.

LEFT Two *Close Encounters* trading cards from Laurent Bouzereau's collection.

ABOVE Steven Spielberg and François Truffaut during shooting of a Devils Tower scene.

RIGHT Truffaut films the scene in which Claude Lacombe demonstrates how hand signals could be used to communicate with extraterrestrials.

from just about any angle they want. But back then, using optical compositing processes, they had to carefully select which shots would be achievable and photorealistic. The lack of options pushed the movie's team to innovate, finding simple yet compelling solutions. That's another reason the film still holds up today. It's a real visual effects masterpiece.

Steven was very particular about the design of the smaller UFOs seen in the film and wanted them to look like a family unit. When they go flying past, it's almost like there's Mom, Dad, and smaller kid UFOs trailing behind. By making these UFOs seem like a family, something incredibly otherworldly and fantastical suddenly becomes relatable. And, of course, Steven calls the main craft the Mothership.

The moment when Neary enters the Mothership at the end of the film is symbolic of him returning to the womb. He is leaving everything, his family, the world, and all his adult responsibilities in order to, in a very real sense, be reborn into an utterly new life within the ship. Maybe this is a second chance for him to learn to be a better person. Maybe one day he might return to Earth, never having aged, and be able to start a new life as a better person, someone who is ready to be a father and a husband. That's a beautiful way to look at the film.

> **" Steven was very particular about the design of the smaller UFOs seen in the film and wanted them to look like a family unit."**

The Rule of Threes

Another notable characteristic of *Close Encounters* is that many elements of the film subscribe to the rule of threes. For starters, of course, it's called *Close Encounters of the Third Kind*. Also, at the end of the film, there are three sequences featuring three different groupings of UFOs—there are two sets of smaller craft that fly in formation and then the Mothership. And when the Mothership opens, three different races of extraterrestrials disembark—a spindly puppet alien with long limbs, a group of little aliens (played by young girls), and the main alien, known on set as Puck, a sophisticated animatronic that makes hand signals to the human characters.

ABOVE Steven Spielberg (*second from left*) works with cinematographer Vilmos Zsigmond (*center*) during the *Close Encounters* shoot.

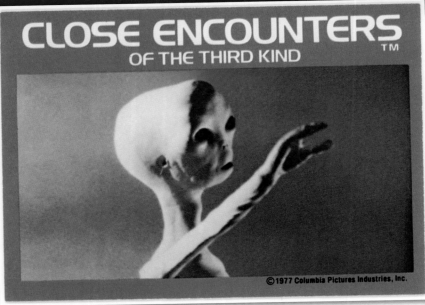

TOP Roy Neary (Richard Dreyfuss) is surrounded by friendly extraterrestrials welcoming him aboard the Mothership.

ABOVE LEFT Puck, the alien designed by Carlo Rambaldi, appears on a *Close Encounters* trading card.

ABOVE RIGHT (*Left to right*) Steven Spielberg, editor Michael Kahn, and cinematographer Vilmos Zsigmond.

There are also three different versions of *Close Encounters*. There's the 1977 theatrical version, 1980's The Special Edition, and the Collector's Edition (also known as the Director's Cut) that was released in 1998. The Special Edition featured new scenes specially shot for that cut, including new footage of Neary inside the Mothership. In 1980, the notion of a director creating a special edition theatrical release of their film was not at all

common, and it speaks to the impact Steven was already having on audiences across the world. The director's cut combined the theatrical release and The Special Edition, but it removed the footage of Neary inside the Mothership. That sequence was something that Steven was pressured into adding to help make The Special Edition marketable, but he always regretted it.

The director's cut was spearheaded by Marty

Cohen at Amblin. The goal was to create the optimal version of the film that Steven would have released in 1977 if he could have. This included adding the best bits from The Special Edition to the theatrical version—for example, the new sequence from The Special Edition in which the missing ship SS *Cotopaxi* is found in the middle of the Gobi Desert—but not the alternate ending that Steven had since disavowed. Steven, his editor Michael Kahn, and Marty oversaw the new cut, and I was there observing it all while making the documentary. I immersed myself in research and watched all the dailies for the film. I was in my office at Amblin just surrounded by boxes of *Close Encounters* material, and honestly, I could have slept in there and been perfectly happy!

When I interviewed Steven for the *Close Encounters* documentary, he was in full production on *Saving Private Ryan* in England. It was incredible to talk to him about *Close Encounters* amid the set of a destroyed French village. That same summer, I was writing a book on the making of George Lucas's *Star Wars: Episode One—The Phantom Menace* (1999). Traveling from one set to another to meet with these

two giants was one of the most exciting times in my entire career. I remember sharing my excitement with Steven about visiting his set and then going off to spend time on the *Phantom Menace* set, and he simply said to me: "You're one lucky guy!"

ABOVE A French lobby card created for The Special Edition featuring Roy Neary (Richard Dreyfuss) inside the Mothership.

BELOW Laurent Bouzereau's copy of the *Close Encounters* novelization autographed by Steven Spielberg.

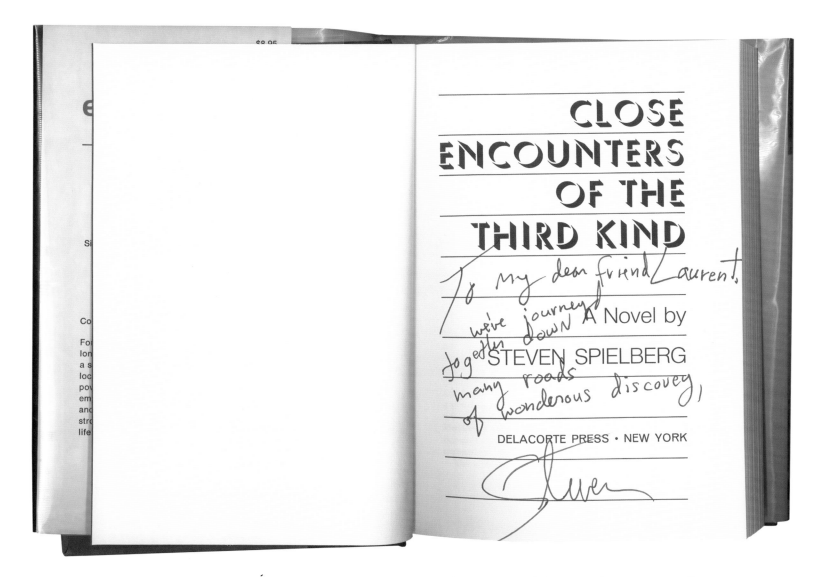

SPIELBERG ON *CLOSE ENCOUNTERS OF THE THIRD KIND*

Close Encounters really starts with a story of your childhood, involving your father.

Yes, that's a good story. I must have been five or six years old, and my dad woke me up in the middle of the night and said, "Come with me." I must say this terrified me—but I followed my dad to his car, and as we drove, he said, "I have a surprise for you." We got to this field. Several people were there but from my child's perspective, I thought there were hundreds; in fact, it must have been several dozens. And I kept asking, "What time is it?" and Dad would answer, "It's the middle of the night." He went and got a picnic blanket—we sat down, looked at the sky, and witnessed this extraordinary meteor shower. Every few seconds, there would be a fantastic streak of light across the sky. And that was my first introduction to the world beyond this Earth and what was the origin of me wanting to tell stories not of this world.

Your film *Firelight*—which you directed in 1964—was in essence your first feature film, done on your own at the age of seventeen. And it does concern UFOs with a plot that bears some resemblance to *Close Encounters*. There's also your love for Kubrick's *2001: A Space Odyssey* [1968]. Are all those things connected and responsible ultimately for *Close Encounters*?

I'm not sure if any of those films really inspired me to do *Close Encounters*. *2001* intimidated me because it was such a phenomenal and patient film, and if anything, I wanted to make a movie set on Earth, not in outer space.

At what point did you start working on *Close Encounters*?

I had been doing some writing on *Close Encounters*

before *Jaws*. My whole concept was UFOs and Watergate and kind of putting those two notions together—basically, a government conspiracy and the UFO phenomenon wrapped into one. It was a movie I was going to make next. I didn't know if I could get it financed because people were balking at financing it before *Jaws*. But I had two producers, Julia Phillips and Michael Phillips, who were very strong. They had produced *Taxi Driver* [1976] and *The Sting* [1973]. They were very supportive of me and pretty much said, "Don't worry. We're going to get the financing for this."

But I had a lot of ideas. One of them was the story about a police officer. Cops make very credible witnesses, and when they say they saw something, you tend to believe them. At one point, I thought the character should be a military person, a debunker, working for Project Blue Book [the US Air Force's UFO study, which started in 1952]. But that made it hard to relate to. I wanted to make this about my own experiences, about my parents, about my friends. I wanted this to be a story that would be accessible to everyone—about a common everyday man who has a sighting that overturns his life, and throws his family into complete upheaval, as he is consumed by the experience. So, eventually, I settled on a man who worked for the power company and is sent out to investigate a blackout. He has a blue-collar job, a utilitarian career, and was easy to identify with.

Did you—do you—believe in the UFO phenomenon?

Let me start by saying that I never thought of *Close Encounters* as a science-fiction film, even when I was writing it. If I had thought of it as a science-fiction film, I wouldn't have taken so many drives out to the California desert, hoping to have a UFO sighting—by

the way, I have never had a UFO sighting. I'm the one person who perhaps deserves a UFO sighting [laughs], and yet, it hasn't happened for me. This was science speculation because I had a real deep-rooted belief that we had been visited in this century. I was a real UFO devotee in the 1970s and was deep into the whole UFO phenomenon from an early age. I was reading books, including Erich von Däniken, who wrote about our world having been visited. For me that was science. I still believe we're not alone in the universe.

But back then, I was reading books on the matter and eventually met Dr. J. Allen Hynek, who inspired the title of the film and was the Project Blue Book debunker working for the military as a civilian consultant, looking into UFO sightings. He was bringing everything down to a terrestrial level until finally he just couldn't explain about 10 percent of the sightings. And that 10 percent presented compelling cases to the point where he eventually resigned his position to pursue the study of the entire UFO phenomenon, through both the physical human and cultural aspects of it. I called him up after I'd read his book, and he's the one who coined the title, "close encounters of the third kind," which initially nobody, not even my producers, liked. They thought I was crazy. They kept asking, "What does that mean?" But I owe a lot to Hynek, to his point of view, and

his research on the subject. He helped me make the movie more credible.

As you started writing the story, what was the theme that emerged for you? What did you think *Close Encounters* was about?

I always thought the theme of the film was based on Jiminy Cricket's song "When You Wish Upon a Star" from Disney's *Pinocchio*. That's how I found my story. If you wish for something, and if you use a star to wish upon, your dreams come true. And I really thought that there was an element of this film that had a lot to do with wish fulfillment and about making the dreams that everybody around you says are impossible come true, no matter who you are or where you come from. So, those lyrics, "When you wish upon a star, makes no difference who you are," were for me the very beginning of everything.

This was a script you wrote—I know there were several drafts. What changed?

I had to cut out scenes involving the government's research, for budgetary reasons. Also, originally in my first draft of the script, I had written that Lacombe goes up the Amazon and through the thick jungle, finds some kind of crop circles, and inside each of them is one of the torpedo bombers from Flight 19 that mysteriously disappeared over the Bermuda

Triangle during World War II. But we couldn't afford to do this. I sort of put that sequence aside, and later, while I was editing the film, I felt there wasn't enough "wow" moments or mystery at the very beginning of the film. I remembered my Amazonian sequence with the missing bombers, transposed it to Palmdale, California, and filmed it with big wind machines. And that became the opening sequence of Close Encounters.

You had such incredible actors in Jaws—how did you approach the casting process for Close Encounters?

What I was really looking for were actors who were still closer to, or in touch with, their childhood memories. Richard Dreyfuss was a bigger kid than the children Roy Neary was raising in his suburban house. François Truffaut was in real life a "wild" child at heart. He was in touch with the things that make children eternally optimistic. Truffaut was that kind of a person. I saw that when I watched his performance in his film The Wild Child [1970]. I recognized that quality in every movie he ever directed. He was my first choice, even though I went to other actors always believing he'd say no.

Everybody in the movie, from Teri Garr and Melinda Dillon to Bob Balaban, had child-like qualities, except some of the more rank-and-file military personnel. For them, I went more for the cynical, more life-hardened adults. And there was of course Cary Guffey, who was only four at the time. But we made this picture in the spirit of childhood and believing in things that only children believe in.

Let's talk specifically about Richard Dreyfuss, who had been in Jaws. Based on the different drafts of your script, Roy was older than Dreyfuss was at the time. What convinced you he was right for Roy?

When we were making Jaws, I told Richard about Close Encounters. It had a different title then [Watch the Skies], but I told him I wanted to make a movie about UFOs and an everyday man. Richard just thought it was a great story and kept hocking me, saying, "I'm your guy! I'm your guy!" At first, I couldn't see it—the more he asked, the more I could only see him as Hooper from Jaws. I couldn't imagine him outside the film we were making at that moment. So, I looked in other directions.

My first choice was Steve McQueen. I remember calling him to introduce myself. I explained I was making this UFO movie, and would he read the script. He was very cool about it—he agreed, and

I sent him my screenplay. Later, through his agent, he asked to meet me. I went to Trancas, California, where he lived with Ali MacGraw, and asked that we meet in a bar called the Dune Room. I'd never been to a bar in my life, and that's where we met. In fact, there was almost a fistfight and Steve wanted to break it up—it seemed wherever Steve went, something of that nature always happened. We talked about the character, and I was convinced I had him. I'd even had several beers with him, and I never drink—I was doing the best I could to keep up and get him onboard. We met several times over a couple of weeks until he said something I'll never forget. He said, "I've decided I can't play this character." I asked him why and he replied, "Because I can't cry on film. I've never been able to do it." I promised him I'd take out the crying, and he immediately said, "No, no . . . the crying broke my heart. I cried just reading the script, but once the camera's rolling, I will not be able to deliver the

ABOVE Richard Dreyfuss prepares for a *Close Encounters* take.

goods." It broke my heart—we became buddies for a while, went skeet and trap shooting and rode dirt bikes together, and I did get to know him a little bit, which was a privilege. I was such a huge fan.

I went to Dustin Hoffman; he turned me down. I went to Al Pacino; I went to Gene Hackman. I went to a lot of actors who said no to this part. And I finally remembered that there was this actor from *Jaws*, Richard Dreyfuss, and how he'd pursued me for the role. In fact, I confided in him the names of the other actors I was pursuing, and he flat out said to me: "They'll either say no or be wrong for the part!" Eventually, I went back to him thinking he'd throw the script in my face, saying, "How dare you come to me after going to so many other actors first." But it was quite the opposite, and he simply thanked me! Richard was great for the part. I saw him in the way I perceived Jean-Pierre Léaud in Truffaut's Antoine Doinel movies. Léaud was sort of Truffaut's alter ego in the same way that Dreyfuss was playing me. In retrospect, through Richard, I felt I was Hooper in *Jaws*, Roy in *Close Encounters*, and that I also was the character he played in *Always* [1989]. I'm not saying

that I'm the actor trying to throw myself into these roles, but when I identify with a character, I like to cast someone who thinks like me. Richard and I agree on so many things about life and work and family.

How did actress Teri Garr come into the picture as Roy's wife?

I saw her selling coffee on television, and based on that commercial, I thought she was the perfect, typical American suburban wife. I had no idea that she was such a gifted actress and comedian. She was full of interesting little quirks, even in that coffee commercial.

Melinda Dillon brought contrast to Teri Garr's character. She played the role with such intensity.

This was a hard part to cast, and I was literally a couple of days from starting to film a scene with that character and still had not cast it. I offered the part to three or four actresses, and they all turned me down. And then, out of nowhere, I got a call from Hal Ashby who told me he had just worked with this remarkable actress named Melinda Dillon, who was the female

lead in his film *Bound for Glory* [1976]. He offered to send me a couple of reels to check her out, and I was blown away by her performance. I didn't cast her because I was desperate—I would have changed the film's schedule until I found the right actress for the role. But luckily, she was the perfect choice.

We have talked a lot about François Truffaut through the years, and I have wondered if he was your first choice for *Close Encounters*.
It was always Truffaut.

How did you contact him?
What happened was that I had written the script for Truffaut, but I didn't have the courage to send it to him because the only acting he had done was in his own films, *The Wild Child* [1970] and *Day for Night* [1973]. So, I figured I would use Truffaut as a role model for the character of Claude Lacombe—Lacombe was named after my friend, Brigitte Lacombe, the photographer. Then I went to Paris to start casting, and I met a lot of good actors. I met Jean-Louis Trintignant, Michel Piccoli, Philippe Noiret, Gérard Depardieu, and other actors. Trintignant was the closest to my image of the character, and I was about to offer it to him, when I thought, before I make the offer, let me just do a Hail Mary and see if I can get François to read the script.

It was a last-second thing, and I got a message to him, which he received through his agent. He said he'd be happy to read the script.

About three days later, I got a telegram, and the telegram said something like, "Dear Mr. Spielberg, I read the script. Where do I report for costume fitting? Sincerely, François Truffaut." I leapt out of my chair, danced around the office, and immediately got him on the telephone, and we had a great conversation. The first time I met him really was in the costume fitting. And later on set, I asked him, "Why did you accept this role?" And he said, "Because I'm writing about the relationship between the director and the actor, and I didn't feel I could legitimately write about it unless I acted for another director at least one time." And I said, "Well, I'm happy I'm a major part of your research." I adored him, and we had a great friendship.

I love that Bob Balaban plays the role of Truffaut's interpreter—he didn't really speak French but got the part anyway!
I didn't know he didn't speak French because I think he told me that he did! He wasn't fluent at all. He did give me a few lines of dialogue in French, and I was impressed. Plus, I had loved his performance in *Midnight Cowboy* [1969]. I'd seen him in other things and always thought he played

ABOVE LEFT Ronnie Neary (Teri Garr) accompanies her husband, Roy (Richard Dreyfuss), on a late-night UFO-spotting excursion.

ABOVE RIGHT Jillian Guiler (Melinda Dillon) heads to Devils Tower looking for her abducted son, Barry.

ABOVE Young Cary Guffey, who plays Jillian's son, Barry, arm wrestles with Steven Spielberg during filming of *Close Encounters'* finale.

quirky parts. Yet I wanted him to be a cartographer who happens to speak French and gets hired to be Lacombe's interpreter. There was something interesting about the way that he and Truffaut looked together. In my mind, they looked like a writing team. Anyway, that's how he got the part.

One of the pivotal roles is the little boy Barry, played by Cary Guffey. I know you hesitated between him and another boy named Zack Bauman.
I was torn between the two because they were both so good. I had to make a choice and was drawn to Cary. There was something about his curiosity and his directness as a three-and-a-half-year-old in making preternatural eye contact with grownups. He responded to visual things more than anything. I would bring gift boxes with toys inside. I would slowly unwrap the gift off-camera. I'd have to be on a step ladder so he would look up. The reason why he is smiling is because he is just waiting to see what's in the box! At some point he says, "Toys!" because that's what he was expecting to see. He always got to keep the toys, by the way. Because he was so spontaneous, you couldn't do a second take—most of the shots of him are take one.

And that's how he got the nickname "One Take Cary"!
Exactly.

And there's the time when you dressed someone up in a gorilla suit for the scene in the kitchen when the aliens are "visiting" his home, right?
Yes, I dressed our makeup man Dale Armstrong in a gorilla suit and someone else as a dog, and I had them in big cardboard boxes. I told Cary to come into the room and to stop at his mark—a line on the floor. He came in, stopped, and I unveiled the dog. First, he looked a bit surprised and then he was delighted. Then we revealed Dale, our makeup man in the gorilla suit. Cary turned his head over to Dale, looked a bit startled again, until I signaled Dale to take off the gorilla mask. He did, and Cary delivered a huge smile because Dale did his make-up. In the film, with the sound effects, you totally get the illusion that Barry is looking at the aliens—and that his surprise quickly turns to joy and genuine curiosity. But yes, Cary was truly the perfect casting for the part and the youngest actor I had ever given lines to say.

What is most striking about the film is a very specific and unique sense of design. For instance,

the way that you approached the UFOs as objects filled with light.

I was fascinated by planes all stacked up out in the sky, coming in to land, one after the other. I wanted a similar effect at the end of the film when all the UFOs show up at Devils Tower. I even sent the visual effects team to the Los Angeles airport to see exactly what I meant.

At the same time, I didn't know what the Mothership would look like. We tried various things. My first concept was saying, the Mothership is just a big pie pan with no lights on it at all. It just blocks out the sky, and I wrote that some big shadow just covers everybody as this silent, black, featureless pie tin comes across the landing zone. I held on to that concept for a long time. My illustrator George Jenson did some early drawings with that in mind. Then I was in India shooting my last couple of days, and I kept passing this huge refinery on my way to the location where we were shooting. I took some pictures of it. Later, when I got home, I noticed how beautiful the San Fernando Valley looked at night, from the top of Mulholland Drive. Eventually, I took this refinery to create the superstructure of the Mothership, and the underbelly of it is inspired by the lights of the San Fernando Valley.

I remember giving that concept to the great illustrator Ralph McQuarrie—he painted a conceptual drawing of my vision, and I don't think I ever varied more than 5 percent from what Ralph gave me. So, these were all things that were floating around in my head. In a way, this was just a process of "hunt and peck" for the right look for the UFOs and the Mothership.

One thing I've wondered about: Why does the Mothership appear to be coming from the ground behind Devils Tower?

Because I wanted it to feel unexpected. I thought it was less predictable to have it rise behind Devils Tower. But you know, a choice like that has no logic behind it. It is just an image from your imagination, and I instinctively go for it. It only falls apart if you become literal and self-conscious about it.

How did you conceive specifically the idea of the communication between the humans and the aliens?

I remember when I wrote the script, I kind of created it backward. I started with the landing and then tried to back the rest of the story into the question, "Well, how did we get here?" I also started to think of an operatic way for humans and aliens to communicate,

ABOVE LEFT A crew member dresses up as a dog, part of Steven Spielberg's plan to elicit a naturalistic moment of awe from Cary Guffey.

ABOVE RIGHT Guffey tries on the gorilla mask originally worn by a *Close Encounters* crew member as part of Spielberg's scheme.

using music. At first, I thought, mathematics would be the way of communicating with another species, but mathematics is also music. I eventually settled on communicating through colored lights and their corresponding musical tones.

How did the idea of Devils Tower as a location come up?

Joe Alves, my production designer, first looked at Shiprock, New Mexico, and Monument Valley [in Arizona], where John Ford had shot his famous westerns. But it all looked too familiar.

Joe came back one day and announced he had found the perfect place: Devils Tower, Wyoming. Joe showed me these amazing pictures and I just knew that was it. That's the place. Then Joe Alves made a model miniature of Devils Tower. Upon seeing it, I remember grabbing a tape recorder and I pretty much just spitballed the entire ending, what would come first, second, third, all the different symphonic movements of light and sound and communion. It was coming to me so fast. Then when I got home, I didn't need to listen to the recording—I remembered

it all, and basically, that night, it all went into my typewriter.

The sort of psychic connection that exists with people who have had a close encounter and are drawn to Devils Tower was truly a bold and brilliant device.

When I was writing the script, I thought, wouldn't it be cool if Richard Dreyfuss's character Roy is so obsessed, he starts seeing the shape of Devils Tower out of a folded pillow or mashed potatoes. I imagined that this image of no apparent meaning could also become the source of his emotional obession and the collapse of his family. But then, when he sees Devils Tower on the news, he realizes that all this meant something. Then I thought, well, what if a lot of other people have had the same close encounter, have been implanted with the same image, and all converge on Devils Tower for their own deliverance and the ultimate encounter of the third kind? That's cool! Let's put that in the script.

After what you had gone through while filming *Jaws*, what were you anticipating on *Close Encounters*?

I remember thinking how much easier *Close Encounters* was from *Jaws* because all the sets in *Close Encounters* didn't roll and pitch. There weren't thirty-five-mile-an-hour winds hitting us in the face, taking the tops off the waves and making our lives miserable. My crew wasn't vomiting. Basically, after *Jaws*, everything seemed easy.

You did have the challenge of finding a space large enough to build a gigantic landing strip! I saw that famous photograph of the outside of the hangar with a banner that read: "Not since Cecil B. DeMille . . ."

We had a set that was the biggest ever built in an interior space at that time. It was a huge hangar where they used to make blimps, dirigibles, in Mobile, Alabama, that didn't have beams in the middle, which allowed Joe Alves to build the entire set under one roof. It was so big that it caused its own weather systems—it would even rain on us at times! To simulate night, Joe had to use tons and tons of black duvetyne, and of course, Vilmos's lighting package was huge. We had generators for the lights within the story as well as our own movie lights. You see, it would have been impossible to shoot those scenes outside—I was too afraid that it

would rain and cause major delays in the production. But yes, every day, I went to work thinking how lucky I was to be off the water. However, had I not made *Jaws*, *Close Encounters* would have appeared to be a much tougher production. Remember, this was my third feature film, fourth if you count the theatrical version of *Duel*, and I was still learning a lot. In fact, *Close Encounters* was a learning curve for everyone involved with the production. I didn't learn so much on *Jaws*, except never to make a film on water again. At the same time, it was the success of *Jaws* that was my ticket to making my passion project. Comparatively, *Close Encounters* was my dream story. I never felt defeated by the technology or the natural elements in the way I did every day on *Jaws* while trying to fight the mechanical shark. *Close Encounters*, in many ways, uplifted me, the cast, and the crew and made us all feel like we were telling stories of our own unique wish fulfillment.

This was the second film you worked on with director of photography Vilmos Zsigmond. Not unlike music and the five notes used to communicate with the aliens, light was also part of the fabric of the story. It's almost as if those two crafts, music and lighting, were serving two purposes: one as tools to score and light the film, and the other as part of storytelling devices.
Light as a character is what I tried to do with *Close Encounters* because, when I wasn't showing the actual source of the light in the earlier parts of the film, the beams of light and colors had to be dramatic. That to me was part of the mystery. A good example is the scene at the railroad crossing, where Neary's truck stops, dies, and everything starts to go haywire. Suddenly, a big beam of light comes over the truck. That light became almost organic and was the main driving force of that entire sequence. Then that light also is what implants the image of Devils Tower in those who have had such a close encounter.

Light also plays a role in the abduction sequence with Barry and his mother.
That event in the house where screws started to turn and rise by themselves, and how the house is bathed in light with everything going crazy, was great fun to stage.

OPPOSITE TOP Steven Spielberg, Vilmos Zsigmond, and the crew shoot Devils Tower in Wyoming.

BELOW The landing site set, built in a gigantic hangar for the film's finale by production designer Joe Alves and his team.

It's very much a red herring in that we think the aliens are malevolent beings, whereas in fact, they're just wanting "contact."

I thought it was a way to create a mystery and to make a promise to the audience that I would fulfill when we got to the landing site at Devils Tower.

You had been so successful in keeping the suspense going in *Jaws* without showing the shark—did you debate revealing the appearance of the aliens?

I knew I wanted to show diversity among the aliens to reflect the way our world really is. It is made of different races and cultures. Same with aliens. So, I had the large puppet alien with long arms and legs, then a multitude of little aliens, and finally Puck, a very sophisticated puppet designed by Carlo Rambaldi, which I shot separately later in Los Angeles. Rambaldi had done the 1976 *King Kong* and I worked with him again on *E.T.*

But my first idea was to use chimps in alien suits and on roller skates gliding down the ramp. That screen test is the closest I've ever come to making a Marx Brothers movie. The next idea for a crowd of aliens was using puppets, but how do you remove the wires? And because I wanted many aliens, how many puppeteers could I get, working all at the same time? That just didn't seem realistic either. The last idea was having little girls in costume. I wanted girls over boys

because they were more graceful and were trained by a dancer to walk and move in an interesting way. They were ultimately backlit so you couldn't tell they were wearing costumes.

What are your overall memories of the production itself?

For me it was a spiritual, connective, cathartic, and wonderful group experience.

And as far as your experience with the cast?

Richard Dreyfuss came to a role he knew intimately. He stuck close to his own sensibilities. Melinda Dillon, Teri Garr, and Bob Balaban were the same way. François Truffaut was in the role of Claude Lacombe but was really playing himself. Cary Guffey as Barry was so young, I don't think he knew to be anyone but himself. He just did what came to him naturally. But frankly, as I said, that applied to everyone in the film. And I think I played myself, too, as the filmmaker— there was no disguise, and we were all working on something that we couldn't wait to show our friends.

***Close Encounters* was the first film on which you experienced an extended postproduction schedule. In a way, production continued with the visual effects and with your collaboration with Douglas Trumbull and with artists like Richard**

RIGHT (*Left to right*) Lance Henriksen, Steven Spielberg, Bob Balaban, and François Truffaut during shooting of a sequence set at the makeshift military base location in Wyoming.

Yuricich and Dennis Muren. Did you worry at all about that specific phase of the project?

I had tremendous faith in Doug Trumbull because of his work on Stanley Kubrick's *2001: A Space Odyssey*. He and Richard created things that I had never seen before. There was also a guy named Colin Cantwell; I think I met him first. For *Close Encounters*, Colin did a CGI test of three discs flying over a football field, all computer generated. It might have been one of the first tests of that nature, ever. It was extraordinary, but it wasn't there yet. It was Doug Trumbull who then said, "Hey, let's get practical and use models. We're going to do this the old-fashioned way but use motion control." I asked him what that meant, and he explained that this system would allow for camera movements, rather than having a locked-in image. That impressed me, I hired him, and he put together a very impressive team. We leased a space for them in Marina del Rey, and nearby, I also found an apartment that conveniently became my cutting room.

Speaking of the cutting room, *Close Encounters* was the first time you worked with Michael Kahn, who went on to edit all your films except for *E.T.* How did you choose him?

I interviewed thirty editors. It was like an audition process. Editors would come to the office, and we talked about movies, about their favorite editors, their favorite directors, their style and approach. When Michael Kahn came in, he was shy. He was reserved. He was very proud of his work on *Hogan's Heroes*. He emphasized that he was fast. We didn't talk about his favorite films or directors; he was a worker bee and he just loved being in the cutting room. But when I first met him, I felt that I had always known him. It was as if we had grown up together, or that we were somehow related. We had so many things in common, including that we had both been Boy Scouts. We talked about where we grew up and how we grew up. So, it was a no-brainer to hire Michael that day. As I've said many times, this was one of the best choices I've made in my entire career.

Earlier, you mentioned filming the opening scene during the editorial process.

After I had a rough cut of the film, I went and shot several new scenes. One good example is the moment when the researchers unscrew a big globe of the world, roll it down the hallway, and discover the latitude and longitude for the encounter of the third kind.

ABOVE Steven Spielberg and *Close Encounters* editor Michael Kahn: their first of many collaborations.

"When I got to the day of the first recording session and John [Williams] started with one of the larger cues for *Close Encounters*, I cried."

Editing *Close Encounters*, especially while waiting for the final visual effects to come in, must have been a logistical and editorial nightmare!
Yes, it was, but Michael somehow organized it all. We edited the film at my Marina del Rey apartment. I just remember that last sequence was the toughest thing we have ever done together. To this day, nothing has been harder than putting together the last twenty-five minutes of *Close Encounters*. Nothing.

Why?
Because we only had the practical effects and the dramatic scenes with the actors—not the final visual effects that Doug and his team were working on. So, as we edited the film, Mike Kahn and I had a lot of "empty" shots with actors and hundreds of extras watching a ball on a string, used as a reference so we could match the eye line with final visual effects. At times, it felt silly, almost comedic, watching people reacting to nothing, especially in those big wide shots.

I remember in those days, of course, everything

was cut on film. He had the film spread out all over the floor. Usually, scenes are stored in white boxes. Smaller trims hang from wire pegs in film bins. In this case, Mike had rolls of film on the floor, with his own labeling system. We would walk across the floor looking for shots. We put that final scene together literally "by eye and by hand."

Of course, part of the identity of the film is the score by John Williams.
Just like in *Jaws*, John's music was a character in *Close Encounters*. John doesn't like to read the scripts very much when I make a movie. He would rather just see the rough cut, and all the impressions that he gets from the rough cut go into his process. His pathway to inspiration really comes from seeing the rough cut. But in this case, I needed a prerecording for the musical duel between the synthesizer and the Mothership. I described to John what I had written in the script, and I might have even sent him that portion of the script to read, so he could come up with those five notes. John explained that it couldn't sound like a song or like a fragment of song. It had to be something in between and he decided mathematically that it would be five notes. Five notes felt like a "hello." Seven might have felt more like a melody. And I remember one day, I came over to his house, and he played me about a hundred five-note combinations until together we picked the one you hear in the film. To both of us, it just sounded right.

He had given you two notes for *Jaws* and you got five for *Close Encounters*!
Exactly! I got seven notes between two pictures— that's great!

In 1977, John scored both *Star Wars* and *Close Encounters*. But given that *Star Wars* and *Close Encounters* were both labeled as science fiction, did you have any worries or concerns?
Listen, I first saw *Star Wars* without John's score, and when I did—and that was before he started to work on *Close Encounters*—I thought it was hands down the greatest score I'd ever heard. But how it played out was, I didn't attend the recording session for *Star Wars* with John conducting the London Symphony Orchestra. George [Lucas] called me from Abbey Road, and I heard the famous *Star Wars* theme as it was being recorded. That's when I started to worry, asking myself, "How is John going to have anything left over for me?" I was having a real hard time thinking how the same person who

had composed that score for *Star Wars* could still do *Close Encounters*.

Then, when John saw my movie and reacted as strongly as he did to it, I worried a bit less because I could see how he embraced the film and how the film embraced him. He played some themes for me on the piano, which I thought were beautiful. When I got to the day of the first recording session and John started with one of the larger cues for *Close Encounters*, I cried. And I cried because the music was right for the film and because it was so beautifully written. But I also cried because I was so relieved that he had more than enough left over after *Star Wars* to give to *Close Encounters*.

In one of the versions of the film, John Williams referenced the "When You Wish Upon a Star" melody at the tail end of the credits.
Yes. In fact, we originally wanted the end credit music to be entirely a musical adaptation of "When You Wish." I previewed the film both ways. Ultimately, we settled on a quick reference only.

Let's not forget the disco version of the main theme of *Close Encounters*. It's not in the film, but it was available as a single back in 1977!
Yeah, disco was alive and well then. Remember, in

competition with us, a month after *Close Encounters*, *Saturday Night Fever* opened! John's little disco theme is worth listening to today. It's really good.

You mentioned sneak previews. What was that experience like, especially after the triumph you had with *Jaws*?
We previewed again at the Medallion Theatre in Dallas. I had to return there after the incredible experience I'd had with the *Jaws* sneak preview, which I attributed to that lucky theater more than I did the film! Again, we had one of the greatest previews. It was almost a religious experience. We had all been so caught up with the production that we had forgotten that we were making the film for an audience. I remember you could hear a pin drop throughout most of the film. There were a few appropriate laughs, too. At the end, there was an ovation. It was so amazing that I decided that no matter what, I would return to that theater for my next sneak preview, which was *1941*. I did and had the worst preview of my entire career. I quit going back to the Medallion Theatre after that.

***Close Encounters* came out on November 16, 1977. What are your memories of the phenomenon that the film became in the United States and eventually all over the world?**

ABOVE *Close Encounters* composer John Williams with Steven Spielberg.

The first thing that I remember was being forced to deliver it before it was really finished. I felt that I was being forced into finishing the movie based on huge corporate matters, which I had no ability to comprehend. Columbia was facing bankruptcy, and *Close Encounters* was going to either break or revive the company. They wanted it for November, and I initially thought it was more fitted to be a summer movie.

While making the film, the studio went through major changes at the corporate level, but all along, I felt they supported my vision. As I was finishing the film, the head of the studio came to me and said, "Look, take your time. I know you've got to finish the film. But what can I do to make your life a little bit better?" He was trying to help with the pressure that the New York office was putting on me to get the movie out in November. The word I got was, "If you can't complete the film to meet our date, then we'll find someone who can."

I had no choice. I didn't know very much about marketing in those days, and I didn't understand why they would take a film that was supposed to make its money back at the very least and release it first only in two theaters, the Cinerama Dome in Hollywood and the Ziegfeld in New York. The miracle was, we sold out for a month in both cities. Then, I kept wondering, who's going to come see the film when it goes wide? And when we went wide, it was almost like a brand-new opening-day release. We had tremendous numbers on the first day. Yet to this day I believe that Columbia would have made even more money if *Close Encounters* had opened wide on the same day and didn't platform the film in two exclusive runs for six whole weeks.

But that was their decision, and because of the deadline, I couldn't shape it properly editorially. Even the visual effects were rushed. They would have been better if we'd had another month or two. So, my memory of the release itself is all about the anxiety of having my baby taken from me before it could take its first steps, at least in front of me, in a private moment. At the same time, the audience embraced *Close Encounters*. They didn't know that it wasn't finished in my view. It worked great for them.

The film was an immense success—it instantly became a classic. How did the experience change you as a director?

For one thing, it gave me something in my contract that I never had before: final cut! That's a power that unfortunately backfired on my next film, *1941*, where I had nobody telling me that I was going over budget. I didn't have a strong producing team like Zanuck and Brown from *Jaws*, or Julia and Michael Phillips from *Close Encounters*. Everybody was too afraid of telling me what to do because of the success of both *Jaws* and *Close Encounters*. And I learned a lesson, which was to keep your friends and advisors close to you, work on making them realize that you're not going to always be right, and that collaboration is essential to a good performance on the job. I have always believed in collaboration. I surround myself with the best and most talented people—when I succeed, it's not just me, it's all of us. The success of *Close Encounters* was a learning experience because it was my acquisition of power, immediately followed by my abuse of power.

In 1980, three years after *Close Encounters* debuted, you released The Special Edition. Were you able to "finish" the film in the way you originally wanted?

Yes. It was closer to my original vision, with a few

more moments of investigating the extremely bizarre phenomenon of a huge ship in the middle of the Gobi Desert. That was a scene that I'd always wanted to shoot but I didn't have the budget or time for it. But the deal was, to get the money to shoot that scene and recut the film, I had to show the audience something that the marketing department at Columbia felt they wanted to see—which was to go inside the Mothership. So, I agreed to that. But then, when I had a chance to revisit the film for the third time, I decided to delete the sequence inside of the Mothership because I really felt that it should have stayed in the audience's imagination. I went there initially to get the money to complete a film that I felt was unfinished. That moment, however, should have never been in the movie. For me, the Collector's Edition is the official version. But even today, although there will never be a fourth version of it, I still feel like *Close Encounters* is a work in progress.

Did you ever have the desire to do a sequel to *Close Encounters* and reveal what happened to Roy? In a way, *E.T.* sort of reverses the premise and has an extraterrestrial visit Earth.

ABOVE Richard Dreyfuss and Steven Spielberg confer during shooting of the sequence in which Roy Neary boards the Mothership.
GATEFOLD IMAGES Spielberg shoots a sequence in which the soldiers evacuate civilians from the area around Devils Tower.

RENCONTRES DU TROISIEME TYPE

> **"When I first wrote it in the script, storyboarded it, then set up the shot, it was always for me symbolic of what only a child can do, which is to trust the light."**

E.T. is really based on two things, the divorce of my parents and, even before that, all my imaginary friends. So, it kind of came at me from a real, personal place. Where there's a slight connection to *E.T.* is through the alien in *Close Encounters* we called Puck, sort of like Pip from Dickens's *Great Expectations*. Puck comes out at the end of the film and does the hand signal with Lacombe. I thought, wait a second, what if that extraterrestrial didn't go back on the ship? What if it was like a foreign-exchange program, where Roy and a few selected others go off in the Mothership, but one alien stays on Earth as an ambassador? I seriously asked myself, *Should I change my movie right now?* Then I thought: That notion really jives with this imaginary friend concept I've been working on all my life, which is why I brought *E.T.* to Columbia first. Of course, the rest is history. They turned me down. They didn't like it.

There's such an interesting and genuine edge to

LEFT Richard Dreyfuss poses for a *Close Encounters* publicity photo.

ABOVE A French lobby card featuring one of the film's most memorable scenes: the abduction of Barry (Cary Guffey).

Close Encounters, **including the ending with a man literally leaving his family to pursue a life in outer space.**
It was risky to create a husband and father like Roy Neary who was either a narcissist, self-involved, or just blinded by his obsession. But I was a kid when I made that movie. I didn't have a family. I wasn't married. I didn't have children. And so, for me, it was relatively easy to have the Roy Neary character follow his obsession at all costs because I was him and he was me. At that time in my life, I followed my obsession to be a filmmaker at any cost, and that came before family, and before any deep personal commitment to a real personal life. I was deeply personally committed to movies and to being a movie maker. Roy was not far from who I was then.

Is there a specific image that sticks with you when you think of *Close Encounters*? One that symbolizes what the experience of that movie means to you?
It would have to be when Barry, the little boy, opens the front door of his house and sees all that orange light outside. It's one of the first scenes that came to me. When I first wrote it in the script, storyboarded it, then set up the shot, it was always for me symbolic of what only a child can do, which is to trust the light. An adult would run and hide and never open the door. So, for me, thematically, *Close Encounters* is all about children opening doors onto beautiful sources of mystery and possibilities and light.

Over the years, and following the many different releases of *Close Encounters*, do you feel that the film has continued to find a new audience?
I've had young people come up to me and say, "I just saw *Close Encounters*. My dad or my mom showed it to me." They get it. They accept it as a movie of their generation, and they forget the cars are period, they forget there are no cell phones, and that it's totally an analog movie. The spirit of the film captures their attention and captures them emotionally. The film has in my humble opinion stood the test of time.

The one scene that feels the most of its time might be the press conference with the army and people claiming they have seen UFOs. One of the journalists says something like: "I've had a camera with me a lot and I've never been able to see a car accident happening right before my eyes." You realize how far we've gone with our cell phones

capturing everything, in the moment, and then instantly sharing it on social media platforms.

When you think of the movie, what does it remind you about yourself, about that time in your life and career?

I was naïve. I see my youth, I see my blind optimism, and I see how I've changed. I grew less optimistic, and I got older because I am dealing with seven children, living in a practical world. On a professional level, in subsequent years, I became a producer and created my own studio. At the time I was making *Close Encounters*, I was just a director and was much more idealistic. So, as I was saying earlier, I look at *Close Encounters* as the odyssey of a man who gives up on everything except the pursuit of his dreams. I would never tell that story the same way today because I am a father, and I would never leave my family behind for any reason. I would never drive my wife and kids out of the house, build a mountain inside my living room, and then egress the terrestrial life to get on a spaceship to who knows where? That was the privilege of youth—in that regard, *Close*

Encounters is the one film that dates me and what I stand for, and it really tells me who I was then and who I am no longer today.

I'd like to conclude with a few more words about François Truffaut. Did you stay in touch with him after *Close Encounters*?

We did stay in touch. We talked a lot, had dinners together each time I visited Paris. Sadly, when he got sick, he didn't really see anyone except for his closest associates. With him, we lost the greatest emotionalist of world cinema and the most personal filmmaker—someone who was in touch with his own feelings and put us closer in touch with our own. I regret that I never had the opportunity to see him direct. I can tell you that he laughed a lot watching me direct because we had such different styles. One thing that amused him, for instance, was when he saw the set for Jillian's small hotel room, which was built in a corner within our big hangar. I remember him saying that this was at last a set he could relate to and that reminded him of his own filmmaking! He is missed but also vastly remembered.

ABOVE Steven Spielberg directs Melinda Dillon as Jillian Guiler on the motel room set, one of the lavish production's most modest builds.

V

1941

(1978)

"My name is Wild Bill Kelso, and don't you forget it!"
—Captain Wild Bill Kelso (John Belushi)

The first time I met Steven Spielberg was when I interviewed him for the *1941* LaserDisc documentary in fall 1994. I wanted all the interviewees in the documentary to be framed with some element of the movie visible in the background. For Steven's interview, I had gone through the Amblin archive and found a *1941* poster concept that had never been used. I placed it on an easel at the back of the shot. When Steven walked in, he saw the poster and said, "Oh my god, I have not seen this in so long. This poster *has* to be used for the LaserDisc jacket of this project. This needs to be the cover." The picture stirred a memory and he instantly knew, "That's the image."

It was a great way to start our interview, which quickly became a conversation. I didn't even feel like I was asking questions; we just chatted. *1941* is infamous for being a box office disappointment, but I wasn't there to focus on the film's failure. Regardless, it turned out that Steven had a great sense of humor about the film's original release, and he even asked me to include all the bad

PAGES 154–155 John Belushi as Wild Bill Kelso in *1941*.

RIGHT A French lobby card features the scene in which Kelso pilots his plane down Hollywood Boulevard.

OPPOSITE Steven Spielberg (*far left*) directs the Hollywood Boulevard scene on the Universal backlot. At center and right (*both wearing glasses*) are *1941* co-writers Bob Gale and Robert Zemeckis, aka "The Two Bobs."

Columbia Films et Universal Films présentent
UN FILM DE STEVEN SPIELBERG
1941
© 1979 Columbia Pictures Industries Inc.,
Universal City Studios, Inc.
All rights reserved.
Visa de contrôle n° 8536

" Sharing the first cut of the documentary with Steven was great."

reviews on the LaserDisc! So, I licensed all these terrible reviews from newspapers and other media outlets that said things like, "*1941* will live in infamy!"

Because I didn't have a big budget for the documentary, I decided to only interview Steven and the main behind-the-scenes team, rather than the big ensemble cast. I spoke with executive producer/story writer John Milius; screenwriters Bob Gale and Robert Zemeckis; the legendary special effects creator A. D. Flowers, who did *The Towering Inferno* and *The Poseidon Adventure* (1972); and cinematographer William A. Fraker, who shot *Rosemary's Baby* (1968). Bob Gale played a huge part in the creation of the *1941* documentary. He still had an office at Universal and had kept all the drafts of the script that he wrote with Bob Zemeckis, and I used those to do a comparative study to trace the creation of the story. I also managed to talk with editor Michael Kahn and composer John Williams,

which were amazing encounters for me given how much I admired them both.

Sharing the first cut of the documentary with Steven was great. It wasn't like a conventional documentary—it was cut in a way that would convey my experience of sitting across from those people. To do that, I avoided the traditional clip montages intercut over the interviews. I had creative freedom. And because I was new to the profession, I didn't have any preconceived ideas of how documentaries were supposed to be done. I felt so privileged to be

Top-left sheet

STUDIO CENTER
WARDROBE PLOT SHEET

PRODUCTION NO. _____ TITLE _____
CHARACTER _Ward Douglas_ CAST _Ned Beatty_

CHANGE	SCENE NO.	SET	D/N	DESCRIPTION
1	23	INT Douglas Home	D	Paint...
	24-25-27	EXT Douglas Home	D	Cran...
	35A	INT Douglas Home	N	eating
	36	" Liv Room		w/ Bett...
	84	" "	N	
	98	" montage "	N	
	124	EXT Douglas Home	N	Losin...
	124C	" " "	N,N	fok...
	124D	" " "	N	Tello...
	124F	" " "	N	
	125	EXT Sickle & Home	N	
	137	EXT Douglas Home	N	in
	158	" " "	N	
	165	" " "		Fi...
	168	" " "		
	170	" " "		
	172	" " "		
	173	Int " "		G...
	174	" " "		
	176	" " "		H...
	198	EXT Douglas Home		
	213-216	INT Destroyed Douglas Home		

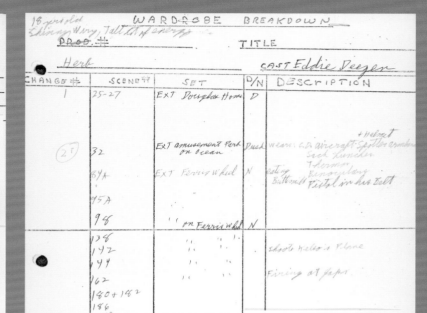

Top-right sheet

WARDROBE BREAKDOWN

PROD. # _____ TITLE _____

Herb CAST _Eddie Deezen_

CHANGE #	SCENE #	SET	D/N	DESCRIPTION
1	25-27	EXT Douglas Home	D	
2	32	EXT amusement Park on ocean	Dusk	wears CD aircraft Spotter armband + Helmet Sick Luncheon Thermos
	84A	EXT Ferris wheel	N	eating Binoculars Buttmilk Pistol in his Belt
	95A			
	98	" on Ferris Whel	N	
	138	" "		
	142	" "		Shoots Nelson's Plane
	144	" "		Firing at Japs
	162	" "		
	180 + 182	" "		
	186			
	188			

Bottom-left sheet

WARDROBE BREAKDOWN

PROD. # _____ TITLE _____

Claude CAST _Murray Hamilton_

CHANGE #	SCENE #	SET	D/N	
1	25-27	EXT Douglas Home	D	
2	32	EXT amusement Pier on ocean	Dusk	
	84A	EXT Ferris Wheel	N	
	95A			
	98	on Ferris whel	N	
	138		N	
	142	" "	N	
	144	" "	N	
	162	" "		Firing at Japs
	180 + 182			
	186			
	188			
	190 + 192	" "		Ferris Wheel Spinning Stunt
	194			
	196	EXT Ocean		
	205			
	213	INT Destroyed Douglas Home	T	

Bottom-right sheet

U.S. ARMY — THE BURBANK STUDIOS

COSTUME DESCRIPTION PLAYED BY: _John Candy_

COSTUME FOR: _Foley_

		SET	D/N	DESCRIPTION
	110		N	Sc 37
	112		N	Overseas Cap: Brown w/ green/yellow Trim
	114		N	
	126	Ext Street	N	Blouse: SB enlisted Brown
	148		N	
	150		N	Belt: Brown Lea
	153 & 156		N	Pants: Brown
	157 & 159		N	Shoes: Brown Ox ford o
	178		N	Next Sc
	201 & 203	Ext Pier E		7
	206			
	208			
	211	Ext Ocean		
	213-216 (7:20am	Ext & Int destr Douglas Home		Sc 65 Helmet, Tee shirt Field Jacket Equip Belt Pants Brown

interviewing these amazing people, and so, when I was cutting with my editor David Palmer, we felt like, "Why cut away from these people? Let's just keep them on screen and don't cut to a photo or a clip." Steven was very supportive of this approach, and his enthusiasm gave birth to all the other projects that I would go on to produce for him. From that day on, I never wanted to leave Amblin.

Loving *1941*

The film is set in the aftermath of the Japanese air force's attack on Pearl Harbor. In California, panic spreads as several wild and wonderful characters anticipate an attack on Hollywood. This triggers total insanity and chaos among the population and the US Army alike. Off the coast, a Japanese submarine captained by Commander Akiro Mitamura (Toshiro Mifune) and carrying Nazi officer Captain Wolfgang Von Kleinschmidt (Christopher Lee), sets its sights on destroying Tinseltown, as Wild Bill Kelso (John Belushi) pilots his fighter plane toward Hollywood Boulevard to join the defense.

I think that to really appreciate *1941*, you have to look at it in its historical context as a piece

of cinema. Steven was very much a part of the new wave of film directors who were coming into Hollywood and shaking things up. But interestingly, *1941* is an incredible intersection of past and present Hollywood, with classic movie actors like Robert Stack, Elisha Cook Jr., Toshiro Mifune, and Christopher Lee sharing the screen with an energetic new generation of actors, including John Belushi,

OPPOSITE Christopher Lee, Steven Spielberg, and Toshiro Mifune during shooting of *1941*'s submarine interior scenes.

TOP Spielberg and John Belushi during filming of the Hollywood Boulevard sequence. The director is holding the Super 8 camera he used to film behind-the-scenes footage.

ABOVE LEFT A French *1941* lobby card featuring (*clockwise from bottom left*) Dan Aykroyd, Mickey Rourke, Donovan Scott, Treat Williams, and John Candy (*center*).

ABOVE The special effects crew films a miniature version of Wild Bill's plane flying over a miniature Ocean Pier Park.

RIGHT Steven Spielberg (*on stepladder*) and his crew film the spectacular scene featuring the miniature Ferris wheel.

Dan Aykroyd, Nancy Allen, Tim Matheson, and others. In addition, Steven's approach to crafting the film embraces old-fashioned techniques, including using miniatures for the special effects sequences. But at the same time, Steven is literally using these techniques to destroy Hollywood on-screen, so there's an interesting dynamic at the heart of the film. It's like old Hollywood and new Hollywood are colliding in front of our very eyes.

1941 is an incredible Rube Goldberg contraption from beginning to end. It's a collection of set pieces, whether it's the elaborately choreographed USO dance sequence, Wild Bill Kelso crashing his plane on Hollywood Boulevard, or the house of Ward Douglas (Ned Beatty) and his family sliding down the hill at the end of the film. It's also an ingenious feat of editing. Despite all the zaniness and the way that 1941 cuts between so many different characters, the geography of it is easy to follow because it's put together masterfully and is so well thought out.

> **One of the greatest things about working on the documentary was getting to meet special effects maestro A. D. Flowers."**

I also love 1941's spectacular special effects. One of the greatest things about working on the documentary was getting to meet special effects maestro A. D. Flowers. His work for 1941, and that of miniature supervisor Greg Jein, is incredible. In one scene, a Ferris wheel breaks off and rolls down a pier, and it looks 100 percent photorealistic, even though it was created with models. 1941 really represents an apex of those classic miniature techniques. Back then, filmmakers had to get inventive and just use whatever they had on hand to make a shot work. For example, the klieg lights seen in the distance in the Ferris wheel sequence are basically light reflected off Scotchlite stuck to pieces of wood. The film is just so inventive.

I also think *1941* is a great tribute to the artifice of cinema. My favorite films are ones that embrace a kind of heightened aesthetic—so that you can tell the

movie is being shot on a set or with miniatures. This approach subconsciously reminds us that we are inside a different world, one that's designed for escapism and not criticism.

A Magnificent Disaster

During filming, Steven used a Super 8 camera to record his thoughts on how the production was progressing. There's great footage of him driving through the gates at Universal Studios and confiding to the camera that he felt the film was out of control. Around this time, many of his contemporaries were experiencing disappointing box office results after enjoying big initial successes. After *The Last Picture Show* (1971) and *Paper Moon* (1973), Peter Bogdanovich made *At Long Last Love* (1975), a musical that was very poorly received. Following *Mean Streets* (1973) and *Taxi Driver* (1976), Martin Scorsese released *New York, New York* (1977), starring Liza Minnelli and Robert De Niro, which proved to be a box office failure, and, in the wake of the huge success of both *The French Connection* (1971) and *The Exorcist* (1973), William Friedkin directed *Sorcerer* (1977), a brilliant thriller starring Roy Scheider that is

now recognized as a classic but was a huge box office disappointment at the time. Those directors had been given the creative freedom to put their visions on the screen and although there were some notable misses, this leeway resulted in some truly singular filmmaking.

1941 is often accused of being self-indulgent. Steven is not a filmmaker who includes a lot of self-referential material in his films, but 1941 is the exception. The film opens with a *Jaws* pastiche in which Susan Backlinie, the same actress who played Chrissie, the shark's first victim, returns for a similar role. This time, however, the underwater menace is a submarine, and she is lifted out of the water on the vessel's periscope. The film also features a reference to *Duel*: John Belushi lands his plane at a gas station that is attended by Lucille Benson, the same actress who played the gas station proprietor in *Duel*. For me, watching the film as a teenager, catching these references was part of the experience. It was exciting to see Susan Backlinie from *Jaws* and to connect the dots to *Duel*. All this contributed to the fun of the film. I had a ball, feeling like I was part of the world Steven was creating, and I went to see 1941 every weekend for as long as it ran in France. With each new viewing came new discoveries.

1941 Redux

After negative feedback from an early test screening, the film was recut and several scenes were removed. For the DVD release, I got involved in restoring a director's cut of the film, working closely with Marty Cohen, Steven, Mike Kahn, and Bob Gale to find outtakes. I remember we could never find one particular moment when two characters, played by Eddie Deezen and Murray Hamilton, are stuck on the Ferris wheel and suddenly switch places with no explanation. I really wanted to find the shot where they switched seats, but I never could. Bob Gale was adamant that the scene was filmed, but we just couldn't locate it. But there was a lot of great stuff that we did find, including John Milius's cameo as Santa Claus and the moment where Japanese soldiers disguise themselves as Christmas trees.

TOP Steven Spielberg with executive producer/story co-creator John Milius, who is dressed as Santa for a cameo appearance that would be deleted from the final film.

ABOVE A French lobby card featuring Murray Hamilton and Eddie Deezen, who play two volunteers, Claude and Herb, respectively, who end up stranded on the Ferris wheel while trying to spot Japanese planes.

BELOW A US lobby card featuring a publicity still of Dan Aykroyd and Jim Belushi in the Hollywood Boulevard sequence.

RIGHT Steven Spielberg (*yellow cap*) and his crew shoot the *1941* finale using the Louma crane on location in Santa Monica.

BOTTOM Spielberg speaks with Murray Hamilton (*left*) and Lionel Stander (*right*), who plays Angelo Scioli, neighbor of Ned Beatty's character, Ward Douglas.

" Although the film didn't connect with audiences as anticipated, the sheer spectacle of it and the attention to detail is incredibly impressive ..."

When I got the opportunity to work on the *1941* LaserDisc, I saw it as a chance to share with Steven my admiration for a film that others hadn't really appreciated. At the time of our interview, Steven was coming off the massive back-to-back successes of *Jurassic Park* and *Schindler's List*, so he could look back at the disappointment and feel at peace with his experience making *1941*. It must have been difficult when *1941* was released to face the negative reviews and the public's response. Although the film didn't connect with audiences as anticipated, the sheer spectacle of it and the attention to detail is incredibly impressive—the costumes, the choreography. Whatever you think of the film itself, you can see the love and attention that goes into every single scene.

And, of course, this was the last time that Steven would make a film so crazy and freewheeling. From his next film onward, he was, by his own admission, much more budget conscious. Steven is always so well prepared that it's easy for him to course

BELOW Spielberg during shooting of the sequence in which Ward's Santa Monica home is destroyed.

correct if something is not working. When he directs the cast and crew, he gives them his all because his initial vision is so strong that he can easily communicate what's required. He'll walk up and give someone a couple of brilliant ideas for solving a problem. It's amazing to witness, and it makes you realize that's what has made him so successful.

End of an Era

The home theme that runs through Steven's early films is also very prevalent in *1941*. The film itself is, of course, about an attack on America—Japanese forces targeting the US homeland. More specifically, the Douglas family home plays a big part in one of the key storylines, and its destruction is the central focus of the film's finale. So, *1941* has a thematic heart that connects with Steven's other films during this period, despite the fact that it seems so different from his other movies.

" Steven stepped out of his comfort zone to make *1941*..."

1941 is much more appreciated in Europe. This could be because Europeans are more willing to consider a director's oeuvre and how a specific film fits into their wider body of work. Steven stepped out of his comfort zone to make *1941*—he took a big risk with it and that's no less admirable when a film fails. There's something liberating about watching a movie that you know is imperfect— you know it's flawed, so you don't judge it the same way.

There's great value in bringing attention to films like *1941* because they tell us so much about cinema at the time. In this case, it's significant because *1941* marked the end of the old Hollywood era. No other film was made that way ever again.

ABOVE Steven Spielberg (*right*) directs Lionel Stander and Ned Beatty (*seated in antiaircraft gun*) during filming of the home destruction sequence.

OPPOSITE BOTTOM Spielberg takes a well-deserved nap in between setups at the Douglas house location in Santa Monica.

GATEFOLD IMAGES A huge crowd of extras gathers on the Hollywood Boulevard set for the scene in which Dan Aykroyd's character gives a rousing speech; Spielberg directs John Belushi as Capt. Wild Bill Kelso.

SPIELBERG ON *1941*

1941 was a real departure for you and wasn't the type of film audiences might have expected from the director of *Jaws* and *Close Encounters*. How did *1941* come into your life?

The first time I heard about *1941* was from my friend John Milius and our then protégés, Bob Zemeckis and Bob Gale—the two Bobs as we called them. They had come up with this crazy screenplay, and I think what got me to want to read the script was they described, at one point, the scene where there's an attack on an amusement park, with the Ferris wheel rolling down a pier and into the water. I remember getting the script and immediately turning to that page and noticing the way Bob and Bob write by putting exclamation marks, underlining, and capital letters; if that isn't

exactly the way it was, that was the impression I got from reading that sequence. I thought, *Well, anybody that passionate is worth reading.* So, I sat down and read the entire script. I must confess, there is a part of me that is probably as crazy and insane as Milius and the two Bobs, and that's what attracted me to the project. I didn't approach it as an experiment. I really thought it would be a great opportunity to break a lot of furniture, see a lot of glass shattering. It was basically written and directed as one would perform in a demolition derby.

My understanding is that John Milius was going to direct the movie, but then instead he did *Big Wednesday* [1978]. Is that what happened?

RIGHT Spielberg with co-writers Robert Zemeckis and Bob Gale on the ruined house set.

OPPOSITE The cover of the Japanese *1941* press kit, featuring art by David McMacken.

Well, I've never had a career plan where I know what my next three movies are going to be. *1941* was just something that came to me. I knew that John was interested in directing it, but then *Big Wednesday* came along, which was truly his personal passion project. That made *1941* available. Then John said, "Why don't you direct it?" I thought, *Well, I don't have anything lined up after* Close Encounters. I really made the decision like that, spontaneously. I was not thinking, *Gee, is this going to be good or bad for my career?* I literally committed to direct the movie based on, *I didn't have any great passion project gnawing at me after* Close Encounters. So, I committed to it. Bob

Zemeckis and Bob Gale came to Mobile, Alabama, several times while I was shooting [*Close Encounters*], and we would talk about *1941*. We would trade ideas and work on rewrites while I was shooting a film that up to that point had been the most personal filmmaking experience of my career.

I read a half-dozen drafts, and it's interesting to see how much darker the earlier scripts were. What do you remember of your journey developing the film?
It's hard to tell because it has been so long since I worked on the script. Also, the experience has been colored by many, many different layers of how difficult it was to make the film, how disappointing it was to release it and have no one in America really enjoy it except for people as crazy as Bob, Bob, myself, and John Milius.

I've got to tell you: I really didn't know what I was doing on this movie. I think one of the reasons *1941* came out so chaotic is I really didn't have a vision for it. I'm convinced that Bob Zemeckis would have done a much better job than me had he been an accomplished director in 1978. In retrospect, that was really the kind of film where the coauthor of it really should have stepped in and directed. Given a few more years, I think Bob Z. would have immediately stepped into the director's chair.

I didn't really have a clear vision or a point of view. I always saw *1941* as an old-fashioned Hollywood musical and had fantasized with John Williams about doing eight musical song-and-dance numbers all based on big band music. You know, Tommy Dorsey, Benny Goodman, and that sort of big band era. I kept thinking, *Why couldn't we make a big band era musical in 1978 or 1979?* What a great opportunity to make the first musical of the old Hollywood tradition in a couple of decades. But I didn't have the courage of my convictions or even the courage of my innermost dreams to prerecord those numbers. I just didn't have the courage at that time in my life to tackle a musical. But inside *1941* we do have a big dance sequence—the jitterbug contest, which is a fragment of what I originally intended to do. In a sense, I will always regret not having made *1941* into a complete, old-fashioned, golden-era Hollywood musical. I remember John was enthusiastic about this. We discussed this big dance number I wanted to do by the Hollywood sign—Hollywoodland in those days. There were other areas in the script where I thought we could cut out twenty lines of dialogue and instead replace them with a musical narrative. In the tradition of great musicals, every song would have advanced the story.

"I've got to tell you: I really didn't know what I was doing on this movie."

So how did you begin visualizing the film?
I brought in Chuck Jones, the famous animation director and creator of *Road Runner*, as a consultant. I wanted him to bring some of that Warner Brothers Looney Tunes value to *1941*. Chuck came up with a great sequence about a runaway torpedo that goes through town with people falling on top of it and riding it for a few blocks, then getting knocked over, as it keeps going under cars, threatening to hit something, and blow up Los Angeles. Chuck came up with something that was so wonderfully "looney" and so "tooney," but it would have been technically and logistically impossible to shoot it with the technology of the time using real sets, even with stunt people.

Maybe today with CGI technology, it would have been much easier to make that sequence come to life, but we couldn't do it with the money I had in the budget in 1978. George Jenson was another artist I worked with. He had been with me on *Close Encounters of the Third Kind*, and he came back for *1941*. We tried to take what Bob and Bob had written to see if we could max out on visual gags. My role models for the film were *Hellzapoppin'* [1941] and *The Fuller Brush Man* [1948] with Red Skelton. I loved the Preston Sturges screwball comedies, or those with Fred MacMurray. And I kept saying, "We're missing a lot of humor, we can make this funnier," but that never came to pass.

What about Stanley Kubrick's *Dr. Strangelove*? Wasn't that one of your inspirations and the reason why you hired Slim Pickens to be in *1941*?
Everything Stanley Kubrick has ever directed has been a personal inspiration for me. I wanted Slim Pickens in the movie so I could do the parody from *Dr. Strangelove* when his character is going through the survival-kit checklist. I wanted to do a parody of that moment when he's been kidnapped and the Japanese are doing an inventory of what's in his pockets. It was both a send-up and an homage to *Dr. Strangelove*.

The thing I love about the cast is that it combines three types of actors. There were actors you

had worked with already, a new generation of Hollywood stars, and then Old Hollywood veterans. How fun was it to be collaborating with this eclectic group?
For me, this was a version of *Hellzapoppin'* and a little nod to Stanley Kramer's *It's a Mad, Mad, Mad, Mad World* [1963] that combined all kinds of generational stars from young and upcoming actors to actors that we basically have grown up and grown old with. I really wanted the cast to be wildly eclectic, and that's why I dipped into three generations for the cast. Also, I had flown to New York and gone as an audience member to the first taping of *Saturday Night Live*, when it debuted in 1975. My generation thought it was about to become a cultural phenomenon before it ever was one. We all knew that something very important was happening. I came back every week for the whole first season—almost every show. I missed about three shows. I flew back every Friday just for *Saturday Night Live*, and I'd go back to LA on Sunday, basically becoming a groupie very early on in my life. It was the first time I was ever a groupie for anything. I became friends with John [Belushi], Danny [Aykroyd], Gilda [Radner], and Garrett Morris. They were the most accessible of the cast members. So I was able to get to know them.

I'm of course curious about your experience working with John Belushi.

Working with John Belushi was a motion picture experience. That's a whole other story. I really loved John Belushi and had a great time working with him. He was great to me and my family. We got along great. He was just an amazing talent. He is still missed today. I have great, sad, and happy memories, very personal memories of John. But as far as working with him, you never knew what he was going to do. You never knew if he was going to stay with the script, make up his own dialogue, or if he was going to include one of the extras simply because she or he appealed to his sense of humor and create a new moment within a scene. The specific moment where John is trying to get back on his plane, he slipped and took a real header. Headfirst. Luckily, someone was there and half-caught John and he didn't get hurt. It didn't even faze him. It looked like a very natural fall, so I kept it in the movie.

Robert Stack played General Stillwell, but I think you wanted Charlton Heston originally?

My first choice for General Stillwell was Charlton Heston, but my real first choice for Stillwell was John Wayne. John Wayne and I had met at Joan Crawford's memorial service at the Academy in 1977. We were sitting on the dais because my first professional job had been directing Joan Crawford in the television pilot of *Night Gallery*. I was very happy to be honoring her because I liked Joan. And of course, John Wayne kept looking over at me, making a bunch of cracks,

saying, "Who is this guy sitting here talking about Joan Crawford? He looks like my great nephew." We met backstage after it was over, and he came over to me and said, "I hope you have a sense of humor. I wasn't trying to hurt your feelings. I couldn't help myself." I replied, "It was great to meet you, and if you had knocked me across the room, I would have still been happy to have met you." At one point, John Wayne sent me a script I think he had co-written that he wanted to do with Maureen O'Hara about an Arabian horse race in Morocco.

When *1941* came into my life about that same time, I mentioned it to him, asked if I could

ABOVE Director Francis Ford Coppola (*left*) joins Steven Spielberg on the set of *1941*.

BELOW Tim Matheson, Steven Spielberg, and Nancy Allen during shooting of *1941*'s final scene.

> **"** And as he proved later in a very funny movie called *Airplane!* [1980], Bob Stack when playing straight with funny material is a wonderful humorist."

send him the script to see if he would consider playing the part of General Stillwell. Well, he knew all about General Stillwell. He went on and on about what a great general Stillwell was, and with great enthusiasm he said, "Please send me the screenplay." So, I did, and I must say he read it immediately because he called me the next day, outraged. He thought it was the most anti-American piece of drivel he had ever read. He said, "I'm so surprised at you. I thought you were an American. I thought you were going to make a movie to honor the memory of the Second World War, but this dishonors the memory completely. It's not even accurate. I was around when those fake bombs fell out of the sky, and there was no panic in Los Angeles. There were some news reports on the radio and that was about it." Then he tried to talk me out of making the movie. He said, "You shouldn't touch this film with a ten-foot pole. I'll be very disappointed in you if you wind up making it because it's really anti-American." I never saw it as an anti-American film, but he took great exception with that.

The next choice was to go to Charlton Heston, who I believe also felt it was a bit of a slap in the face of America, or a big pie in the face of America. And

that's how I used to always think of *1941*. It was like a big pie fight. Chuck Heston didn't think it was funny. I didn't talk to Heston. Milius did because he had the relationship with him, and John just reported that Chuck had passed, in no uncertain terms. Of course, our next choice was Robert Stack, who probably turned out to be the greatest General Stillwell because he looks a lot like Stillwell, especially with the haircut and the glasses. He was the spitting image of Stillwell. And as he proved later in a very funny movie called *Airplane!* [1980], Bob Stack when playing straight with funny material is a wonderful humorist. He's such a fine actor anyway, but he really knew how to handle the comedy in *1941*. I was so happy to have him in the film.

Let's talk about Toshiro Mifune. Milius had this great story about him really getting into character.
He was acting like a Marine Corps drill instructor. A lot of the soldiers were not professional extras and were hired because they were Japanese. They had never been in the military. We were filming in a tank on stage 27 at MGM, and they had to look and perform like disciplined sailors. Mifune did not like the way they were play acting, so he asked me for permission to take over the direction of all

the Japanese extras in the film—I gave him that permission, and he proceeded to act as director, drill sergeant, and disciplinarian. Within two hours we were ready for the first shot and his submarine crew looked as though they had been through several wars!

You had all kinds of interesting ideas for cameo roles, including casting Meyer Mishkin.
He was Richard Dreyfuss's agent. Meyer Mishkin, a very famous talent agent. I wanted him to play himself in the movie and to appear as a talent scout at the jitterbug contest. I asked him and he said, "Ahh, I like the job I've got. I'd rather stay at the office. Hire somebody else but you can use my name." And so we got Iggie Wolfington for the part.

There are a lot of cameo appearances in the movie, including Penny Marshall, Gray Frederickson who produced *Apocalypse Now* (1979), Sam Fuller, David Lander and Michael McKean, James Caan. . . .
This was a no-holds-barred experience, a sort of free-for-all, as in that great Cole Porter song "Anything Goes," which I would use at the opening of *Indiana Jones and the Temple of Doom* [1984] several years

ABOVE A French lobby card featuring Robert Stack as General Stillwell.

later. I've always loved that song, and that was my philosophy when I made *1941*. Anything goes, which meant it was okay to put our friends in the movie. It was a good opportunity for Penny Marshall, who was a very close friend of mine. Gray Frederickson was John Milius's friend as well, and yes, Lenny and Squiggy from *Laverne & Shirley* had a small cameo. Milius ran through Hollywood Boulevard as a crazed Santa Claus firing a gun in the air. It was hysterical, but it was so "inside" that only he, Bob and Bob, and I knew it was funny. The big secret as it turned out with *1941* is that Milius, Zemeckis, Gale, and I were among the few who thought the movie was really funny.

And your dog, Elmer, was also in the film.
He had been in *Jaws* and in *Close Encounters*. He came out of the Mothership at the end. So yes, Elmer was also in *1941*.

One of my favorite scenes is the opening, which is literally a self-parody of *Jaws*.
Independently from the script, I thought it would be funny to start the film with a take-off on *Jaws* and use the same actress, Susan Backlinie, swimming out, doing a little bit of a water ballet, and then suddenly, bubbles form, but instead of the shark, it's a submarine. I even used the score from *Jaws*. It was a fun way to start the film. And at the sneak preview it was one of the few set pieces that got any laughs.

Of course, you had the Louma crane, which was invented by Jean-Marie Lavalou and Alain Masseron. It was the first remote telescopic camera. I remember seeing it used on the set of *Moonraker*. The operator was on the ground, the camera was at the end of an arm on a gyroscopic head, and he would turn wheels to have it do all kinds of pans. You were the first American production to use it.
I attended the Deauville American Film Festival in France with Bob Zemeckis and Bob Gale for their first film, *I Wanna Hold Your Hand* [1978], which I had produced for them. We saw a demonstration of the Louma crane on the front lawn of our hotel. It was this incredible crane contraption that had this long pole with a remote camera. Bob and I played with it, and I said, "We've got to use this. It's probably the greatest invention since the Fisher dolly!" So, I leased it and used it every single day on *1941*. It was our "A" camera. It allowed me to get some amazing shots that I couldn't have realized with a conventional Chapman crane, for instance, and in a lot less time.

One of the two inventors was on set to help educate us on how to use it best.

I really like all the inside references in the film—including the nod to the gas station scene from *Duel*. That made the film appear to be a lot more of a personal experience than it seems on the surface.
Yes, we used a similar gas station to the one from *Duel* where Dennis Weaver goes to make a phone call, in the middle of a snake farm. The truck attacks him, knocks all the snake cages over, and Dennis gets a tarantula on his leg, a rattlesnake snaps at him, and luckily, he manages to escape. Not only that, but I cast Lucille Benson to reprise her role. Only real aficionados of *Duel* would understand what I was trying to do with *1941*. In fact, I should've spent much more time concerned about my main characters, the overall narrative, and "comedy comedy comedy" than all these homages I kept throwing at the wall. It's a real good indicator of where all my nervous energy was going at the time. I wasn't concerned with it

OPPOSITE The crew shoots Susan Backlinie for *1941*'s opening sequence.

ABOVE Legendary special effects artist A. D. Flowers with Steven Spielberg.

making sense. I wasn't concerned about making the story work. I was just adding to the chaos by creating damage through melee.

One of the most memorable scenes is the jitterbug contest.

What was most satisfying about the entire production of *1941* was shooting the jitterbug contest, which Paul De Rolf choreographed for me. I had never really shot a musical number before, and I had been a big fan—I still am a huge fan—of the Busby Berkeley and the Gene Kelly and Stanley Donen musicals. I wasn't trying to rival those. I just wanted to experience what it was like to choreograph and film a dance number. It took five days, and those were the best five days out of the entire production of 178 days of principal photography on *1941*.

There's a cool bit that's not in the film, where Bobby Di Cicco dances on a table.

We did a switch. Bobby Di Cicco was well trained, but he couldn't do all the gymnastics. So, we came up with this contraption that allowed him to travel off-screen to the end of the table, while we filmed a professional dancing on the table, and then Bobby jumped back into the shot. Once again, these were the old days before all the CGI tools we have today. It was more fun to try to figure out, like home cooking instead of microwaving.

1941 also followed the great tradition of miniature work.

1941 had some of the greatest miniature work I have ever seen since the A. Arnold Gillespie days at MGM. Greg Jein and his team of artists did the most amazing job re-creating not only Pacific Ocean Park but re-creating Hollywood Boulevard. The details on the miniature buildings were incredible. One thing I suggested was to film the explosions using air mortars in slow motion, and I came up with the idea of adding glitter and tiny pieces of balsa wood, as well as flashbulbs of different colors. It really made each explosion last longer.

The Douglas home by the cliff, overlooking the ocean, was built for the film.

We built it near Nicholas Beach Road, off the Pacific Coast Highway. We constructed it so it could roll off the cliff. Interiors, of course, were shot on stages. We used several cameras to film the house go off the cliff. Initially, I wanted the house to fall off the cliff when the sub shot at it, earlier in the film. And Bob

Gale said, "We don't have a great ending. The movie sort of tapers off and goes into a lot of dialogue. Why can't we end the entire film with the house falling off the cliff?" So, that's what we did.

For all the physical special effects, it was so great being able to make a movie with A. D. Flowers, who was one of the most revered and talented special effects artists in the world. He did *Tora! Tora! Tora!* [1970], *The Poseidon Adventure* [1972], *The Towering Inferno*. A. D. was most known for full-size physical effects, and he is the one who came up with putting miniature planes on wires to fly over Hollywood Boulevard and created a system to have them do numerous flips and rolls. A. D. and the legendary special effects technicians Logan and Terry Frazee collaborated very closely together on the explosions, the rigging of the tank running over the cars, the plane landing on Hollywood Boulevard, the tank going through a paint factory and through walls, and yes, the rigging of the entire house rolling off the cliff at the end. They were responsible for everything that was full-size and physical. They did brilliant work on that movie. A. D. retired after *1941*. He suggested that I retire with him. He said, "You're as worn out as I am. And this movie may retire us both anyway."

OPPOSITE TOP Steven Spielberg directs one of *1941*'s most exciting sequences: the jitterbug contest.

OPPOSITE BOTTOM Two French *1941* lobby cards featuring scenes from the jitterbug contest: (*above*) Wendie Jo Sperber and Treat Williams; (*below*) Bobby Di Cicco, Williams, and Dianne Kay.

BELOW Steven Spielberg and the *1941* crew shoot in Santa Monica at the Douglas house location.

Watching deleted scenes, I learned that the gag in *Raiders of the Lost Ark* where Toht [Ronald Lacey] pulls out what looks like an instrument of torture but is in fact a coat hanger was created in *1941*!

I got this idea for a side gag where I had Von Kleinschmidt, played by Christopher Lee, as he is threatening Slim Pickens, who swallowed the compass, to pull out this contraption which looks like a torture device but turns out to be a collapsible coat hanger! But when I previewed the film in Dallas nobody laughed, so I cut it out. Now, that was probably because nobody had been laughing for the past forty-five minutes. The biggest laugh, at least in the sneak previews that I experienced, was in the beginning with the *Jaws* parody. But after that, the audience began to titter and people began watching the film with their mouth wide open, in total disbelief! But I was determined to put the coat hanger gag in some movie, someday. So, in *Raiders of the Lost Ark*, which was my very next picture, I repurposed the gag, and this time the audience burst out laughing.

This was your second film working with your editor Michael Kahn.

Mike Kahn, who had just cut *Close Encounters*, followed me on *1941*. It was one of the most challenging jobs he's ever had. We had over a million feet of the film exposed on *1941*. That's a lot of filing and cataloging and cutting.

How did it feel to start showing the film and realize people were not connecting with it?
I had only done two sneak previews prior to *1941*, both at the Medallion Theatre in Dallas, Texas. *Jaws* was a through-the-roof phenomenal preview that I'll always remember, as was *Close Encounters*, with a standing ovation at the end of it.

Naturally, I wanted to go back to the Medallion Theatre for good luck's sake. But as I said, people just quickly stopped laughing. I looked over the entire audience midway, and at least 20 percent of the audience had their hands over their ears because the film was so loud. I had seen audiences covering their eyes during *Jaws*, but never their ears. That was a whole new experience for me. I knew we were in trouble at that point.

Of course, with nobody laughing, you realize that you are in a little bit of hot water. At the end of the preview, Sid Sheinberg, to his credit, came over to me and put his arm around me and said, "I think there is a movie somewhere in this mess. We should go off and find it." The executives from Columbia and Universal didn't even talk to me [the studios co-produced the film]. They were on the other side

of the lobby sort of in a huddle but certainly not the kind of huddle you get from a winning team. It was a very unhappy experience for all of us, I think, at that sneak preview.

What about the reviews? Did you feel hurt by the way the film was being treated?
I didn't read any of the bad reviews on *1941*. The only one I read was the good review by Pauline Kael, which George Lucas faxed me in Hawaii, as I usually would leave the country when I had a movie coming out. Then he faxed me his own review, which was quite extraordinary. But I knew the reviews were bad because people let you know. It's almost unavoidable. I read all the reviews about five years later, and I was fascinated with them. I thought they were very interesting. I was almost sorry I hadn't read them closer to the time of the film's release.

> **❝ I looked over the entire audience midway, and at least twenty percent of the audience had their hands over their ears . . . ❞**

OPPOSITE TOP The special effects crew shoots the climactic dogfight on their miniature version of Hollywood Boulevard.

OPPOSITE BOTTOM Director of photography William A. Fraker (*far left*) consults with Steven Spielberg on the miniature Ocean Pier Park pier set. Producer Buzz Feitshans is second from left.

BELOW Spielberg, Christopher Lee, and Slim Pickens at the Ward house location shooting the film's finale.

When I first met you almost thirty years ago, it was to talk about *1941,* **and we chatted about the fact that it was your first film that was perceived as not as successful.**

It took years for *1941* to become a break-even success story, but the success of *1941* was denied by everybody because it was just too much fun to talk about my first major failure [laughs]. It did do great at the box office in Japan.

At the time you were making *1941,* **Francis Coppola was doing** *Apocalypse Now* **[1979], and everyone expected that to fail. Meanwhile, directors like Peter Bogdanovich with** *At Long Last Love* **[1975], Martin Scorsese with** *New York, New York,* **and William Friedkin with** *Sorcerer* **[both 1977] had experienced box office failure.**

Yeah, I felt we were all in it together—these brothers of cinema—we were all failing upward at the time. When I say failing upward, we got our next jobs immediately. We kept working. And the best defense against failure is to just keep shooting.

Did you like *1941* **after you saw it all put together and done?**

No, I never really liked *1941* after I'd put it all together because it was, for much of the audience

and myself, too much of a demolition derby. But I liked the craftsmanship, not just on my part, but Bill Fraker [the director of photography] did a great job lighting it. And it had great sound design, a great music score by John Williams, and zany performances. The script was quirky, and completely representative of Bob Gale and Bob Zemeckis and my sensibilities at that time in our lives. I was proud that we had done the film together, but I was a little squeamish. For one thing, I did not want the title of the movie to be as it had originally been called, *The Night the Japs Attacked.* I was already squeamish about that and changed it to *1941.* The original title was politically, culturally, and morally disrespectful. For the most part, it took me a while to acquire a taste for the movie. It was only because of the rabid fanship that the picture garnered several decades later, and as I started looking at it through the eyes of its die-hard fans and could recognize what they liked about it, that I realized that the Bobs, Milius, and I were not such outliers after all. The next gen caught up with what we had done and thought we were mavericks, anarchists of sorts, and saw value in the damage path *1941* left in its wake. After that, I started to like it, too.

ABOVE Composer John Williams visits Steven Spielberg on the jitterbug contest set.

OPPOSITE A one-sheet poster for *1941* with art by David McMacken.

VI

RAIDERS OF THE LOST ARK

(1980)

"Snakes . . . Why did it have to be snakes?"

—Indiana Jones (Harrison Ford)

I went to see *Raiders* by myself on the Champs-Élysées the weekend it came out. The theater was packed, and I was sitting so close to the screen I was practically pressed up against it. Having already read the novelization and listened to the score, I had certain expectations, but the movie itself was a whole different experience, and I was genuinely stunned.

You could immediately sense that *Raiders* was a benchmark film. The way Steven treated the hero of the movie was so fresh and unpredictable. Much like Roy Neary in *Close Encounters*, intrepid archaeologist Indiana Jones (Harrison Ford) is a guy who pursues his dream, the search for the Ark of the Covenant, no matter what. In that respect, he's kind of another man-child. Just like Neary, he loves his toys above all else—whether it's the idol we see at the start of the film, the Staff of Ra he uses to find the Ark, or the Ark itself.

Indy is a guy who appears to have no family and no home. He has a house, a physical space he can return to, but you get the sense it's a waystation for his adventures rather than a home. In *Raiders*, Indy does have a love interest, Marion Ravenwood (Karen Allen), but even that relationship is complicated. We learn that Marion's father, Abner, was a parental figure to Indy, but it's suggested that the relationship soured after Indy left Marion some years earlier. He's a man alone. In subsequent films in the series, Steven would give Indy family members, including a surrogate son in *Indiana Jones and the Temple of Doom*, a dad in *Indiana Jones and the Last Crusade* (1989), and a real son in *Indiana Jones and the Kingdom of the Crystal Skull* (2008). But at this stage, Indy is a man without familial attachments.

In contrast, friendship is a very important part of Indy's world in *Raiders*—he might not have family, but he relies on close friends, including museum curator Marcus Brody (Denholm Elliott) and his contact in Cairo, Sallah (John Rhys-Davies). There's a sense of deep-rooted bonds that he's built up through his many adventures over the years, and that very much reflects the friendship between Steven and George Lucas, who was the executive producer on *Raiders*, wrote the story, and presented Steven

ABOVE Director of photography Douglas Slocombe (in beige jacket) shoots Harrison Ford on the temple set.

OPPOSITE Steven Spielberg during shooting of the Peruvian temple scene that opens *Raiders of the Lost Ark.*

❝❝ Indy is a very fallible, and hence relatable, hero which sets him apart . . .❞

with the initial idea for the film.

Indy is also surprisingly vulnerable. In an echo of Brody's fear of water in *Jaws*, a major phobia gets in the way of Dr. Jones's mission: snakes. We also see him get hurt and we see him fail. In the iconic Peruvian temple sequence that opens the film, the booby traps are unleashed because Indy miscalculates how much sand he'll need to offset the weight of the idol he is stealing. And though he makes it out of the temple with his prize, it's stolen straight out from under him by the film's central villain, René Belloq, played by Paul Freeman. Indy is a very fallible, and hence relatable, hero which sets him apart from Roger Moore's James Bond and other similar kinds of movie heroes audiences expected at that time.

If Indy is an unconventional hero, Marion Ravenwood is an even more unusual heroine. Steven introduces her in the middle of a drinking contest at the bar she runs in Nepal. She's as tough as Indy, and very smart and funny, certainly not a typical female character in filmmaking of the late seventies and early eighties. As Marion says to Indy, "I'm your goddamn partner," and that's exactly what she becomes, holding her own during the search for the Ark, and becoming much more central to the story than most female romantic leads of the time. It's also interesting that, when we first meet her, she is costumed in a way that's not conventionally feminine, especially given the 1930s setting of the film: She favors pants and a shirt, with her hair tied back. And nothing is typical about the romantic relationship between Indy and Marion. Their big love scene isn't even a love scene—Indy falls asleep mid-kiss. And this is after she accidentally hits him in the face with a mirror!

An Icon Is Born

The introduction of Indiana Jones at the beginning of *Raiders* is so iconic that it gave Harrison Ford's character instant mythic status. I worked as a documentarian on the fourth Indy film, *Indiana Jones and the Kingdom of the Crystal Skull.*

Filming started in Las Cruces, New Mexico, and when Harrison Ford arrived on set the first day in that costume, complete with fedora and whip, I really had to pinch myself. I hadn't experienced something like that since I saw Roger Moore playing James Bond on the set of *Moonraker*.

But Harrison is such a funny guy and so laid-back. When I was working on *Kingdom of the Crystal Skull*, at one point he called me into his trailer because he wanted me to film him delivering a message for a charity. I arrived at his trailer, opened the door, and there he was, dressed as Indiana Jones. As he spoke to me, it was hard to remain professional and not geek out like a fan.

Of course, when Steven was making *Raiders of the Lost Ark* at the start of the 1980s, nobody knew anything about Indiana Jones. His introduction in *Raiders* has parallels with the way that George Lazenby's James Bond was revealed in *On Her Majesty's Secret Service* (1969) and is extremely effective: Indy's face is kept in shadow or off-screen for several shots before he comes into the foreground for his close-up. The director of

photography on *Raiders* was Douglas Slocombe, whose filmography is so impressive. He made his name working on classic British comedies including *Kind Hearts and Coronets* (1949) and *The Lavender Hill Mob* (1951), and later went on to work on a wide variety of high-profile projects including *The Italian Job* (1969), *The Great Gatsby* (1974), and *Julia* (1977). Steven loved his work and gravitated to him, and their creative collaboration defined the look of not only *Raiders* but all the subsequent Indiana Jones films.

James Bond was a big influence on Steven, and the sequence that opens *Raiders* is very much in the tradition of the mini adventures that start 007 movies—standalone scenarios that often have little to do with the main plot and serve to plunge the audience straight into the action. In the case of *Raiders*, though, the opening temple sequence goes a long way toward establishing the character and his world.

I remember talking to *Raiders* screenwriter Lawrence Kasdan about his approach to that sequence and the way in which he and Steven

included so many little moments that pay off later in the film. Indy's fear of snakes is introduced when he finds one on the escape plane that spirits him away from Belloq's Peruvian allies. Later, Indy's snake phobia will pay off when he discovers that the Well of Souls, the resting place of the Ark, is filled with the slithering creatures. Steven is a master at layering in details that take on much greater significance later in the story.

The huge number of snakes they used when shooting the Well of Souls scene in Raiders is legendary. If you look very closely, though, you can see that a lot of snakes in the scene are not moving. But the fake snakes are so cleverly intercut with the real ones that you don't focus on them. And it just looks so gross that you don't even consider the possibility of subterfuge—you just accept the illusion.

Opening the Ark

I love the way the opening sequence introduces Belloq. Like Indy and Marion, Belloq is an unusual character and not a typical baddie. He's a "champagne villain"—he works with the Nazis in pursuit of the Ark but he's not ideological, just an opportunist. In contrast, Steven also introduces real Nazi zealots—Toht (Ronald Lacey) and Dietrich (Wolf Kahler)—who are much more detestable. Belloq is

TOP Steven Spielberg, Harrison Ford, and Karen Allen rehearse the "I'm your goddam partner!" scene that introduces Allen's character, Marion Ravenwood.

ABOVE A photograph signed by Karen Allen for Laurent Bouzereau during the making of his *Raiders* documentary.

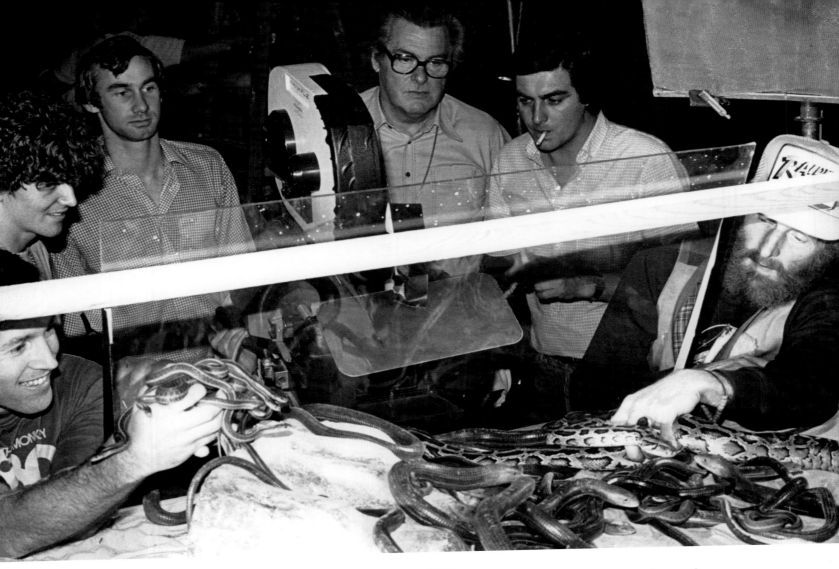

> ## "The huge number of snakes they used when shooting the Well of Souls scene in *Raiders* is legendary."

TOP The *Raiders* crew prepares to shoot a writhing mass of snakes for the Well of Souls scene. Producer Frank Marshall can be seen getting to grips with the reptiles at far left.

ABOVE During shooting of the Well of Souls scene, Harrison Ford demonstrates that, unlike his character, he has no fear of snakes.

OPPOSITE Actor John Rhys-Davies (*left*), who plays Indy's Egyptian friend Sallah, and Harrison Ford, prepare for action on the Well of Souls set.

set up to be almost like Moriarty to Indy's Sherlock Holmes—there's a sense that they are peers, and Belloq himself makes a comment to that effect. Paul Freeman delivers a great performance, but even so, it's clear to me, as a Frenchman, that he's not actually French. This isn't a problem, though, because the film is pure fantasy, a knowing tribute to movie serials of the 1930s and pulpy action-adventure films.

I find it interesting that *Raiders* is the first of

Steven's features to deal with supernatural horror, a genre he would explore further, just a few years later, in *Poltergeist*. *Raiders* doesn't reveal its supernatural elements until the very end of the film, when the Nazis open the Ark of the Covenant and all hell breaks loose: Spirits shoot out from within the Ark and kill all the villains in spectacular fashion, leaving Indy and Marion unharmed.

The visual effects in this sequence—created by George Lucas's company Industrial Light & Magic (ILM)—are stunning, even today. In the finale, Belloq, Toht, and Dietrich are killed by the Ark spirits in different ways: Dietrich's head collapses inward, Toht melts, and Belloq explodes, although for ratings reasons ILM used effects to hide the

TOP Steven Spielberg (*left*) directs actors Wolf Kahler and Paul Freeman, who play villains Dietrich and Belloq, respectively, in the film's stunning finale.

RIGHT A French lobby card for *Raiders* features Freeman's Belloq leading the ceremony that precedes the opening of the Ark of the Covenant.

OPPOSITE TOP Harrison Ford films the famous swordsman scene with actor/stuntman Terry Richards playing his adversary.

OPPOSITE BOTTOM All tied up: Steven Spielberg directs Karen Allen and Harrison Ford in the *Raiders* finale sequence.

gore. It's a very satisfying comeuppance for these B-movie villains.

It's funny to me that in the subsequent scene—the debriefing where Indy meets with the government guys who sent him after the Ark—nobody really talks about the fact that they opened this big box and a bunch of ghosts came out and

killed all the Nazis. The government agents, played by Don Fellows and William Hootkins, are portrayed in a similar way to those in *Sugarland*—essentially, they seem ineffective. Steven's next film, *E.T.*, takes a similar approach to government types, although there's a twist in that instance. But we'll get to that later . . .

Fast and Loose

The pacing of *Raiders* and the flow of the storytelling provide an absolute master class in filmmaking. The beauty of *Raiders* is that you never question any lapses in logic. The movie has a kinetic energy that carries the audience onward. Watching behind-the-scenes footage from the set of *Raiders*, it's apparent that the energy on-screen in the final film is a direct result of the energy that Steven brought to the shoot. Because of his experiences with budget and schedule overruns on his previous movie, *1941*, he shot this one very quickly and efficiently. There's a sense of constant forward momentum not only in the story, but also in the way that Steven approached the production; the energy and efficiency are obvious in every shot.

And that's pretty much the Steven we know today—he still has that energy, and he's so inspired during shooting that he's constantly coming up with new ideas and making decisions on the fly. There's a famous behind-the-scenes story about the scene in which Indy is confronted by a swordsman in Cairo who does some elaborate twirls with his blade before Indy shoots him dead. The original idea was that it would be a conventional fight scene. But Harrison Ford was sick on the day of the shoot, and because he wasn't well enough to do the fight, the moment

through the water all the way to the island. Steven shot a scene just like this, with Harrison looking very bedraggled as he hangs on for dear life, but it didn't make it to the final film. It's another classic example of Steven's approach to cinematic reality—as long as the audience is swept up in the moment, the logic comes second.

It almost goes without saying that John Williams's score is a huge and vital part of *Raiders of the Lost Ark*. The main theme, "The Raiders March," is certainly one of his most famous compositions of all time. It's an incredibly stirring piece. But my favorite cue is "Marion's Theme," which is stunning and romantic and gives life to the love story in the film. There's so much pathos in the piece that seems to fill in the backstory of the romance between Marion and Indy. Steven has always said that John Williams's scores complete his films. The shark from *Jaws* might not have worked in the way Steven had wanted, but John's cues brought it to life in such a vivid way that the audience believed in the shark before they even saw it. And in *Raiders*, John's score really adds layers to Indy and Marion's relationship and gives the film a sense of romance that wouldn't be there without it.

TOP Shooting the submarine scene in La Rochelle, France. The submarine replica was borrowed from director Wolfgang Petersen's *Das Boot*, which was filming in the area at the time.

ABOVE A French lobby card for *Raiders* shows the submarine dock from the film's final act.

when Indy shoots the guy was improvised. As to who actually came up with the idea, there are several versions of the story, but it is nonetheless indicative of the kind of energy and creativity that propelled the making of *Raiders*.

The film's fast and loose approach to logic is also evident the scene in which Indy hitches a ride on a Nazi submarine that's traveling to the island where Belloq intends to open the Ark. In the *Raiders* novelization, it's explained that Indy attaches his whip to the submarine's periscope and gets dragged

Indy Filmmaking

I was very fortunate to work on the first release of the Indiana Jones films on DVD, which featured the three original films. It was a huge event, with a lot riding on it. I remember being called in to meet with the head of marketing at Lucasfilm at the time, who told me, "This is a big responsibility! Don't screw it up." It was a high-pressure situation, and I really needed to deliver.

I was so excited to connect with everyone involved. I had met producer George Lucas earlier, on a documentary I made about *American Graffiti*, his second movie. I'd also written a book called *Star Wars: The Annotated Screenplays*, so he also knew me from that. George is a very interesting guy, and very generous. There's a respect between him and Steven that I think is evident in the final film.

Raiders hasn't aged at all. The fact that it's inspired by old movie serials is a key reason for that longevity: It doesn't matter if something looks artificial in *Raiders*, because it's supposed to be a B-movie. There's a moment during the big chase sequence in Cairo when a Jeep full of Nazis goes flying over a cliff and you can tell the background is a matte painting. There's really something to be said for celebrating the artifice of a film.

Raiders was, in a sense, a new beginning for Steven after the disappointing reaction to *1941*. Its ultimate success showed he could still deliver a highly successful film without spending the same

kind of time or money he had poured into *1941*. In a way, it was almost a return to his days on *Duel* and *The Sugarland Express*, when he was working with strict budget and time constraints and finding creative solutions daily. On his first two movies, it's amazing how much he accomplishes with so little—he squeezes all these great moments out of the material, despite his limited resources, and creates something magical. *Raiders* is very much like that.

SPIELBERG ON *RAIDERS OF THE LOST ARK*

What is the history of your friendship with George Lucas right before *Raiders*?

George and I have known each other practically forever it seems. I met George when I was in college, at Cal State Long Beach, at a film festival at Royce Hall at UCLA. He was introducing his short film *THX 1138: 4EB* [1967], and we met at a backstage party after the festival was over. I believe George won first prize.

We became friends; we were film enthusiasts, we loved movies. We loved the same kinds of movies even though we had a different approach to the process of filming them. We really came out as brothers in the end because we cared about the same kind of stories, and our films were very character-driven but relied on very big ideas. In fact, we were both criticized by film critics for capitalizing too often on high concepts and lavish Hollywood productions. George used to hate hearing that because he decried Hollywood.

As we began working on *Raiders*, I was of course concerned about what would happen to the friendship if we had a disagreement. So, we kept reminding each other, it's only a movie.

Was *Raiders* more nerve-wracking for you because of budget concerns?

Yes, because I had done three movies—*Jaws*, *Close Encounters*, and *1941*—prior to *Raiders* with horrific cost and schedule overruns. I could've made three movies for the amount of time I [used to shoot] *1941*, maybe four. So, I wanted to prove something to myself, and I didn't want to pull George into a financial fight with me. George did not want to get into a financial fight with me, either. So, I made a vow to George that I would bring this picture in under budget and under schedule. And George said, "I'm going to hold you to that." And he did, and I brought the film in fifteen days under schedule and several million dollars under budget.

How did you start discussing Indiana Jones?

George and I had planned this vacation together. He wanted to get away from the *Star Wars* opening, and I joined him in Hawaii. I was completing *Close Encounters*. We were just waiting for the *Star Wars* grosses to come in, kind of like waiting for election returns. It turned out to be a landslide for George [laughs]. It was this mega success, and we got the word very early that the film was going to become a landmark, not just a classic, but a cultural phenomenon. George at that point just breathed

RIGHT "I'm making this up as I go." Indiana Jones (Harrison Ford) rides after the Ark.

OPPOSITE Steven Spielberg and executive producer George Lucas don desert headgear for the Tunisia shoot.

a sigh of relief and then changed the subject from *Star Wars* to asking what I was doing next and what I wanted to do. I mentioned I'd always wanted to direct a James Bond picture. And George said, "I got that beat. I have a better idea, and it's called *Raiders of the Lost Ark.*"

He pitched me the story, which he had been developing with Phil Kaufman—not the full-on plot but the general concept about this archaeologist who's also a bit of a grave robber, who goes around hunting for religious and sometimes supernatural antiquities all around the world. He wears a fedora hat and has a leather jacket and carries a bullwhip. That's pretty much all George told me. But it amounted to this globe-trotting adventure, and that was good enough for me. So, I signed on and we began developing the actual story for *Raiders of the Lost Ark.*

At that point in time, I was also looking back at the films I had done. My films had all been set in America, and I wanted to somehow find a movie that would take me all over the world. I had also expressed to George my desire to make the type of

BELOW Steven Spielberg wears a *Raiders* T-shirt during promotion of the film.

movies like the Republic serials I had been raised on.

Did you have a sense that audiences would be interested in that type of film?
Very much so. At the time, I was obsessed with making films for the audience. The moviegoing public was my collaborator, and it was important that Indiana Jones be accepted. Interestingly, I had very little commercial hope for *E.T.*, which I did after *Raiders*. It was a very personal story that had been haunting me and I just had to get out of my system. But *Raiders* was intended to be a movie for everybody.

How did Lawrence Kasdan come to collaborate on the script?
I brought Larry into the picture because I had just bought a screenplay of his called *Continental Divide* [1981]. I liked the script a lot, and I gave it to George as a writing sample, saying Larry should be writing *Raiders*. George agreed and we started having story meetings, spent three days with a tape recorder outlining the whole plot, defining the set pieces. Then Larry went off to put it on paper.

> " Harrison was a great collaborator and on board to create a living, breathing, three-dimensional character."

Was the final script very different from what you had initially discussed in the story meetings?
Larry's a great writer, and he added his own style, wit, and humor to the mix. It was like Preston Sturges meets Michael Curtiz, with shades of Humphrey Bogart in *The Treasure of the Sierra Madre* [1948]. He pretty much took the story we had discussed, but he brought it all to life.

At what point did you start thinking about the actor who was going to play the role?
George and I tested a lot of potential Indiana Joneses, from Tim Matheson to Peter Coyote, Tom Selleck, and a number of other people. Coyote is in *E.T.* because we met on the *Raiders* auditions.

It wound up that George and I liked Tom Selleck the best of all the people we had screen-tested. We

especially liked the idea of Tom because he looked almost like the early concept illustrations that [comic book artist Jim] Steranko had done for George. We went after Tom, and then a man who became a very close friend of mine, Bob Daly, who was at the time the head of CBS, said, "Wait a minute, we have a series commitment with Tom called *Magnum, P.I.*" So CBS preempted Selleck. Tom had a television series that took him to great heights, fame, and fortune, and we had nothing.

Another month went by and we're searching, and then, independently of our work on *Raiders*, George showed me a cut of *The Empire Strikes Back* [1980]. At the end of the screening, after telling George how incredible the movie was, I asked, "What about that guy? You know, Han Solo, for Indiana Jones?" And George said, "Harrison? Yeah, he'd be great." We met with Harrison, he read the script, loved it, and said he'd do the film.

What qualities do you think Harrison brought to the part?

Harrison was a great collaborator and onboard to create a living, breathing, three-dimensional character. He was sort of the next draft of the screenplay. A lot of

his ideas went to my notepad and then into the movie. Harrison was a big component of that process of creating this character. He gave Indy something that is now considered the archetypal action-adventure hero. A guy who is tenacious and foolhardy, even if it means getting hurt. And he gifted Indy with his dry sense of humor.

TOP In Kairouan, Tunisia, Harrison Ford works with the group of children who played Sallah's kids in the film.

ABOVE Harrison Ford in the iconic Indy hat and leather jacket during shooting of the film's opening sequence in Hawaii.

Karen Allen was so memorable as well. Were you familiar with her work?

I first saw her in *Animal House* [1978] in which she played Peter Riegert's girlfriend, and she was always sort of there, in a sea of many possible Marions. We met with several actresses, tested many of them—I'm talking about dozens. Finally, it was obvious after about two months of screen tests and interviews, Karen was the clear favorite because she had spunk. She was a firebrand and reminded me of those '30s

actresses like Irene Dunne and Carole Lombard. I could see directors that I had admired like Cukor and Sturges putting her in one of their classic films. She just seemed like such a natural fit with the genre.

While you were casting, what else was happening with preproduction?

One of the things that George and I talked about in Hawaii when I said I wanted to do *Raiders* was the fact that my films *Jaws*, *Close Encounters*, and *1941* had gone widely over budget and over schedule. George said, "Steve, you can't have a gigantic budget to shoot *Raiders*. I don't want to spend that kind of money on the movie." George is a great producer and asked me to figure out a way to make the film in eighty-seven days. I agreed on the sands of the Big Island of Hawaii that the film's schedule would not go over ninety days.

Also, to keep the budget in check, I storyboarded every single shot I intended to put in the movie, following the continuity of the script right down to people in dialogue scenes. Once that was done, I began to edit what I thought was extraneous or superfluous or indulgent. For instance, instead of planning to shoot three master shots, I decided I

would do it in two for one scene. Instead of those extra five inserts, I would shoot two inserts. I brought the movie down to what was truly needed, without compromising the big action sequences. Another step I took was to put together a solid second-unit team, headed by Mickey Moore, who was able to follow the storyboards I had worked on with Ed Verreaux and other artists.

I really was ready to turn over a new leaf, and *Raiders* was my chance to prove to myself that I could make a movie responsibly, economically, with a little help from my friend George Lucas, who gave me a lot of tips on how to be prepared. I became obsessive-compulsive about getting *Raiders* in under budget and under schedule, so looking back brings memories of kicking myself in the butt every single hour of every single day to make a very lean movie and trying to be a responsible friend to George.

I'll never forget that Paramount took out an ad saying *Raiders of the Lost Ark* had come in fourteen days under schedule, basically applauding George and I for being fiscally responsible. I saved and framed that ad, thinking, *I'm a born-again director, now that I've learned how to make a big, epic movie that doesn't have to cost a fortune and doesn't have*

to take forever to complete.

The sets designed by the great Norman Reynolds were spectacular.

This is the very first picture I ever directed in the UK. I first assumed we would go to the most famous studio there, Pinewood, the home of James Bond. But George had had good luck at Elstree Studios, having done *Star Wars* and *The Empire Strikes Back* there.

I went ahead and visited the studio but was told that one of the stages that we were going to use for the Well of Souls was currently being used by Stanley Kubrick for the Overlook Hotel from *The Shining* [1980]. I got a chance to meet Stanley Kubrick that day, and of course, the rest is history. Stanley and I were friends for nineteen years until he passed away in 1999.

Norman Reynolds, who had done *Star Wars*, was there with me. I was very excited to work with the guy that did *Star Wars*, and he was excited to be doing something completely different. He shared with me models and sketches for the different sets. He did a lot of research, used all sorts of real places for inspiration, and created the world of Indiana Jones.

ABOVE Steven Spielberg and legendary director of photography Douglas Slocombe.

ABOVE In Tunisia, the *Raiders* crew shoots Sallah actor John Rhys-Davies on the dig site set.

RIGHT Steven Spielberg (at top sitting) with the crew in Tunisia.

OPPOSITE TOP A wide view of the expansive dig site set created by production designer Norman Reynolds.

And I think you used the models to create your shots and plan out camera placements ahead of filming, correct?

Yes. Not only did Norman do models for me, but he did large topographical layouts of the areas where we were going to shoot exteriors of the archaeological dig site. And I used to get my little 35mm view finder and lie down on that model trying to find my angles and map out my shots.

How did you come up with the signature look for Indiana Jones?

It all came from the original concept paintings before anybody was hired. But our brilliant costume designer Deborah Nadoolman really refined the look and made it more lived in, more "fitting" to Harrison's persona. He inevitably became the only possible Indiana Jones—you couldn't swap him with another actor. But I loved what she did for Belloq, and the dress that Marion uses to seduce him. She also wanted to make the Nazi uniforms authentic to the period and to history. She just did an amazing job putting it all together. I had worked with her on *1941* and had been impressed by her commitment. *Raiders* felt like an epic costume picture.

> " *Raiders* is one of those films that I can look at with my kids, distance myself from all that went into making it, and appreciate it as an audience member."

Who came up with the idea of opening the film with the Paramount logo dissolving and revealing a similar-looking mountain?
I just thought it would be fun to start with a shot of a mountain that looked like the Paramount logo. When I was a kid, my first film company was called Playmount Productions. "Playmountain" is my name in German, and I shortened it to Playmount. For *Raiders*, I sent people all over Hawaii looking for a mountain that bore some resemblance to the Paramount logo. What they eventually found was a close likeness.

At the same time, the opening scene might lead you to believe that you're about to enter a film noir—the jungles were so dense in Hawaii, it was very hard to get any light in. But I kept telling Douglas Slocombe that I wanted to see everybody's eyes, just like in those 1930s swashbucklers.

It is so fun to see Alfred Molina as Satipo in those early scenes—how did you find him?
Alfred Molina was just one of the many actors who came in to meet during the casting process in the UK. I liked him, I thought he was great—he had never made a movie before. This was his first picture. I remember him saying to me, "Is this what picture making is all about? You stand around, people put tarantulas all over your body, and then shoot compressed air to get them to scurry about?"

To that point, you took a lot of care with the secondary characters. All were so well-written and cast that they stood out as immediately memorable.
It's a tradition that goes way back, something I was aware of from watching the great movies of Bogart and Bacall, James Cagney. Look at the supporting cast

TOP Indy (Harrison Ford) flees a booby-trapped boulder in one of *Raiders'* most iconic moments.

ABOVE Steven Spielberg and George Lucas pose with the extras who played Belloq's Hovitos warriors in *Raiders*.

of *Key Largo* [1948], or Cagney's mother in *White Heat* [1949]. Tremendous efforts were made in selecting secondary cast members and to have them leave indelible impressions on audiences. So, we set out to have every character surrounding Indiana Jones be as memorable as possible.

There were a lot of fun practical effects in that opening sequence. Today, it would all be done in

CGI, but then, it all felt real, which contributed greatly to the film's realism.

The boulder rolling after Indy is something I came up with during our story meetings with Larry and George, when we were spitballing ideas for set pieces. It may have come from some old serial I saw when I was a kid. But I didn't know it was going to look as good as the day when Norman Reynolds showed me the set. The boulder was extraordinarily large, and in fact, for the first couple of shots, I used a stuntman until I felt it was safe enough for Harrison to then step in and do it.

As Indy escapes with the idol and out of the cave, you introduce the villain, Belloq, played by Paul Freeman. Weren't you going to cast a French actor for the part?

I was going to cast [famous French actor and singer] Jacques Dutronc at one point, but we couldn't work out his schedule. I really wanted to cast a French actor to play a Frenchman, but then I saw this British actor named Paul Freeman on British television. I met him and immediately noticed he had striking eyes. He was charming and witty and had the elegance of a champagne villain in a film noir.

You set up so much in that opening sequence, including Indy's fear of snakes. Yet, aside from the

encounter with Belloq, it's purely done to establish the character of Indy, and his quirks, which all pays off later in the story.

We all agreed that Indy had to be vulnerable. He had to be a real person. He had to be relatable. We wanted the audience to say, "I could be that guy because he's really getting really hurt here. He's not invulnerable and is more human than most superheroes." In fact, I didn't want him to be a superhero. I wanted him to be a little more of a curmudgeon, and we immediately identified his vulnerabilities and phobias. I don't remember which one of us said that he should hate snakes and be afraid of them. But we all agreed that was going to be his Achilles' heel.

Once he is back home and resumes his duties as a professor, he sort of becomes a different type of guy. Almost like Superman's alter ego, Clark Kent!

He's professorial, wears a tweed, three-piece suit, and all the girls are in love with him. David Tomlin, my first assistant director, came over to talk to me on the morning we shot the classroom scene, and he said he had come up with an idea I may like. He suggested that one of the girls had written something on her eyelids, so when she closes her eyes, Indy can read the word "love" on one eyelid and "you" on the other.

This is also where you introduce Indy's friend Marcus Brody, played by the great Denholm Elliott. What a great choice.

I had always been a big Denholm Elliott fan, from his early work in British productions like David Lean's *The Sound Barrier* [1952] and *The Cruel Sea* [1953], among many others. I think he was our first choice, and he lent a kind of paternal warmth toward Indy. He is also the voice of reason. Although it's a small part, Denholm

BELOW Museum curator Marcus Brody (Denholm Elliott, *left*) prepares to send his intrepid friend Indy (Harrison Ford) on another adventure.

Elliott made it memorable and worth expanding on in the third film, *Indiana Jones and the Last Crusade*.

Marion is not your typical leading woman. Having her enter the story through a drinking contest was both unusual and memorable.

Yes, the drinking contest establishes so much about Marion: Not only can she drink anyone under the table, but she is also any man's equal, including Indiana Jones.

Her punching Indy's face when they're first reunited was a genius introduction into their dynamics.

That was a nice way of letting the audience understand the nature of the relationship between Indy and Marion. We didn't need to explain too much after that. In a very few, economically written Kasdan lines, we were able to paint an entire backstory between those two characters, including

the relationship Indy had with Marion's father, Abner Ravenwood.

I loved how Indy enters that scene with his shadow projected onto the wall of the bar.

I loved shadows for this movie. I don't have any intellectual justification for it. I just thought it worked. I had shadows appearing throughout the film, most memorable being when Indy and Sallah carry the Ark through the Well of Souls. In that case, the Ark was such a huge, religious icon that I wanted to treat it reverently.

How did you find Ronald Lacey for the notorious role of Toht?

Ron had a solid history of playing different character parts in British films and on stage. When I first met him, he reminded me of Peter Lorre, the iconic actor from Fritz Lang's *M* [1931] and Hitchcock's *The Man Who Knew Too Much* [1934], among other classic

films. We shaved Lacey's head, but mistakenly, not completely, and at some point in the film, he takes off his hat and you can see exactly where his hairline is hiding. But Ronnie had fun doing his version of Peter Lorre.

You talk about the film being an homage to serial films, and the maps tracing Indy's journeys across the world were a staple of cinema in the forties. So many films start with maps, even *Casablanca*.
That was George's idea from the very beginning. He wanted to trace Indy's travels with a lined map. It was nothing new, but we reintroduced that concept to a whole new generation of moviegoers.

Filming in Tunisia I know was a challenge.
The film was made before the days of easy digital removals, so we had to physically remove the television antennas from the rooftops in Kairouan, Tunisia—and we had to put them back up when the shot was complete. We must have removed two or three hundred antennas, especially for the wide panoramic shot on the rooftop of Sallah's house. It's amazing that this is something you wouldn't have to worry about today.

That sequence introduces John Rhys-Davies as Sallah. Again, he was a very inspired piece of casting.

ABOVE Steven Spielberg directs actor Wolf Kahler (sitting) who plays Dietrich in *Raiders*.

LES AVENTURIERS de L'ARCHE PERDUE

I first went to Danny DeVito, and I offered him the role. We had become friends, and he was dying to play Sallah. Unfortunately, due to conflicts in the schedule of his TV show *Taxi* [1978–1983], he was unable to do the film. Then, I saw John Rhys-Davies in the hit miniseries *Shogun* [1980], and I thought he was like Falstaff. He had a great basso profundo voice and a tremendous sense of humor. I immediately thought he would be perfect as Sallah.

The street fight is one of the standout scenes from the film.

One of the memorable moments is the idea I had about Marion being in one of the baskets and being carried away. Indy runs after her and finds himself surrounded with a crowd carrying similar baskets and tips them over, looking for her. I remember we spent an hour and a half laying out something like five hundred marks on the ground for five hundred extras who had to be in certain places and positions. It was all choreographed, and when lunch came, the extras, unaccustomed to film production, looked down and they all picked up their marks and went off to lunch with them. I was left with an empty square with nothing on the ground for the extras to come back to after the break.

In general, there was so much stress shooting in Tunisia—we just wanted to get home. I had six weeks scheduled in Tunisia but managed to do it all in four. It was so hot that it was hard to breathe, especially in the afternoon. You almost felt claustrophobic like the air was closing in on you—like the air was a solid wall of heat. Plus, we all began getting sick, except for me because I subsisted on canned food. That's all I ate.

The rest of the crew would go to restaurants or eat at the hotels, and they all got sick. Harrison himself got terribly ill one time, same with John Rhys-Davies. So I tried to simplify the basket sequence, for instance, and limited the number of shots to move the production along faster.

I have a lot of favorite scenes from *Raiders*, but one that stands out for me the most is that entire sequence with the basket chase through Indy just shooting the swordsman.

That's how the scene with Indy shooting the swordsman came about, right? Harrison was so sick, he just pulled out the gun on him!

Harrison and I have a friendly running feud over this. My memory is that Harrison told me I basically had him for a short amount of time to get that sequence, and I basically replied to him, "Just shoot the guy!" The crew laughed, and we filmed it. Harrison feels he came up with the idea. It doesn't really matter—it got the biggest laugh in the movie.

What's interesting is that each of the action scenes have their own identity. To your point about Indy getting hurt, there's this amazing fight that he has with stuntman and actor Pat Roach in the Flying Wing sequence as Indy and Marion are trying to escape.

I remember that was an interesting scene, and it might be the first time I'd ever done anything like this as a director. I began storyboarding the fight, then threw it all out and choreographed it in continuity, shot by shot, one punch at a time. I basically made that scene up as we shot it. Originally, it was only meant to be a couple of punches, but I kept expanding the scene. It took, I think, about two days to shoot, and it played nicely in contrast to Indy just pulling out his gun on the swordsman in Tunisia, which we shot in just a few hours! By the way, my producer Frank Marshall has a nice cameo appearance in that scene [as the pilot of the Flying Wing who shoots at Indy]!

Of course, before the Flying Wing scene, one of the most memorable sequences takes place in the Well of Souls with the snakes!

That scene was not improvised. It was all storyboarded and meticulously planned out, months before we started shooting. What I didn't realize was that in our sketches, the ground was completely covered in snakes. We had thousands on set, but they barely covered the ground, and I couldn't really get wide shots. I had to use a 35mm lens to

get close and give the impression that snakes were everywhere. But that's when I said to Frank Marshall, "We need more snakes!"

And thousands of snakes began coming in. I'm not afraid of snakes, but seeing all of them being untangled and spread across the set made me nauseous. At one point, David Tomlin got bit by a python, and he just stood there with the python not letting go. The snake was fine, David got medical

attention, and we carried on under the supervision of the Royal Society for the Prevention of Cruelty to Animals and handlers. When it came to the cobra, we had antivenom serum and filmed with a glass separating the snake from Harrison.

What happened to all those snakes once you were done with filming?

Probably some escaped—although not the

ABOVE Shooting the flying wing sequence: (*clockwise from top*) Harrison Ford and Karen Allen; a huge explosion is detonated on set; Steven Spielberg.

RIGHT Filming with Karen Allen and Harrison Ford on the Well of Souls set: (*top left to top right*) Steven Spielberg, Douglas Slocombe, and David Tomblin.

cobra or the python! I remember at times, out of nowhere, a snake that had been hiding would show up on the next set. But seriously, they were all safely attended to and returned to reptile stores.

One of the most amazing stunts in the film is when Indy goes underneath the truck.

It was inspired by the famous scene in *Stagecoach* [1939], in which the legendary stuntman Yakima Canutt went underneath horses and wagon going at full speed. He had been hurt doing that stunt, yet stuntman Terry Leonard said he wanted to go underneath the truck and come back out the other side. I said, "My God, I wish I had thought of it. That's an amazing idea."

There was a great camaraderie between the stunt team with Vic Armstrong, Glenn Randall, and Terry Leonard.

I had three of the greatest stuntmen in history working on *Raiders* with me. When Harrison would let him, Vic Armstrong did most of his stunts because they looked so much alike. In fact, I remember mistaking Vic for Harrison one day! The resemblance was uncanny.

TOP A stuntman playing a German soldier is left in the dust during shooting of the sequence in which Indy chases after the Ark.

ABOVE Indy jumps from horse to truck in another classic stunt from the film.

The scene aboard the ship the *Bantu Wind* is just classic thirties and forties romantic comedy.

We shot that whole sequence in La Rochelle, France, and used a submarine from the German production *Das Boot* [1981]. I came up with the mirror gag during which Marion inadvertently hits Indy—and I specifically wanted his scream to be heard outside the ship, way out in the ocean, to underline comically how much this hurt. But when we first previewed the movie, I was really upset because Marion flipping the mirror and hitting Indy got such a huge laugh that nobody heard the scream over the next shot

of the ship. The first time I think audiences really experienced that gag was when the film was first on TV or on videocassette! That scene ends with Marion kissing Indy and him falling asleep, which I thought was also very funny. I love Marion's line there: "We never seem to get a break, do we?"

The climax of the film with the opening of the Ark is an amazing blend of practical effects and magic shots from ILM.

Again, I storyboarded every single shot so the actors could understand what was happening, what the final shots would be. They could come up to me, check out the drawings, and be influenced about what they were being asked to react to that was only on paper.

How did you decide whose head to shrink, which one to melt, and whose head should explode?

You know, I don't remember when and how that was decided. The melting head was an actual head made of wax and was filmed practically by ILM, using time-lapse photography. The shrinking head was the least successful for me. The exploding head had to be covered over by a large pillar of fire to avoid an R rating.

ABOVE Steven Spielberg and Harrison Ford in La Rochelle, France, with the vessel that doubled for the *Bantu Wind* in the film.

LEFT Karen Allen, Steven Spielberg, and executive producer Howard Kazanjian during the filming of the *Bantu Wind* sequence.

> ❝ George and I were back on the beaches of Hawaii waiting for grosses and building our traditional, good luck sandcastle.❞

I think that last scene between Indy and Marion on the steps was additional photography.

By the time I showed the movie to George, we realized we didn't have any resolution for Marion Ravenwood. So, we went to San Francisco and shot that on the steps of the city hall.

The last shot of the Ark being stored away features one of the most famous matte paintings in cinema.

That shot has become part of the mythology of *Raiders of the Lost Ark.* All those boxes stacked up recalled the ending of *Citizen Kane* [1941], but the irony is in all the effort that went into possessing the Ark and how it's basically become the property of government bureaucracy.

Again, with *Raiders*, John Williams created an amazing score.

John saw the movie, loved it, and went off to write the music. He called me one day and previewed all the themes on the piano. He'd written two separate *Raiders* themes, and my only contribution was to have him merge both because I loved them both.

Editor Michael Kahn has told me that this movie was an opportunity for him to do things he'd never done before.

We were coming off *1941*, and *Raiders* was a very different kind of film. We also had to streamline the editorial process to save money, and we didn't have as much coverage as we'd had on *1941* and *Close Encounters.* But it was fun to meet those challenges.

I've been fascinated with Ben Burtt's sound design. His work on *Raiders* is insanely creative.

Ben Burtt is just such a sound savant, and I loved what he had done on *Star Wars.* He was part of the George Lucas and Skywalker Sound family with Gary Summers and Gary Rydstrom, whom I worked with in subsequent years. I remember the first time I was impressed by something Ben did on *Raiders.* It was a sound he included in the opening jungle scene, when Barranca [Vic Tablian] and Satipo [Alfred Molina] talk about a poisoned dart Indy pulled out of a tree. I don't know where Ben got that sound, but it suddenly made that entire jungle scene so frigging alien. It almost sounded like something out of *Star Wars.* When I first heard that, I said, "We are in for a great adventure in sound."

At what point did you realize that you were making history again with this film?

I didn't think we were making film history. In fact, I thought we failed, despite amazingly good reviews and the *Newsweek* cover. We didn't have a spectacular opening. George and I were back on the beaches of Hawaii waiting for grosses and building our traditional, good luck sandcastle. Then after the weekend, we got a call from the studio with the good news that the Monday numbers were unusually great. I remember I flew

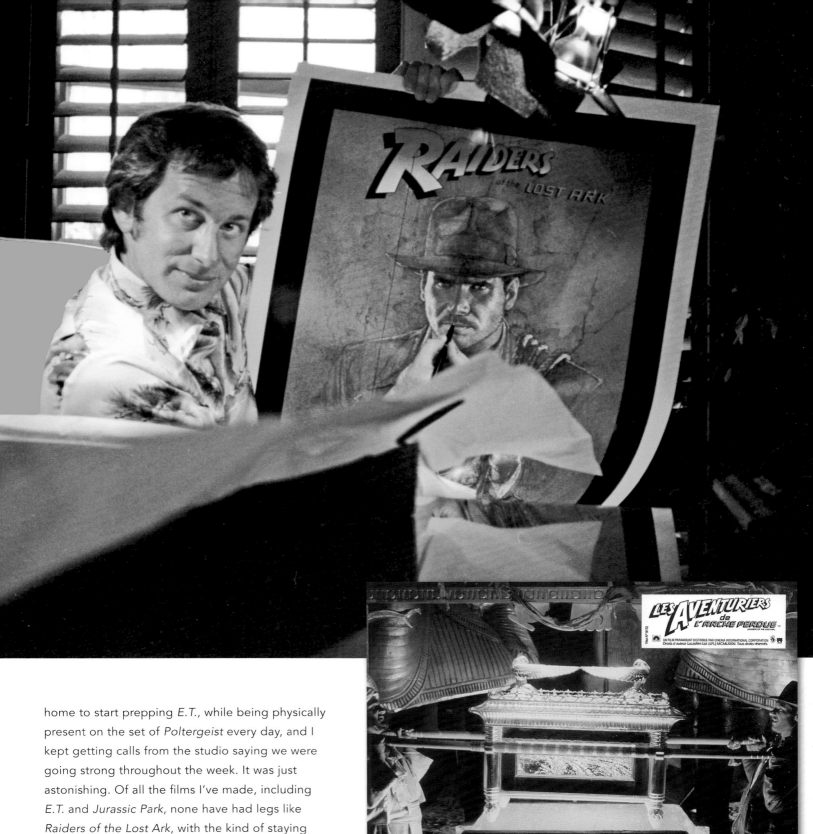

home to start prepping *E.T.*, while being physically present on the set of *Poltergeist* every day, and I kept getting calls from the studio saying we were going strong throughout the week. It was just astonishing. Of all the films I've made, including *E.T.* and *Jurassic Park*, none have had legs like *Raiders of the Lost Ark*, with the kind of staying power and durability over its first theatrical run. So, it wasn't the immediate gratification over the opening weekend, but it's the longevity it garnered with audiences over the following weeks that made the film such a megahit.

You were nominated for a Best Director Oscar for both *Close Encounters* and *Raiders*. How does it feel to look back at *Raiders* and that experience, following *1941*?
I can't go back and look at a lot of my movies without flinching and going, "I could have done that better." I have a handful of films I directed that

I can watch objectively, as if I didn't have anything to do with them. *Raiders* is one of those films that I can look at with my kids, distance myself from all that went into making it, and appreciate it as an audience member. That's what's fun about that picture. The gift that *Raiders* gave back to me is that I can still watch it objectively all these years later.

TOP Steven Spielberg showcases the one-sheet poster for *Raiders*, designed by Richard Amsel.

ABOVE A French lobby card featuring the moment when Indy (Harrison Ford) and Sallah (John Rhys-Davies) lift the Ark of the Covenant.

VII

E.T. THE EXTRA-TERRESTRIAL

(1982)

"E.T. phone home."

—E.T.

The thrill surrounding *E.T.*'s release was unparalleled. It was a true cultural phenomenon. Personally, *E.T.* symbolized everything that I loved about America, like the massive home that Elliott (Henry Thomas) lives in with his family. There is always a huge amount of food in the refrigerator and these big packages of groceries. It felt so American, so typically big. It was almost like a documentary about American suburbia.

Like a lot of people in the early eighties, I had a Walkman, and I bought the John Williams *E.T.* soundtrack on cassette so I could listen to it wherever I went. I also had composer Jerry Goldsmith's score for *Poltergeist*. I wore out both tapes quickly because I was constantly fast forwarding and rewinding them to listen to my favorite cues again and again. In my memory, the summer of 1982 was the summer of *E.T.* and *Poltergeist*. I always find it very interesting to compare those two movies as they were created

at the same time. Steven did not direct *Poltergeist*, but he was heavily involved as both writer and producer, and as a result it's a very Spielbergian film. Thematically, both *E.T.* and *Poltergeist* deal closely with dying and the notion of loss. These parallels are more than coincidence. They speak not only to who Steven was at the time but to who he was becoming.

Through the Eyes of a Child

Written by screenwriter Melissa Mathison, in close collaboration with Steven, *E.T.* is, of course, the story of an alien who, after becoming stranded on Earth, befriends a young boy, Elliott. It's a film that's very much told from a child's perspective. Steven took pains to frame the adults in the film—except for Elliott's mom—from the waist down for most of the film to give the sense that the story's events are being observed from the viewpoint of kids. Despite this POV, *E.T.* is not a childish movie. It's a very adult and mature film that deals with some very dark themes. The story is essentially a rite of passage from childhood to adulthood, with Elliott, over the course of the movie, learning about the pains and responsibilities of being a grown up in the absence of his father. His mother, Mary (Dee Wallace), is separated from Elliott's dad, who is never seen in the film, only discussed.

Steven uses this extraterrestrial visitor as a way for Elliott—a surrogate for his own childhood self—to experience life as an adult and help him make the transition from boy to man. For example, through the telepathic connection that E.T. forges with Elliott, the boy gets drunk for the first time and experiences his first kiss. The film also deals with loss in a very powerful way through the death and resurrection of E.T. It's through experiencing this trauma that Elliott grows beyond his childhood. In the final shot of

ABOVE Filming the home escape sequence: Steven Spielberg (*center*) composes a shot featuring (*left to right*) Peter Coyote, Henry Thomas, and Dee Wallace.

> ❝ [*E.T.* is] a bold and edgy portrayal of childhood but executed with sentiment.❞

the film, as Elliott watches E.T. leave, he is forever changed—he's no longer a naïve boy. Unlike man-child Roy Neary in *Close Encounters*, he doesn't choose to leave Earth—he knows his place is with his family and his vulnerable mother, who needs him. Elliott has become the man of the house. I think this also represents a new maturity in Steven's thinking about the responsibilities of adulthood.

In essence, *E.T.* is a sophisticated coming-of-age story, and its success with adults can be attributed to its hidden depths. *E.T.* is sometimes considered highly sentimental. I find this to be an oversimplification. Rather, it's a bold and edgy portrayal of childhood but executed with sentiment. The kids in the film are just like real kids in their imperfection—they use vulgar language and are quite mean to one another at times. But they are

incredibly endearing because they are painted in an authentic way that we instantly recognize. In the hands of another director, *E.T.* would have been another kids' film, but Steven avoids the pitfalls of simplistic storytelling and cliché.

As previously discussed, *E.T.*, like *Close Encounters*, features a slow-burn reveal. Over the course of the story it becomes apparent that forces initially presented as sinister are benign. In *E.T.*, the government agents—led by Peter Coyote's character, Keys—appear to be nefarious at first. But when E.T. falls sick and seems to be close to death, there's an intimate conversation between Keys and Elliott that leads to an intensely hopeful and humane connection. Keys reveals to Elliott that he would love to have made contact with the extraterrestrial himself, and there's a real pathos to the moment. You get the sense that the adult world and the world of the child are not so distant—Keys is just like Elliott, in a way, and has the same hopes and dreams. It's a profound sequence that speaks to adult regret and the importance of embracing experiences in life. It really brings the adult audience into the fold because it's a moment to which we all can relate.

Playing by the Rules

The thing that I love about Steven's storytelling is that the mythologies he creates always have rules. Because he follows the rules that he establishes, it doesn't matter if the movie has an outlandish, fantasy premise, as everything makes sense within the boundaries of the fictional world he has created. In *E.T.*, there are several things we learn about the alien. He has a glowing finger that can heal, he can levitate objects with his mind, and so on. These rules are all very vividly realized, despite being pure fantasy, and pay off later in the film in spectacular fashion. By setting rules and sticking to them, Steven creates a little ecosystem that the audience believes in 100 percent. In *E.T.*, the familiar suburban setting also makes these more fanciful elements of the film feel more real. The film is grounded in so many real-world elements that it's easy to relate to, most notably E.T.'s desire to "phone home."

Of course, the famous catchphrase "E.T. phone home" embodies the home theme that runs through all of Steven's early films. Apart from the fact that E.T.'s main quest is to return to his home planet, much of the film takes place in Elliott's family home. Elliott's house feels very homey and lived in, and a

large part of that comes down to the exceptional lighting. Cinematographer Allen Daviau and Steven carefully orchestrated the use of light in the house, slowly revealing each part of it. It is also important in some very literal ways—E.T. himself has a heart that lights up, as does his finger when he heals Elliott. Light is a key theme throughout the film.

TOP In the studio, director of photography Allen Daviau (*with viewfinder*) and Spielberg (*standing next to Daviau*) call the shots during filming of an *E.T.* forest scene.

ABOVE Spielberg and Daviau on location in Crescent City, California, to capture exterior shots for *E.T.*

E.T. Comes Home

I got to work on the 2002 twentieth-anniversary rerelease of *E.T.*, which featured some digitally augmented elements and new scenes. For the home-entertainment release of this updated version of the movie, I organized a reunion of the original cast—including Henry Thomas, Drew Barrymore (Gertie), Robert MacNaughton (Michael), Dee Wallace, and Peter Coyote—plus Steven, writer Melissa Mathison, and producer Kathleen Kennedy. It was crazy—they were all sitting in front of me, and I had to conduct this mass interview. I remember opening by saying,

"Well, this isn't too intimidating. . . ."

The DVD was my second adventure with *E.T.* because I had worked on the LaserDisc, which was released in 1996. That was an amazing project. One of the challenges was to track down the cast and crew, and with some help from Amblin, it all came together. One of my favorite things about that project was the research I was able to carry out. There was this little vault at Amblin filled wall-to-wall with VHS cassettes. I was sorting through those looking for *E.T.* footage, and I remember pulling one with a handwritten label, "Henry Thomas screen test." I popped it into the VCR, and there it was—the legendary moment when Steven cast Henry as Elliott on the spot after his audition. Steven often tells this story, and the tape completely backs it up, including when Steven, off-screen, says, "Okay, kid, you got the job." And, to this day, that screen test is so heartbreaking and powerful.

When working on the *E.T.* LaserDisc, I also discovered that there had been a huge amount of behind-the-scenes footage shot on set that had never been seen before. It was filmed by John Toll, who would go on to become a very accomplished cinematographer, winning Oscars for his work on *Legends of the Fall* (1994) and *Braveheart* (1995).

E.T.
20TH ANNIVERSARY EDITION

Research Consultant
LAURENT BOUZEREAU

The footage that John shot for *E.T.* was so real and genuine. When I started watching it, I was immediately transported back to that time and how exciting the *E.T.* shoot was for Steven. It's funny; there's absolutely no difference between that Steven from 1981 and the director who made *West Side Story* and *The Fabelmans* (2022). He has the same energy, joy, and passion for filmmaking that he had back then, and it's absolutely infectious.

Watching the John Toll footage, I was stunned at the level of emotion that Steven brought to directing the children in *E.T.* There's a moment where he talks to Henry Thomas about the scene in which Elliott says goodbye to E.T. after the alien appears to die. In an incredibly moving way, Steven explains to Henry how Elliott feels. The worst thing you can do when directing young actors is to talk down to them like they're children. Steven understands that completely and speaks to them like adults, but at the same time, he enters their universe. For instance, he dressed up

ABOVE A framed image of Laurent Bouzereau's credit on the 20th anniversary edition of *E.T.*, a gift presented to the author by Amblin.

LEFT A magazine advertisement for the LaserDisc version of *E.T.*, featuring a documentary directed and produced by Laurent Bouzereau.

in costume while directing the kids on Halloween. Steven was able to create a fun, safe environment in which the younger actors could do their best work while being treated like equals.

Drew Barrymore was so incredible in the film as Elliott's little sister Gertie. Watching the footage of her on set, you can tell that Steven really fed off her sense of humor and energy, and he found a way to channel those qualities into the Gertie character. Just six years old, Drew was barely acting in the film—she was just being herself—and it's remarkable. Her performance was not just a product of Steven's direction but of the family atmosphere created on set by producer Kathleen Kennedy and writer/associate producer Melissa Mathison.

Kathy was associate to Steven on *Raiders*, and on *E.T.* he made her a producer. It was also Kathy who helped bring Melissa Mathison onboard. They'd gotten to know each other on the set of *Raiders*, since Melissa was dating Harrison Ford at the time. Melissa co-wrote the screenplay for the family film *The Black Stallion* (1979), which Steven and Kathy both loved, and she seemed like the natural choice for *E.T.* I first met Melissa through my *E.T.* documentary. There was something so special about her. She was so talented and smart and very sweet. Just a brilliant person. Melissa passed away in 2015, but I feel very honored that I got to work with her a little on *The BFG* (2016), Steven's adaptation of the Roald Dahl book.

> ❝ Steven loved to have Melissa [Mathison] around on *E.T.* and made her an associate producer on *The BFG*, knowing she would bring so much to the shoot.❞

Melissa was very involved with *The BFG* in the same way that she worked on *E.T.* I've observed many writers on set with Steven, and how much he loves the collaborative spirit that comes with working with them on a script. Melissa was no exception—on set, she entered the world of the film and was an integral part of the production on all levels. Steven loved to have Melissa around on *E.T.* and made her an associate producer on *The BFG*, knowing she would bring so much to the shoot. Melissa was extremely generous and dedicated, but also modest. She gave so much to each project. You felt the love she carried for each of the characters.

Steven likes to surround himself with dynamic

creative women, and *E.T.* was very much the product of a strong female team. On *E.T.*, not only was he working closely with Kathy and Melissa, but also his amazing editor Carol Littleton, who would go on to win an Oscar for her work. Before that, he'd had an extremely successful collaboration with editor Verna Fields on *The Sugarland Express* and *Jaws*, and these experiences set him on a lifelong trend of working with talented female creatives.

OPPOSITE LEFT A selection of autographed *E.T.* images from Laurent Bouzereau's collection: Dee Wallace, screenwriter/associate producer Melissa Mathison, and Drew Barrymore.

OPPOSITE BOTTOM RIGHT Mathison in costume as a nurse for a cameo that did not make the final cut of the film.

TOP Producer Kathleen Kennedy (*far left*) and Allen Daviau (*second from left*) with Steven Spielberg (*behind camera*) on the living room set.

ABOVE Steven's father, Arnold Spielberg (*right*), at an *E.T.*-related event in 1982.

I'll Be Right Here

E.T. is really a beautiful way to end this book because it truly is a summation of everything that Steven was building toward during the first ten years of his career. After the immense success of *E.T.*, I think he transitioned into another phase and became a new Steven Spielberg. During this period, Steven explored deep human emotions through entertaining and often fantastical stories, and with *E.T.*, it felt as if he had reached a new level of humanitarian and spiritual storytelling. I'm sure that for many *E.T.* fans it was frustrating that Steven didn't win an Academy Award at the 1983 Oscar ceremony. *E.T.* was a benchmark movie that touched the heart of the entire world—it is a cinematic masterpiece, perfect on all levels. There was a sense that, because it was a commercial juggernaut, the film's success was reward enough and there was no need to honor Steven with an Oscar. Also, because it was fantasy, some felt it didn't deserve the same plaudits that might be given to a film based in "the real world." But *E.T.* has proven that the true award comes in transcending generations—today, the film retains its powerful and timeless message and continues to win new fans.

The image of E.T. flying across the moon became emblematic of Steven's production company Amblin and its promise of a new brand of entertainment, one that was uniquely recognizable. Filmmakers such as Robert Zemeckis, Joe Dante, Richard Donner, and Chris Columbus flocked to the Amblin banner and created Spielberg-produced classics like *Gremlins* (1984), *Back to the Future* (1985), and *The Goonies* (1985). This unique moment would shape American cinema for years to come. Meanwhile, Steven became focused on exploring other genres he hadn't yet tackled, directing the historical dramas *The Color Purple* (1985) and *Empire of the Sun* (1987). Steven likes to say that *E.T.* gave him the courage to make other types of films, and as he began to move into an exciting new phase of his career, it was clear that the first ten years were only the beginning.

OPPOSITE TOP Steven Spielberg works with Henry Thomas on set.

OPPOSITE BOTTOM Spielberg directs Thomas during shooting of *E.T.*'s emotional final scene.

ABOVE Action begins on a heart-wrenching scene featuring Thomas.

SPIELBERG ON *E.T. THE EXTRA-TERRESTRIAL*

It feels like making *E.T.* was the culmination of the first ten years of your career. Could you summarize how you came to it? Had it been gestating for a while?

I always wanted to do a picture about a disenfranchised, lonely boy and his relationship with his siblings. I had three younger sisters, but I imagined that boy would have a brother and a sister. I also wanted to tell a story about the divorce of my parents. In fact, for a while, I'd been thinking about making a movie on a child's reaction to his parents splitting up when he's still only about ten years old and how that impacts him for the rest of his life.

E.T. specifically was on my mind maybe for fifteen, twenty years before I decided to make it. It might have been there subconsciously way before that, as a fantasy of mine, to make myself feel less alone in the world. I thought it could be the story between a boy and a special friend who rescues him from the sadness of the divorce of his parents. So, *E.T.* sort of came about in stages for me, including toying with the idea of the alien from *Close Encounters* staying behind on Earth, while Roy, the character played by Richard Dreyfuss, goes off in space, as some kind of foreign exchange between earthlings and extraterrestrials. But I really couldn't find a way to justify this, and it was frustrating not being able to realize that concept. Maybe that was really the reason why I eventually made *E.T.*

I had the idea when I was a kid starting to make movies wondering how to fill the need that all young, lonely kids have growing up. And I filled the need with an imaginary creature from outer space. I think *E.T.* was probably like a ping-pong ball, just bouncing from the left side of my brain to the right side of my brain ever since I was a child.

I intended it to reflect my childhood without

being very articulate about it. At the time when I did the press junket and met reporters, I never once said this was inspired by the divorce of my parents. But it always had been in the back of my mind to someday be able to just come out and confess where the basis for the story came from. All the kids in the movie are combinations of myself and my own family growing up.

You explored variations on the story, including a screenplay written by John Sayles called *Night Skies*.

The script that John Sayles wrote for me was a whole different concept. It was loosely based on a story I had read in one of J. Alan Hynek's books about a family on a farm that was terrorized one evening by gremlin-like extraterrestrials. They apparently surrounded the house and kept trying to come inside. The family managed to escape and brought the sheriff, who found no evidence of the extraterrestrial attack. After he left, it happened all over again, until the sun came up. That was an interesting story, and John Sayles wrote a screenplay based on it. But when I read it, I just didn't feel that was a movie that I wanted to make.

And that's when you turned to Melissa Mathison to write the screenplay. She was dating Harrison Ford and visiting the set of *Raiders*.

I shot *Raiders* so quickly, there wasn't a lot of time to think between shots. But there was a particularly long setup, and I walked out into the desert, trying to figure out how I could tell the story of this lonely boy. At the time, I was feeling a little bit separated from myself, which often happens when you're directing. You can go into a kind of fugue state to make a movie, and I was in one of my fugue states, when suddenly, bang, this concept hit me. I knew exactly how to tell

OPPOSITE A publicity photo of E.T. created to celebrate the film's stellar box office success.

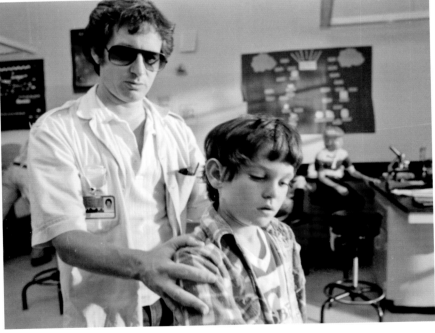

the story of *E.T.*, and it began to flood into my mind. For the next couple of days, during the shooting of *Raiders*, *E.T.* pretty much had a beginning, a middle, and an end. I had the opening, I had what happened at the end. I knew *E.T.* would have to go home. I knew *E.T.* would come into the life of a little boy who didn't have a father, who needed friendship, affection, the paternal guidance he wasn't getting from his mom,

and that he would make friends with the alien. I had some of what happened in the middle of the movie: the government chasing the little boy and his new best friend, how he would somehow help the creature back to his ship at the end.

So, the bones of the story began to fall into place in the middle of the Tunisian desert. It took me two or three days, and then I remembered loving this movie called *The Black Stallion*. I remember loving the way Carol Ballard directed it, and then realizing that Melissa Mathison, who was on the set with Harrison Ford, had co-written the script. I went to her one day, told her the story I had in my mind, and asked if she would write this movie for me. And she said, "No, I don't like science fiction. I'm also down on myself. I don't think I'm a good writer. I thought *Black Stallion* could have been better." And I said, "How could that movie have been any better? That's already an American classic!" But she was very critical of her writing and didn't really want to think about writing again. So, I worked on her, I kept nagging her. I went to Harrison, asked him to talk to her. Then Kathy Kennedy tried to talk her into it. And between Kathy and Harrison Ford, Melissa agreed to at least write a first draft for me. That's how it all got started.

ABOVE Producer Kathleen Kennedy and Steven Spielberg on location in the Redwood National Park, Crescent City.

ABOVE Drew Barrymore and E.T. pose during a publicity shoot.

mime artist Caprice Roth.

ABOVE Steven Spielberg directs Harrison Ford in the school principal's office scene from *E.T.* that would ultimately be cut from the final film.

ABOVE In the principal's office deleted scene, Elliott (Henry Thomas) is levitated by E.T.'s powers while the principal (Harrison Ford) remains oblivious.

ABOVE Filming the *E.T.* bike chase: (*foreground*) director of photography Allen Daviau and visual effects supervisor Dennis Muren. Steven Spielberg can be seen at right.

ABOVE The *E.T.* camera crew during filming of the bike chase: (*foreground left to right*) second assistant camera Rick Fee, first assistant camera Steven Shaw, "A" camera operator John Fleckenstein, "B" camera operator John J. Connor, and director of photography Allen Daviau. Steven Spielberg can be seen on top of the camera car holding a bullhorn.

ABOVE While filming *E.T.*, Henry Thomas, Robert MacNaughton, and the other young actors had to attend classes to avoid falling behind at school.

How did the film end up at Universal?

I was going to do *E.T.* for Columbia, where I had made *Close Encounters*. They liked the script, but the rumor is that they chose another movie they had in development called *Starman* [1984] that eventually became a wonderful movie starring Jeff Bridges and Karen Allen, directed by John Carpenter. When they decided not to make *E.T.*, they told me I could shop it to other studios. I took it immediately to Sid Sheinberg, my mentor, my friend, and the head of Universal Studios. I showed him the script, and at that point I believe I had a prototype of E.T. in clay, as well as some visual concepts that Ed Verreaux had done. I sent it all over to Sid, and the next day he called up, said it was a very good idea for a movie, and to go ahead with it. So, at that point, we set off to make the film.

While developing the script, you had a lot of different concepts and ideas, including a villain or bully named Lance as a threat to both E.T. and Elliott.

Yes, there were a lot of silly ideas that I came up with in an attempt initially to turn the film into something closer to the Disney movies of the late sixties, like *The Computer Wore Tennis Shoes* [1969]. I eventually drew more upon the *Close Encounters* experience of having no real villains whatsoever in that story.

As substitute, the adults who don't have the same pure understanding that children have about a situation like this played that role. I conceived that the adults, science, and government would be the threat. But a lot of ideas came and went, and anything that didn't feel natural to my original concept didn't make the cut.

How did you collaborate with Melissa?

I was editing *Raiders* in Marina del Rey and Melissa came over a lot. We'd sit there with a tape recorder and we just talked. We both liked the single-parent concept, the fact that Elliott didn't have a dad or a mom—we weren't sure which at first. Melissa felt that gave an edge and a real raison d'étre to the story. But ideas would go back and forth. I think I had the idea about E.T. healing people and having a heart light or a center of him that could heal. I was also very interested in E.T. being able to communicate psychically, and how he could reach out to Elliott while he was in school. So, if E.T. got drunk, Elliott got drunk; basically, Elliott would start becoming E.T. and feeling his psychic spirit inside of him. That was all very interesting, but Melissa didn't know where

it was going to fall into the structure of the movie. All those ideas were part of a wish list as we tried to figure out if we could put any of it in the movie. At one point, we almost had too much for a hundred-minute film, but we knew we had a good plot, and within the first three or four days of meeting, we basically came up with the story. Melissa contributed immeasurably to giving the character of E.T. an emotional heart and core. Melissa put herself into E.T.'s own being and really found that spiritual center to him. And for the kids, she based them on Ben and Willard, who are Harrison's two eldest sons [from his previous marriage].

❝ I conceived that the adults, science, and government would be the threat [in *E.T.*]."

What did you think of the first draft Melissa wrote?

I've struggled through a lot of first drafts in my career. Often the first drafts are pretty good, then you do a second draft, which is always a lot worse. Then the third draft is as good as the first draft, and the fourth draft is finally the draft that's better than the first draft. It's so painful going through drafts, but a much better process if you can do it with the same writer throughout. Sadly, that's rare, and it can get confusing. That's why so many films never get made. They just go into what we call development hell. With Melissa, I knew from the beginning that she would be the only writer on *E.T.* We had such comprehensive meetings about the structure, the story, and the characters that I pretty much knew what the movie would be like. I read the script in about an hour, and I was just knocked out. It was a script that I was willing to shoot the next day. I didn't really have any notes. It was honest, and it came from both of our hearts. Melissa's voice made a direct connection with my own.

Her dialogue was honest, edgy, brilliant, and reflected the way kids really talked in those days. I went to Kathy Kennedy, who was having lunch at the commissary, and I said, "Kathy, don't bother ordering dessert—I have it right here!" And I handed her Melissa's script. I asked her to cancel all her meetings that afternoon, to focus on the script and make sure I wasn't crazy. Kathy read it and later came over to the office and just said, "You're not crazy. I love it, too."

ABOVE Legendary creature creator Carlo Rambaldi with one of his E.T. puppets.

Kathy has played such an important role in your career. She was assistant to John Milius on *1941*, became your associate on *Raiders*, and jumped right into producing with *E.T.* The rest, as they say, is history.

Kathy was my secretary for a while, or today we would refer to her as my assistant. As an assistant, she couldn't handle making tea, but she was so smart about movies that I started inviting her to my story meetings. I really saw a kindred spirit in Kathy. On *Raiders*, she came on as my associate, and when *E.T.* came along, I knew I had found a great producing partner. I turned to her and said, "Look, how would you like to produce *E.T.* with me?" Her mouth dropped open. I told her I was serious, and that was the beginning of a wonderful partnership and friendship.

So much relied on the audience connecting with E.T., the alien. At what point did you start designing him?

When I was developing *Night Skies*, the John Sayles script, I hired Rick Baker, undoubtedly the best creature designer of his era. He designed some incredible aliens, but what I needed was one special character. I remember I went to Rick and told him that we were switching projects and overall approach. I explained we were no longer doing a bunch of aliens but focusing on one, and Rick was disappointed. We decided that this wasn't a film that we should do together. I said that *E.T.* was not going to make a lot of money and that I was making it for kids. We parted ways, and I went off to try to find a designer for my singular creature.

I knew I wanted it to look like an organic alien, not someone in a rubber suit. I wanted it to be about three feet tall, with a neck that could stretch out, like a turtle coming out of its shell, but that the head would otherwise just sit on the shoulders. The neck would have a behavior of its own and would defy anyone being inside a suit. That was the prerequisite that I

brought to every designer.

I first went to Stan Winston, who did an interesting design. It was really a curious creature, but I was "shopping." At the same time, I went to Carlo Rambaldi, who had done the Puck alien in *Close Encounters of the Third Kind*. My illustrator Ed Verreaux had been sketching E.T.'s face with me at my beach house on weekends, and we gave Carlo several of the sketches we had done, explaining that was the direction we had been developing. I said, "I want his eyes to be very wide. Here are some pictures of Albert Einstein, Ernest Hemingway, and Carl Sandburg. I love their eyes. Can we make E.T.'s eyes as wizened and as sad as those three icons?" Carlo worked in clay for many weeks. I have actual video footage of E.T. in different stages of development spinning around on a small turntable. I would light him from different angles to try to see how the skin, the cheekbones, his very thick, almost simian brow caught light in relation to his eyes. Carlo did several versions; I stood over him and worked with him. I'm not an artist, so I didn't touch the clay, but I would say, "Too scary, too cute, too Disney, too sweet." Finally, this creature did emerge from clay after a few weeks that became E.T.

My biggest fear was that the audience would not love E.T. and would find him off-putting. My hope was that they would love him within fifteen minutes

of meeting him. I wanted them to have the same journey as Elliott—to be scared at first and then embrace E.T. completely.

What other references did you study?
I wanted E.T. to give the impression of a thousand-year-old wizened life form. Carlo took directions the same way an actor would—but it's of course really the actor who creates the performance, and in that sense, it's really Carlo Rambaldi who created E.T.

I also remember saying to Carlo that E.T. should kind of waddle when he walks like Chaplin with his cane, that he should look like Bambi on ice. When E.T. starts to walk on Earth, he is ungainly, and he is insecure. Several times in the movie, we showed how awkward E.T. is and how funny he is when he falls over.

You turned to Ralph McQuarrie to design the spaceship.
Yes. Ralph contributed to the entire design from scratch. He wanted to do a different kind of spaceship and got this idea of it being a complete oval shape, with a surface that would reflect nature, trees, and the night sky. It was a wonderful concept, and he drew the ship to look a bit like E.T. It would squat when landing—it had legs—and I just fell in love with the design and didn't question it. I just said, "That's it. Let's build it."

ABOVE A team of puppeteers operates E.T. off-screen.

Ralph also did some sketches of E.T., I believe.
He did a whole series of drawings of E.T. As I said, I was "shopping" and looking for the perfect design. His drawings were perhaps too "science fiction-y," but he really scored with the spaceship. I still have the model in my conference room at Amblin.

I believe the idea of showing E.T.'s heart light was inspired by *Alien* (1979) when John Hurt's character discovers the translucent eggs before the "facehugger" springs out at him.
I was really impressed with the insert work on Ridley Scott's movie *Alien*, and I just said, "I want to be able to see E.T.'s organs. When he turns on his heart light, I want to be able to see the organs around it." I think it was Craig Reardon and Robert Short, who worked on E.T.'s puppetry, who said that based on the script, E.T. was a plant. I agreed. I didn't think he was anything like a mammal, a bird, or a fish, but more like a plant or a vegetable. They came up with the idea for his organs to be plant-like, and I thought that was fantastic.

Did you think E.T. had a gender?
I never thought that E.T. was a boy or a girl. I thought

more a cross between a pomegranate and an avocado. Gender was never a consideration.

How did you come to hire Beverly Hoffman from the Jules Stein Eye Institute to paint E.T.'s eyes?
I was not happy with any of the eye work that we were doing on E.T. The eyes didn't have any life to them. So, I just kept asking Kathy Kennedy to find somebody who made real glass eyes. It was Kathy who found Beverly, who worked at the Jules Stein Eye Institute and did this wonderful job of making rather oversized glass eyes for us.

Let's talk about Caprice Rothe, the mime who performed E.T.'s arms and hands.
This is technology back in the early eighties, where the mechanical arms were very jerky. The fingers would move but almost too thoughtfully, and the arms always had what I called "waga-waga," meaning they would stop and go in the most unnatural way. E.T. had to have almost balletic arms and the hands of a mime. So, I thought we could fit a mime with E.T. prosthetic gloves and make the movement realistic when reaching out to things or touching the kids. This is where this wonderful mime

artist came to work with us, and she really added an entire layer of humanity on top of the contribution that Carlo Rambaldi and his team had created.

I remember one wonderful moment in one of the earlier scenes with the kids where Caprice had had too much coffee in the morning, and her hands were shaking. I thought she had found something about E.T.'s character, and I said, "My God, that's great. He's terrified, he's afraid," without realizing that Caprice had had too much caffeine and that the shaking had happened naturally. In that same scene, there was a wonderful moment where E.T. is eating some watermelon, and there was a little bit of it on the lip. Caprice always had this monitor that she could look at. She noticed the piece of watermelon and naturally picked it out. That was so real—only someone like her, a mime, could have thought of making this a moment.

She really had a great understanding of the way the human body moves, what we do with our hands and our face. This was just a tiny moment that most people didn't notice, but I'm proud of what she brought to that scene just by taking a little piece of food off the lip. It brought E.T. to life. He was alive in that moment, completely alive. Nobody was running him. There were no wires, there were no server motors going. That was really someone from somewhere else.

But the whole concept wasn't new. There's a film called *Humoresque* [1946] with John Garfield where he plays a violinist. [The scenes where he plays violin were] shot using the hands of two professional musicians and a recording of Isaac Stern's performance. That had always stuck in my mind, and I thought we could use the same trick with E.T.

You did end up using little people, and a boy with no legs, inside E.T. for certain shots.

We never could figure out mechanically how to get E.T. to walk. I think even today it would be hard to do unless you did CGI. *E.T.* would have been a lot easier to make today, but what was more magical was the fact that the special effects were done for real. So, I knew we had to have actors in an E.T. suit for specific scenes, while keeping the integrity of E.T.'s neck, for instance. The person who did most of the work was Pat Bilon. He made the strongest contributions and was the most used in all the walking scenes of E.T.

Pat was a little person who really identified with E.T., loved E.T., and loved being E.T. When he was inside, E.T. was completely alive. But there were things that others contributed to E.T. coming to life. A young boy, Matthew De Meritt, who didn't have

> ❝ I thought we could fit a mime with E.T. prosthetic gloves and make the movement realistic when reaching out to things . . .❞

legs, was able to walk on his hands and did the scene where E.T. is drunk, for instance. It was what Doug Trumbull had done on his film *Silent Running* [1972] with his robots Dewey and Louis. Matthew—what a kid. What a great spirit, and he came to work with the greatest enthusiasm. And that scene with E.T. fumbling around after he's had too many beers was all Matthew's contribution.

Then Tamara De Treaux, who was like Pat, a little person, did the scene where E.T. comes out of the woodshed and places the Reese's Pieces on Elliott's sleeping bag. And she did the scene where E.T. walked out aggressively and then collapsed on his feet, waited, and was breathing fast. That was Tamara's breathing, too. This was hard work, carrying heavy equipment, especially inside the head. Tamara also did the last scene in the movie where E.T. walks up the gangway holding the flowers that Gertie had given him.

There were several different mechanical E.T. puppets as well. There was the wire-controlled one; you could make it smile, move its forehead. My favorite E.T. is the one that touches his heart and looks up when he sees the spaceship descending through the trees at the end of the movie. It was completely operated by wires that even stretched the latex of the skin and gave E.T. his look of wonder

ABOVE Steven Spielberg gives E.T. a scrub down during shooting of a bath scene that would be deleted from the theatrical release and reinstated for the 2002 special edition of the film.

with his brow going up and his mouth opening.
We used Caprice's hands on E.T.'s heart. Then we
had just a couple of E.T. heads. We had E.T. hands
by themselves, and then we had the bodysuits for
Matthew, Pat, and Tamara.

Didn't you call the operators the twelve hearts of E.T.?

I always felt that E.T. had twelve hearts, and each
heart belonged to one of the operators who was able
to move E.T.'s arm, his face, create a smile, a blink, a
pulse. They were all E.T.'s fathers, or as I used to call
them, E.T.'s hearts.

Did you do E.T.'s voice when you were shooting the movie?

Yes, I had to give off-camera dialogue, rather than
having the script supervisor read the dialogue, as
is usually the case. I began to say things like, "E.T.
phone home," or "El-l-iott, I'll be right here." It was
great fun to do and that became the temp track.
But one day, I was filming the Halloween scene, and
Debra Winger came to visit. She has this beautiful
husky voice, and I asked her to record lines. So,
anyone who saw the rough cut heard me and Debra
Winger as E.T. Later, sound designer Ben Burtt found
a woman named Pat Welsh at a camera store. He
overheard her speak. She was a cigarette smoker and
had a raspy voice, and she made the final and most
lasting contribution to E.T.'s voice.

And Debra Winger has an unusual role in the film.

That day, I told her to throw on a Halloween costume
and mask, and you can see her as a zombie nurse.
So, she had a cameo appearance, but so did Yoda,
for that matter. I just had this idea, which was not
originally in the script, where E.T. would run toward
Yoda and say, "Home, home," recognizing him
because the galaxy is a rather small place among
filmmakers. I didn't tell George Lucas about it.
When the film was done, I organized a big preview
screening for him and everyone at ILM, since they
had done the visual effects.

I was sitting next to George, and when Yoda
came on screen, he roared with laughter and gave
me a nudge—that was his way of saying that was
cool. At that same screening, just as the kids literally
took off on their bicycles, the whole audience burst
into applause—at that point, George leaned over
and said, "It's okay, you can be number one. I'll
be number two. This is going to beat *Star Wars*.
Mark my words." I thought George was just being
supportive. I had no idea at that point that it would
happen.

Incidentally, when *Jaws* came out, it became the
number-one film of all time until *Star Wars*. And I
took an ad in the trades with R2-D2 fishing the shark,
symbolically meaning *Star Wars* had surpassed the
box office gross of *Jaws*. So, without telling me,
when *E.T.* surpassed *Star Wars*, George took out
a similar ad showing the characters from his film

congratulating *E.T.* It's been fun being a partner, collaborator, and friend with George all those years and how we honored each other's success.

There was also another tribute to George when Elliott introduces E.T. to his *Star Wars* toys.

There's even a nod to *Jaws* in that same scene when Elliott shows E.T. a toy shark. From talking to Henry, I know how much he was into *Star Wars*, so that must have come naturally to him. And of course, the casting of Henry Thomas as Elliott is part of the mythology of the film. I watched his audition, and I simply can't imagine what that day must have felt like.

Henry Thomas was a real gift. I feel he was always meant to be Elliott. Before him, I had not been able to find Elliott. I looked for a long time. Now it was only about, I'd say, four or five weeks away from shooting the movie, and I still did not have my Elliott. I remember hearing from Jack Fisk, who had just made a movie called *Raggedy Man* [1981] with this kid named Henry Thomas. He recommended that I look at him. He sent me over a scene from the movie with Henry and Sissy Spacek. I liked it, but I couldn't really tell if Henry would be right for *E.T.*

So, my casting director, Mike Fenton, brought him in for a screen test. I told Mike to explain to Henry that Elliott is hiding an extraterrestrial in the closet. It's his best friend, and it's being taken away from him. Then, I went over to Henry and told him how

much he loves this friend, that it's the most important part of his life, and that he cannot let it be taken away. I said, "Don't let it happen!" I got behind the video camera, turned it on, and with Mike off-screen playing the government agent, the magic just happened.

That's who Henry was, and that's how Henry convinced me that he was Elliott. What was amazing about the audition was that Henry didn't do small talk. He launched right into the emotions of losing his friend. "You can't take him away, he's mine . . ." And he cried. Some of those moments I mentioned to Melissa so she could incorporate them into the script when the government people invade Elliott's home.

In the screen test, I just love how we can hear you say off-screen: "Okay, kid, you got the job!" Such a powerful moment.

I gave him the part right there through tears. I was crying, Mike Fenton was crying. We were all just in tears.

Then of course, Drew Barrymore!

I met a lot of Gerties, but when Drew came in, she had the part the minute she stepped into the room because she began to make up stories, saying she was a punk rocker with a band and going on the road! She's six years old and she's telling me that she is going on a twenty-city tour in America with

ABOVE Steven Spielberg works with the version of the E.T. puppet that was created for the scenes in which the alien rides in Elliott's bike basket.

ABOVE At the Royal Premiere of *E.T.* in London, Steven Spielberg goofs off with his young stars, Henry Thomas, Robert MacNaughton, and Drew Barrymore.

her punk rock band. She kept making up stories, and they got bigger and bigger and wilder and wilder. She just blew me away. There was no second choice. It was fate. She was meant to be in this movie. She got the part and then she became my best friend during filming.

Did you associate her name with the great Barrymore acting family—Lionel, Ethel, John?
I did not. Nobody told me, and I didn't find out until later. The acting DNA obviously runs deep in the Barrymore family.

Robert MacNaughton as the older brother was also quite fantastic.

I thought Robert was a really good actor. He was solid. He had a great attitude as the big brother. He was a typical teenager who liked to torture his younger brother. I only had sisters, but I put a lot of myself in the character of Michael.

And then there's Dee Wallace as Mom!
I chose Dee Wallace because she was herself like a kid. I didn't feel I was violating my rule not to have adults in the film until the very end because Dee was one of the kids. She was, as Mary, trying to get her life back together. She was devastated about the fact that her marriage was over, as Elliott was upset that his father wasn't there anymore. I found Dee to be wonderfully honest and pure of heart and childlike

and a very natural actor, too. She was my first and only choice for the role.

It was interesting because you see Peter Coyote's character, known as Keys, pretty much from the waist down for a large part of the film. At what point did you decide not to show any adults—except for Mary, the mother—in the early part of the movie?
That came at the very beginning. I never wanted to show grown-ups in the movie until the third act, when they invade the house. I wanted to suggest them, show them from the waist down, kind of like in a Tom and Jerry cartoon. I grew up watching television and cartoons, and I applied that convention where you pretty much saw adults from the waist down to E.T.

You brought in Allen Daviau as your director of photography. What did you have in mind for the overall palette of the film?
I wanted E.T. to have a warm look. Allen Daviau had shot my short film Amblin' in 1968. I always kept up with him, but Allen couldn't get into the union. It was his big problem. I remember he did a television movie that Jerry Freedman, another person who helped my career get going in the early days, had directed, called The Boy Who Drank Too Much [1980]. I loved the lighting in that television movie, and what I knew about Allen's work was that he didn't use a lot of back or side light, and he shot a very, very rich, rich negative. I

remember calling him up about A Boy's Life, which was one of the "cover" titles for E.T., and offered him the job. He was ecstatic, and we worked together on my next two movies as well.

You shot the film at Laird Studios in Culver City, and James Bissell was your production designer.
Jim Bissell did wonderful sets. Every choice Jim made was an extraordinary one. We were not doing a period piece or historical fiction. This was an ordinary suburban house, and we had to make every angle look realistically lived in, and Jim did all of that for this movie.

E.T. is a love story between two friends because that's what it had to be, and it's a story of suburbia because that's all I know. I was raised in suburbia. My formative years occurred in suburbia. I began my filmmaking career living in suburbia, making little 8mm movies, and showing films to my neighborhood. A filmmaker can only really reflect what he or she knows. A director can be a chameleon, but the real personal films are the ones that are about something you know about. With E.T., I knew about suburbia. Those were my roots. And the sets and the overall look and approach reflected what I knew best.

How did you work with the kids—how did you direct them?
Melissa did something that no one's ever done for me. She put every day's work, basically the description

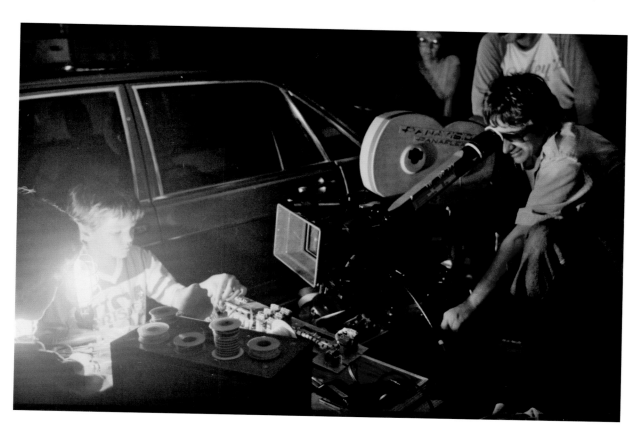

LEFT Steven Spielberg shoots Robert MacNaughton (*left*) and Henry Thomas in a garage-based scene in which Michael and Elliott discuss their absent father.

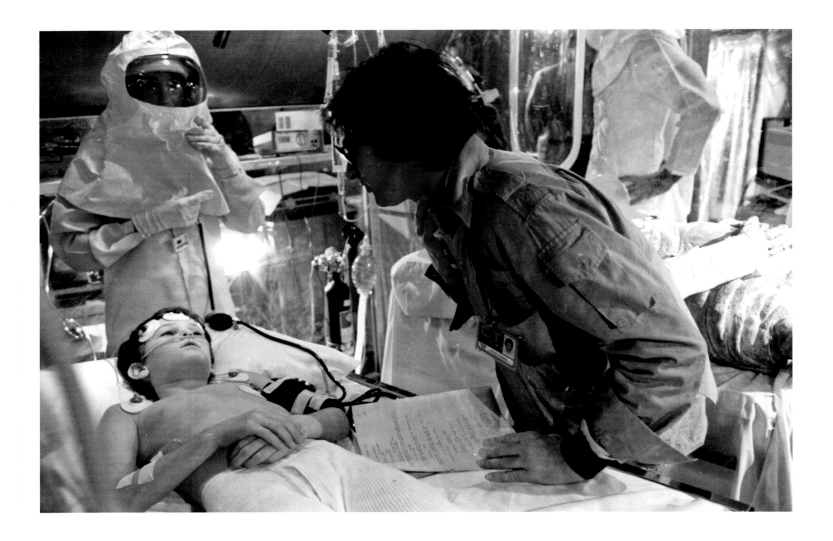

of the scenes with dialogue and stage directions, on
cards. She transferred the script to small form, and
these cards gave me amazing confidence. Rather than
searching for pages in the script, I had these little cards.
I felt liberated. I'd carry the cards in my pants pocket,
and I'd pull them out and say, "Okay, this is what I'm
shooting right now." The cards somehow gave me the
freedom to go to the kids, discuss the scenes, and go
over the dialogue. I'd ask them, "What would you say
if this was really happening to you?" And I'd get new
lines from them. When Gertie says, "I don't like his
feet," that's Drew's line. When Gertie says, "Don't be
pushy, pushy," that was Drew's line as well. There were
several good moments in the film that the kids came up
with on their own.

**I remember Henry telling me he had a real problem
saying lines like "penis breath" and "holy shit."**
Henry was raised properly, never knew bad words,
and didn't want to say bad words. He eventually did.
But the toughest thing Henry didn't want to do was
to kiss a girl [actress Erika Eleniak] on the lips, on the
first day of shooting. At that moment I saw him giving
up his entire career. We were all saying, "But it's just a
little kiss, and you don't have to hold it long." Henry

eventually said he would do it. And after he kissed her,
he started spitting. The young actress burst into tears
and ran out of the room—it just broke her heart that
after the kiss, he would spit out of the other side of
his mouth.

So, on the first day of shooting, I was thinking,
"Oh my God, I'm a father!" I didn't have children
back in the early eighties, and suddenly I was
becoming a father. Every single day I felt like I was
Drew, Henry, and Robert's father and it felt good. I
think I have a big family now because it felt pretty
good having three kids back then. But those issues
like Henry struggling with saying bad words, or
kissing a girl, were always there because we were
dealing with real life. We were dealing with an alien
that all three young kids believed was real. Despite
seeing the operators, the special effects technicians
in the background, they believed that E.T. was real.
It was like having Santa Claus in the room. That's the
way these kids thought about E.T., and I did my best
not to burst that bubble.

One thing I did was shoot most of the film in
continuity because I did not want any of them to
get near that last scene until it was time for Elliott,
Gertie, and Michael to say goodbye to E.T. And the

same for Dee Wallace and Peter Coyote. So, I pretty much scheduled the movie as much in continuity as I possibly could, except for the exterior scenes in the redwood forest. For instance, when E.T. got sick and almost died, that was filmed very close to the ending of the production schedule. It cost us a bit more to make the film that way, but I was never going to start with the last scene and end with the first one.

You couldn't have explained that to the kids. I wanted them to be so caught up as their characters that by the time they said goodbye to E.T., whatever emotion happened there would happen on take one and be genuine. Every single shot you see of Elliott crying, hugging E.T., and saying, "I'll be right here," that's all take one. We'd do a second take for protection, but I know we only used the first take on all the children at the end of the movie.

Aspects of Elliott, like putting a thermometer on a lamp to make it look like he has a temperature, or letting frogs out at school, are based on things you did as a kid.
Sometimes when I wanted to stay home to cut my little 8mm movies, I'd take the thermometer and hold it under a heating pad. I never wanted the temperature

to get into what I called the red zone, where my mom would have to call the doctor, but enough for my mother to let me stay home for the day.

Speaking of Elliott pretending to be sick to stay at home with E.T., there was a scene you deleted for the original theatrical release of the film.
Yes, and I was sorry to lose it. It showed E.T. in the bathtub and immediately sinking underwater—Elliott thinks E.T. is drowning when in fact E.T. can exist underwater and loves to be underwater. E.T. is trying to blow bubbles, while Elliott is talking to his mom on the phone, still pretending to be sick. That was a very fun scene. Another moment that took place in the bathroom had Elliott measuring himself up against E.T. and that was the reveal of E.T.'s neck extending up. I was sorry to lose those moments.

Why did you cut them?
It had to do with the rhythm and tempo of the movie. At the time, those moments just didn't seem to advance the story. But I was proud of those moments.

What about the deleted scenes with Melissa Mathison and the one with Harrison Ford?

ABOVE Under Steven Spielberg's direction, Henry Thomas and Erika Eleniak re-create a classic moment from John Ford's *The Quiet Man* (1952) for the frog escape sequence.

There was a scene that Melissa wrote where Elliott is taken to the principal's office. Harrison Ford played the principal, but you never saw his face and only heard his unmistakable voice. While he is talking to Elliott, looking out the window, E.T. is at home, levitating things up the stairs—and because they're psychically connected, Elliott's chair starts levitating. Luckily, the principal never notices. It was a way to show how Elliott and E.T. share the same energy, but again, the scene did not advance the story, nor did a moment with Elliott and a nurse played by Melissa Mathison! In that scene, Elliott was doing all these equations. Once again, E.T. is telepathically just thinking about how he's going to build his communicator. And Elliott starts drawing on the walls of the holding room he's in before the principal comes to see him. Melissa played a nurse who was coming to check on Elliott to make sure he was okay. She was a little self-conscious about going on camera, so I shot her in silhouette.

In another interesting deleted scene, where kids run riot on Halloween night, you had Wagner's *Ride of the Valkyries* playing in the background echoing the way Francis Ford Coppola used it in *Apocalypse Now.*
I liked that scene. The dark side of Halloween was late at night with kids putting toilet paper in trees

and shaving cream on the windows. There were fireworks and flares going off. It was an aggressive and angry scene that would have scared E.T., and it was part of the sequence where Mary cannot find her own children. She's going from neighborhood to neighborhood, still in her Cat Lady outfit, looking for her kids, and she's really panicked. That was an interesting sequence.

John Toll, who went on to become an Oscar-winning director of photography, shot behind-the-scenes on *E.T.* and documented the production. There's some great footage of you directing, dressed up as a lady on Halloween to amuse the kids.
Henry Thomas kept thinking of me as both his new best friend and his schoolteacher because I talked to him all the time. I was basically always coaching him, even talking to him during takes to help him find emotions. In fact, when he first saw E.T. at the sneak preview, he said to me: "The film's okay, but you've got to cut your voice out of it!" As Henry saw the film, he still kept hearing my voice directing him, and it spoiled the entire first screening of the picture for him. I'll never forget him turning to me, saying, "You have to cut your voice out!" and me arguing back that my voice wasn't in the film. But he was insistent to the point where I thought I might have left my voice in!

BELOW Steven Spielberg welcomes Harrison Ford to Tujunga, Los Angeles, where the exteriors for Elliott's house were shot. Ford performed a cameo as Elliott's school principal, but it was deleted from the final cut.

This is the first time I ever really experienced what it was like to really be a dad. Henry, Robert, and Drew introduced me vicariously to fatherhood. And I think, bless their hearts, made me ready to be a father in real life only four years later.

Originally, you were going to have the climax of the movie take place in a hospital, but then you decided to cover the whole house in plastic.

The early script had the hospital in it, and I had a lot of people from the crew, who don't usually get involved in story development—they were reading the script, and one after another came to me saying it was great until the moment when they leave for the hospital. Elliott's house was its own world. Two good friends of mine, Hal Barwood and Matthew Robbins—who have consulted on several of my other films—had read E.T. and made some comments, including on the hospital sequence. Matthew is a passionate man, and he literally grabbed me by the lapels and said, "This is a potentially great movie, but the hospital ruins everything. Take it out." So, I just said I give up, and I cut out the hospital. Instead, I wrapped the whole house in a kind of Saran Wrap, so to speak. It made a lot of sense that the house would be the place that the government would seal up, shut down the neighborhood surrounding it, and do their work there.

Incidentally, I wanted to hire real doctors for the scene when E.T. is dying. It's hard to believe actors who have to learn all these terms and then spit them out as if they'd known them ever since medical school. So, I got my doctor, my internist, to get a bunch of his friends, who are all surgeons at USC Medical Center, to come down and be in the movie.

I saw the alternate ending for the film, showing the family after E.T. left.

I liked that ending, but I thought it was too much like a TV movie, with the tag saying, "They lived happily ever after." It was too conventional, and Melissa agreed that we didn't need this, that it was much more emotional just to simply go out on the spaceship leaving the trace of a rainbow, and Elliott, looking up to the sky. That was the perfect ending.

The score by John Williams is a classic. I really loved how, very much like in _Close Encounters_, the music matches the tone of the story. At first, we're not sure if we should fear E.T., and then the music takes on his benevolent spirit and the beauty of the friendship with Elliott.

Johnny can take a moment and just uplift it, and he

can take a tear that's just forming in your eye, and he can cause it to drip. When he saw E.T., I immediately saw he was happy. And I can always tell when John's happy with a film because we don't have a lot of musical discussions. He already has themes running through his mind. On E.T., I remember that I left him alone. And then one day he called me, asked me to come over to Fox, where he had offices. I went over, and he played some of the music on the piano. And it was just more than I could ever hope for. It was just on the piano, and I had tears rolling down my face.

I was sitting there at the piano sobbing. I kept saying, "It's beautiful, don't change a note." I'm embarrassing myself in front of him. I loved it. It was great. And I could not wait for the scoring session. I just couldn't wait to hear the orchestra playing what I had heard on the piano. I was just in seventh heaven.

What was the experience of the sneak preview on E.T.?

If the sneak preview of _Jaws_ was a popcorn fest, the one for E.T. in Texas was a religious experience. It was emotional. It was generous on the audience's part. And it was a love fest, it really was.

But you never know what you've got until you show it to an audience for the first time. I didn't pretend that E.T. was anything other than a kids' movie about kids for kids, made by kids, because I was still a kid then. I still am a kid now. But I had no expectations for E.T., and my biggest fear was that if the preview didn't go well, the studio would not back the film with a big campaign. Look, I made the movie for $10 million. It was a very small and low-budget movie, even back in the eighties. So, when the preview started, I didn't know what was going to happen.

The lights went down, and the movie began.

ABOVE Steven Spielberg (*far right*) and his young cast celebrate Halloween during the production of *E.T.*

Everybody paid complete attention. And there was a real feeling of identification. You could just slice the atmosphere.

The audience was responding to every nuance of the picture. They were picking up every laugh I didn't think they would ever understand or ever get. They were appreciating, they were applauding. We had six spontaneous rounds of applause during the movie. And probably about three minutes of sustained applause, almost through all the end credits at the end. It was a wonderful tender experience I'll never forget, possibly one of my favorite experiences watching any of my own films in front of an audience.

The response was extraordinary, and we all came out of the theater hugging each other. A couple of the guys from marketing told us the score cards were amazing. And this is the first time in my career that I got 98 percent in the top box for "Excellent." The 2 percent were in the "Very Good" box. Yet the marketing team didn't think we'd open that well. They kept saying, "It's a great picture, plays great, but how will we get an audience interested? It's still a kid's picture." Sid Sheinberg was the only one who said the film would be number one.

But it wasn't until the world premiere at the Cannes Film Festival that we got a taste of the film as a phenomenon. We took the film there to be presented out of competition on closing night. I'd never been to the Cannes Film Festival before—what a way to go for the first time! I got this telegram from François Truffaut, which meant so much to me, saying, "You belong here more than me," echoing one of his famous lines in *Close Encounters of the Third Kind*: "You belong here more than we." That just broke me up. At the end of the screening, we had like a fifteen-minute standing ovation. I remember I kept standing up and sitting down, they kept clapping, and I would stand up and sit down again, until it became a bit intimidating. We all took a final bow, and I saw this little flame in

the middle of the crowd. Someone was holding their lighter—and I realized it was Jerry Lewis, smiling. That will never be equaled.

Despite the gigantic success of *E.T.*, you never made a sequel?

I never did because I could never make another *E.T.* movie as good as the original. *E.T.* isn't a mechanical cottage industry that invites further chapters. To do two, three, or four movies based on that one character is creating a franchise that I didn't frankly think was the right thing to do. This was a one-time event in my life and for audiences. So, I've just held out all these years and I don't ever plan to make a sequel to *E.T.*

Can you discuss what you envisioned as the "brand" for Amblin movies?

I didn't quite know what Amblin was going to be, but I did know that I wanted a brand and a shingle I could hang outside of my door that didn't just say Universal, Columbia Pictures, or Paramount. I wanted something

that represented the work that I was doing inside the mothership of those other huge corporations and film studios. I had always admired other filmmakers of my generation who had their own brands. George had formed Lucasfilm, and I just thought, well, I should have my own brand at this stage in my life.

In 1981, the same year you launched Amblin, you were also directing and producing *E.T.* and co-writing and producing *Poltergeist*. How challenging was it to work on both films at the same time?

Well, fortunately, I had two scripts that I was secure with. I had written *Poltergeist* in five days, working from eight at night to eight in the morning, with Kathy Kennedy, Frank Marshall, and Tobe Hooper, who were hanging out with me all night long. I pretty much wrote it stream of consciousness. I hardly had an outline. I knew where it was going end . . . I knew how it had to begin. It kind of wrote itself. I did that because the script written by Mark Victor and Michael Grais, that I previously committed to produce for Tobe to direct,

ABOVE A publicity still for the 2002 *E.T.* special edition: (*left to right*) Robert MacNaughton (*standing*), Henry Thomas, Dee Wallace, Steven Spielberg, Kathleen Kennedy, Drew Barrymore, and Peter Coyote.

wasn't 100 percent there. So I started from scratch, and in the process, found different ways of telling the story, and I just started writing furiously until, five days later, I had 118 pages. We were in production within six or seven weeks of finishing the script. We'd already been building the Freeling family's house, so the film was on its way to being ready.

At the same time, I had confidence in the script that Melissa Mathison had written for my story of *E.T.* You can't shoot two movies that close together unless you are completely secure with what's on the page. If I had to scramble to improvise any one of those two movies, I never would've been able to be so creatively attached and associated with both films. I only had three weeks after finishing *Poltergeist* to the first shot of *E.T.* It was only a three-week break between both those productions. I had tremendous control over both productions.

How disappointed were you that you didn't get an Oscar for *E.T.*?
I wasn't. I was young—I figured that my day would come. I was very philosophical about it. But I'll tell you, when I was at the Director's Guild Awards, I was nominated for *E.T.*, and Richard Attenborough had been nominated for *Gandhi* [1982]. I'll never forget when the envelope was opened, and they announced Richard Attenborough's name—instead of walking up onto the stage to accept his award, he came to my table, threw me into a huge bear hug, and he whispered in my ear, "It should've been yours."

What a great story!
I've never forgotten that, and we became acquaintances, and then later friends, when I cast him to play John Hammond in *Jurassic Park*.

E.T. is now forty years old. How does that feel?
You know something? I've never felt time passing.

I've never felt myself aging except for an occasional tweak in my lower back and a little sciatica down my leg and taking a second and a half longer to get up from having been in a chair for two hours watching a movie. But aside from that, I feel that my life and my family and my children are kind of timeless. It certainly doesn't feel like forty years have gone by. But I certainly respect the test of time that *E.T.* has withstood, and it remains a very, very popular choice of families all over the world to show their children when they've come to the right age.

While we're celebrating *E.T.*'s fortieth, John Williams has just turned ninety!
Ninety is young for a person like John Williams, with an ageless outlook on life—and a love for movies, but especially a love for serious music. It's his fountain of youth and will take him as far and as long as he wants it to go. But John certainly has threatened retirement, and I think he means it. He's going to turn to writing symphonies and concertos. He cannot stop. The music comes from the sky and envelops him. The kind of art that comes out of John Williams is the purest form of art I've ever experienced from any human being. I remember going to John after he said he was retiring and saying, "But what if I have another movie and I want you to do it?" And John turned to me and said, "Well, I'll be very hurt if you don't at least ask me." [Laughs.] So, I think there's hope.

Who do you think Steven Spielberg was during those first ten years of his career?
I think the person doing the first ten years was the same person I am now as a filmmaker—not as a human being because I've changed a lot, principally because of my children and my marriage. But I had the same feeling going onto *The Fabelmans*' set in 2021 that I had going onto the set of *Duel* in 1971. I have the same excitement about what magic is going to happen in the next eleven hours of a shooting day, and that hasn't waned. It hasn't dissipated; it has only increased in value for me. That's my goal.

For me, the thing that has been interesting in rewatching the films from your first ten years is the realization that they all seem to be about "home." Like E.T., many of your characters are trying to find or return home. It's amazing that all those movies share that notion.
I guess all I can say to that is, I've never been far from home.

ABOVE A hair-raising scene from *Poltergeist*.

OPPOSITE Steven Spielberg and his extraterrestrial star.

EPILOGUE

Writing this book has been an adventure, full of discoveries and rediscoveries, that has allowed me to look back with fresh eyes at the genesis of Steven Spielberg's cinematic career. It has also given me the opportunity to revisit my own modest career; one which brought me from France to America, driven by my unquenchable passion for the moving image.

When I left France for good to move to New York in the early eighties, I remember my parents asking me bluntly: "What are you really going to do there?" My ambition, in fact, was not just to find a job. It was to meet a person: Steven Spielberg. I didn't mean it literally, but, in my heart, the idea of getting to meet my favorite filmmaker and somehow participate in his world in whatever capacity I could was the dream. I will always feel indebted to Steven for igniting in me a passion and curiosity for the magic of film, which paved the way for my dedication to documenting his cinema.

Revisiting the movies that have forged my own taste and appetite for filmmaking was thrilling, and returning to the many interviews I have conducted with Steven over the years has cemented my appreciation for him not only as a brilliant filmmaker but also as someone who can discuss his craft in compelling and inspirational terms. I remember when I was working on my documentary for *E.T.*, I started telling him what I had discovered during my research. He immediately stopped me and said, "I want to be surprised. Let me discover it when I watch the cut." That exchange pretty much sums up how we've worked together on each documentary project I've produced and directed for him since. In fact, we used the same method for this book: Steven generously gave me permission to write it, allowed me access to his archive, and

kindly sat for additional questions on his early films. And then I later "surprised" him with the book. I am so grateful for his enthusiastic feedback, guidance, and loyalty.

When I first met Steven, he was exactly the person I thought he would be—a modest and passionate filmmaker, filled with love and respect for his profession and collaborators. Creating this book was a reminder that Steven's artistry has been a genuine part of him from the very beginning; he is and remains a phenomenon that has never been equaled or surpassed. Those first ten years of his career informed the years that followed—the humanity, complexity, and thematic depth of his stories becoming a constant in his work. And of all the recurrent themes in Steven's oeuvre, the one I kept returning to when writing this book is the concept of "home." Not only is "home" such an important part of the films themselves, but it also speaks to Steven's own approach to his work. On set, he creates a family spirit; a "home" for everyone involved. Privately, he is a family man who cherishes his home life. These values make his work relatable to us, the audience; he presents us with a world we want to exist in, a world that is our "home."

Moving to America and being gifted with a career that gave me the opportunity to work with Steven Spielberg was like finding home. I am forever grateful for how his films changed my life and then literally guided me in everything that came after. In his cinematic masterpiece *Day for Night*, François Truffaut, who directed the movie and played the role of a director, says, "Films are more harmonious than life." At the conclusion of this book, and in the case of the movies of Steven Spielberg, I would say that cinema *is* life. Cinema is home.

INSIGHT
EDITIONS

PO Box 3088
San Rafael, CA 94912
www.insighteditions.com

 Find us on Facebook: www.facebook.com/InsightEditions

 Follow us on Twitter: @insighteditions

Published by Insight Editions, San Rafael, California, in 2023.

ISBN: 978-1-64722-517-9

Publisher: Raoul Goff
VP, Co-Publisher: Vanessa Lopez
VP, Creative: Chrissy Kwasnik
VP, Manufacturing: Alix Nicholaeff
VP, Group Managing Editor: Vicki Jaeger
Publishing Director: Chris Prince
Editorial Assistant: Emma Merwin
Managing Editor: Maria Spano
Senior Production Editor: Katie Rokakis
Senior Production Manager: Joshua Smith
Senior Production Manager, Subsidiary Rights: Lina s Palma-Temena

Project Manager: Jerry Schmitz

Designed by Amazing15
Jacket and title page art by Rich Davies

ROOTS of PEACE

REPLANTED PAPER

Insight Editions, in association with Roots of Peace, will plant two trees for each tree used in the manufacturing of this book. Roots of Peace is an internationally renowned humanitarian organization dedicated to eradicating land mines worldwide and converting war-torn lands into productive farms and wildlife habitats. Roots of Peace will plant two million fruit and nut trees in Afghanistan and provide farmers there with the skills and support necessary for sustainable land use.

Manufactured in China by Insight Editions

10 9 8 7 6 5 4 3 2 1

ACKNOWLEDGMENTS
from author Laurent Bouzereau

This book would not have been possible without the collaboration, support, and enthusiasm of Steven Spielberg. I am eternally grateful for this book and for the many amazing opportunities Steven has given me for nearly thirty years.

I was so moved that the extraordinary John Williams and George Lucas agreed to write such profound words about Steven's first ten years, exclusively for this book. Their contribution is truly insightful, generous, and inspired.

This book summarizes the friendship and support I have received, particularly from the incomparable Kristie Macosko Krieger.

And, at Amblin Partners: Jon Anderson, and Matt Andrée Wiltens, who read many drafts of this book and offered invaluable comments and editorial guidance.

Brittani Lindman, Emma Molz, Dan Berger, and Marvin Levy, who are always there for me.

Holly Bario, Jeb Brody, Christine Burt, Justin Falvey, Darryl Frank, Mark Graziano, Andrea McCall, Elizabeth Nye, and Jeff Small.

At the Amblin Hearth Archive: Rachel Rohac-Bernstein, Morgan Cuppet-Michelsen, and Michelle Fandetti.

I want to thank Kathy Kennedy, Frank Marshall, and Kate Capshaw who have been constant support in all my endeavors with Steven.

The amazing and passionate Chris Prince at Insight Editions whose creative contributions have elevated the narrative, structure, and overall look and content of the book. Many thanks also to Martin Stiff at Amazing15 for the book's fabulous design and to Maria Spano, Katie Rokakis, and Emma Merwin at Insight for their support throughout the project.

Jerry Schmitz, who got this journey started on all fronts and introduced me to Raoul Goff, master publisher.

Steven Awalt and my longtime friend Steven Asbell for generously accepting to read this book and for their invaluable editorial notes.

Michael Gorfaine, Jamie Richardson, and Connie Wethington for all their assistance.

Michael Dawson for his wonderful *Raiders of the Lost Ark* images and Jamie Benning for leading us to them.

My literary agent, Mark Falkin, of Falkin Literary, as well as Ryan McNeily at WME, and Derek Kroeger.

My family unit: My amazing husband, Markus Keith, who never stops believing in me and my crazy dreams; my parents, Daniel and Micheline Bouzereau, and my sisters, Cécile and Géraldine, who have been at my side through my lifelong obsessive passion for movies (but did they have any other choice?); my childhood movie buddy, Laurent Hagége, who provided illustrations and a friendship that began over forty years ago.

At Steven's generous request, and with the invaluable recommendation of Harold A. Brown, copies of this book are being donated to libraries for under-privileged readers.